JN092424

他者をめぐる人文学
グローバル世界における
翻訳・媒介・伝達

大橋完太郎
トーマス・ブルック編

ADAPTATION, MEDIATION AND COMMUNICATION OF OTHERNESS IN A GLOBALIZING WORLD:

PERSPECTIVES FROM JAPAN

THOMAS
BROOK
&
KANTARO
OHASHI

目　次

CONTENTS

謝　辞

本書は、2017 年以降、神戸大学大学院人文学研究科で行ってきた共同研究の成果を形にし、広く公開するためにまとめたものである。2018 年に開催したワークショップの場で論文集の刊行を提案してくださった増本浩子先生（当時研究科長）はそのとき、このようなバイリンガル図書となることを恐らく想定していなかったと思われるが、この手間のかかる実験的な試みをあえて実現まで運ぶことができたのは、絶えずこの活動を肯定し、距離を保ちつつ励まし続けてきた先生のおかげであるといっても過言ではない。この場を借りてお礼申し上げる。

本研究を行う上で、同研究科から様々な支援と、ここで全員の名を挙げられないほど多くの教員の高配と助言をいただいた。特に、企画の途中から共編者として加わっていただき、本全体の形式から、出版に関する現実的な課題まで相談に乗ってくださり、刊行まで導いてくださった大橋完太郎先生には大変お世話になった。この活動の母体となった大学院生主体の「他者をめぐる人文学研究会」のメンバーを代表してお礼申し上げる。しかし、ここで「代表して」と書いてよいか不安を覚えるほど、実はこの研究会に参加してくれた方々の意欲と、研究方針が定まらないなかでの困難な状況に対する忍耐力の強さに助けられるばかりであった。共同研究を行う難しさと楽しさを分かち合えたことに心より感謝している。特に、本書の表紙カバーをはじめ、デザインのことで多大なご協力をいただいた中村紀彦氏にお礼を伝えたい。

2011 年から 4 年間、私はロンドン大学 SOAS に在籍したが、その当時はグリゼルディス・キルシュ先生から指導を受ける機会に恵まれなかった。2017 年 11 月の第 1 回ワークショップから計 4 回、先生が神戸大学までの長旅を実行してくださったおかげで、大学院に入学した当初に想像もしなかった豊かな国際的共同研究に関わることができた。ワークショップでの的確なご指摘はもちろんのこと、会場の外で言葉を交わせた際は常に先生の先入観の介在しない冷静で開かれた態度に驚かされた。それは、「他者」の存在にどのように向き合うかという根本的な問いの長期的な継続によって培われたもののように思われた。私にとって本国であるイギリスで日本文化に関する教育研究活動に従事するキルシュ先生と研究情勢の現在や外国の地に住むこと、多言語状況への向き合い方などについて語り合うことができたのは、揺れ動く世界の中で「人文学」なるものとの関係を模索する自分にとってかけがえのない経験となった。

本書には、21 世紀の「グローバル社会」の中で人文学研究が面している課題に対する決定的な「答え」は書かれていない。しかし、この書物がそれを手に取ってくださる読者にとって同じような模索の手がかりとなってくれるならば、キルシュ先生をはじめ、この企画をサポートしてくださった皆さまへの細やかな恩返しにはなると思いたい。

トーマス・ブルック

（神戸大学大学院人文学研究科博士課程後期課程）

Acknowledgements

The present volume is the result of a collaborative, interdisciplinary research project carried out at the Graduate School of Humanities, Kobe University, for approximately four years beginning in 2017. The project was led by a group of graduate students based at the faculty who met on a monthly basis as the "Others in the Humanities Research Group". With the encouragement and assistance of Professor Hiroko Masumoto, we invited Dr Griseldis Kirsch of SOAS, University of London to act as commentator and speaker at a workshop held on November 1st, 2017, titled "Others and Othering in Modernity". The success of this first meeting led to a series of workshops in May 2018, July 2018 and July 2019, which have culminated in this collection of papers.

Professor Masumoto first suggested we consider publishing our research on the occasion of one of the 2018 workshops. Although she probably did not envision the eventual bilingual format of the book, its realization in print is a testament to her continued encouragement and belief in the value of the project and the students who led it. The publication was also made possible by the measured guidance of Dr Kantaro Ohashi, Associate Professor of Art Theory, who helped us to coordinate our efforts and maintain our focus, especially in the later stages of the project. On behalf of all of the students involved, I thank Masumoto sensei, Ohashi sensei, and the many other faculty staff who assisted throughout for their enduring support and encouragement. I also, personally, must express my deep gratitude to the participants of the "Others in the Humanities Research Group", who showed themselves always able to adapt to the changing format of the workshops while also consistently contributing thought-provoking material in their research presentations. I especially thank Norihiko Nakamura for his assistance in designing the book cover and page layout of this volume.

My greatest thanks must be reserved for Dr Kirsch, who made the long journey from London to Kobe four times in only three years, devoting much of her limited time to taking part in our workshops. Although I was a student at SOAS between 2011 and 2015, I did not directly receive her tuition during that time. However, from our first meeting at JR Rokkomichi station in November 2017, I was frequently struck by Dr Kirsch's unassuming attitude and genuine interest in both individual presentations and the discussions she helped to moderate. If the content of this book succeeds in showing appropriate sensitivity towards questions relating to "the Other", it is in no small part a reflection of the model she provided via her participation and engagement. It has been a true privilege to work together with her on this project, and I thank her sincerely for her goodwill and commitment to seeing it through to completion.

Thomas Brook

(Ph.D. Student, Graduate School of Humanities, Kobe University)

第一部

グローバル世界の人文学研究における
学際的研究と他者性の媒介

PART 1

GLOBALIZATION, INTERDISCIPLINARY RESEARCH
IN THE HUMANITIES AND THE MEDIATION OF OTHERNESS

序論：ワークショップ開催から出版まで

トーマス・ブルック

はじめに

本論文集『他者をめぐる人文学―グローバル世界における翻訳・媒介・伝達―』（*Adaptation, Mediation and Communication of Otherness in a Globalizing World: Perspectives from Japan*）は、神戸大学大学院人文学研究科の博士課程に在籍する大学院生（当時）が主導した共同研究の成果を広く公開するとともに、「グローバル化」する現代社会における人文学の学際的ないし国際的共同研究の意義、可能性、および難点を反省的に問うものとして構想された。

この共同研究にとって相応しい形式を考えた結果、たどり着いたのは日本語と英語の両方による二言語併用を積極的に取り入れた二部構成である。この序論も含まれる第一部の「総論」では、現役大学院生の視点から「グローバル化」という現象または状況が「他者」をめぐる問題系にもたらす影響と、その展望を捉えようと試みた。特に、この序論では、論文集実現に至るまでの経緯を振り返りつつ、「グローバル化」が、とりわけ現代日本の文脈において、人文学の分野における学際的共同研究に課している試練について詳しく論述する。

続く第二部「各論」では、より一般的な学術誌の特集形式に倣い、ワークショップでの口頭発表に基づいた個別論考を収録している。これらの論文では、「他者」および「他者性」が翻訳、媒介、伝達という動的な作用において交渉され、変容する様相を捉えようとした。「日本」と「グローバル化」は必ずしも全編におけるテーマとして扱われないが、「グローバル化」が盛んに言われるなか、日本の大学において、日本にとっての「他者」とも言える外国人日本学研究者との交流の中で成立した研究であることは事実である。この二部構成をもって、そうした現代的な状況を前景化させ、第二部における独立した論文の文脈化を試みた。なお、完全な二言語併用を採用したのは第一部のみであり、第二部は巻末の要旨を除き英語による論考のみからなる。なぜこのような特殊な形式を採用したかという問題について、以下に続く本序論の部分で述べる。

他者（性）と差異は、人間の条件の多様性と、自と他をはじめとする差異に

Introduction: From Planning to Publication

Thomas Brook

Introduction

The present collection of papers titled *Adaptation, Mediation and Communication of Otherness in a Globalizing World: Perspectives from Japan* has been planned with the aim of publishing the results of a joint research project chiefly organized by Ph.D. students of the Graduate School of Humanities at Kobe University, and call into question the significance, possibilities and difficulties of international or interdisciplinary collaborative humanities studies in a "globalizing" world.

After careful consideration of the appropriate form for this joint research, we actively adopted the present bilingual style in English and Japanese as the format of this two-part work. In the first section "Outline", which includes this introduction, we attempt to grasp how the phenomenon or situation of "globalization" affects the problematique of "others" and comprehend its future prospect from our perspective as Ph.D. students. In particular, this introduction will look back on how the project has come to realization and expatiate upon the trials of interdisciplinary collaborative research in the field of humanities imposed by "globalization", especially in the context of Japan.

On the other hand, the second part, which follows the more common format of a scholarly journal, contains papers based upon individual presentations that were given at workshops. These papers aim to contribute to the understanding of how "others" and "otherness" are negotiated and transformed in the active processes of translation, mediation and transmission. "Japan" and "globalization" are not necessarily the central theme of the papers, but these papers were certainly generated in a Japanese university, through academic exchange between Japan-based scholars and foreign researchers of Japanese studies, who might be defined as "others" to Japan. Through this two-part structure, we try to foreground such current circumstances, and contextualize the individual papers in the second part.

It must be noted that it is in the first part only that we adopted a completely bilingual style, while part two consists of papers written solely in English except for abstracts in both languages at the end of the volume. The rest of this

基づく区別が人間の経験に及ぼしてきた破壊的な暴力と構築的な可能性を考慮する人文学研究においては避けては通れない問題である。今日、自と他の間の線が改めて引かれ、極めて濃密で多方向的な文化間接触、ネットワーク化および標準化が技術的な発展を促すとともに、文化的固有性と個人の主体性を脅かしてもいる。グローバルまたは地域間の変化と局地的な固有性を対象として扱うことにより、本論文集はそんなグローバル化時代をめぐる議論へ寄与すべく考案した。

論文集企画の経緯

本企画が本格的に始動したのは2017年11月1日に神戸大学大学院人文学研究科で開催したワークショップ「近代における他者と他者化——自文化と他文化の表象をめぐって」（“Others and Othering in Modernity: Representation of own and other cultures”）においてである。これは、「他者をめぐる人文学研究会」という名称の下で集まった大学院生が1年以上に渡る準備期間を経て、ロンドン大学東洋アフリカ研究学院（SOAS）で日本のメディア表象に関する研究と教育に携わるグリゼルディス・キルシュ（Griseldis Kirsch）准教授を招聘し、実現させたものである。ワークショップでは、キルシュ先生に大学院生による研究発表についてコメントをもらった上で、自身の研究に関する講演をしていただいた。研究発表と講演は研究科内で告知し、学部生と大学院生も参加した。

この基本形式は、「メディアの諸相」（“Aspects of the Media”）と題される、2018年5月24日（副題「媒体・ジャンル間における題材の転用」“Adaptation from One Medium to Another”）、同7月27日（副題「媒介作用とメッセージ」“Mediation and Message”）、2019年7月4日（副題「局地的・地域間の潮流」“Local and Global Currents”）の計3回に渡り開催した一連のワークショップに継承された。すべてのワークショップにおいて、「他者」をめぐる問題を前景化させつつ、日本の中に研究活動の拠点を置く若手研究者と日本の外に研究活動の拠点を置くベテランの日本学研究者が知的交流を行う場を構築することが主な目的であった。

それぞれのワークショップ題目が示すように、「グローバル化」は私たちの

introduction will centre upon the reasons why we adopted such a unique form.

The issues of other(ness) and difference cannot be shunned in the field of the humanities, particularly in research which explores the diversity of the human condition and how discrimination based on differences (e.g. between self and other) has brought about both destructive violence on the one hand and constructive possibilities to human experience on the other. In the present day, lines are being drawn afresh between “self” and “other”, and extremely dense and multi-oriented cultural contact, networking and standardization are promoting technological development while at the same time threatening the cultural identity and subjectivity of individuals. This collection of papers was conceived in order to contribute to the ongoing discussion surrounding the age of globalization, by focusing on global/interregional fluidity and local specificity.

The history of the publication project

We launched this project on a full scale in a workshop titled “Others and Othering in Modernity: Representation of own and other cultures” held at the Graduate School of Humanities, Kobe University on 11 November 2017, which was hosted after more than a year of preparation by postgraduate members of the “Others in the Humanities Research Group”. In this conference we invited Dr. Griseldis Kirsch, Reader at SOAS, University of London (the School of Oriental and African Studies), who researches and teaches Japanese media representation. She gave feedback on the presentations given by the graduate students in the workshop, and then lectured on her research. The student presentations and keynote lecture were advertised in the faculty, and undergraduate students and graduate students participated as audience members.

We kept this basic style in the following three workshops, all under the main title of “Aspects of the Media”, namely, “Adaptation from One Medium to Another” on 24 May 2018, “Mediation and Message” on 27 July 2018, and “Local and Global Currents” on 4 July 2019. In all of these workshops, we aimed at foregrounding the problems surrounding “others”, and also generating opportunities for intellectual exchange between young researchers based in Japan and senior scholar(s) based outside of Japan.

As shown in the titles of the workshops, “globalization” was not our initial theme. However, this research activity offered a rare opportunity to face the issue of “globalization” for the organizers, who were mostly graduate students

当初からの問題設定ではなかった。しかし、「グローバル化」が一般社会や教育の文脈においてしばしば議論されるなかに、主に日本の人文学研究分野の博士課程に在籍していた本企画の実行委員にとって、この研究活動は「グローバル化」に向き合う稀有の機会となった。しかし、それは常に困難な試行錯誤を伴うものでもあった。その困難は何よりも、言語をどのように使う（使い分ける）かという問題と深く関わるものであった。

全プロジェクトを通じてワークショップの基本形式を継承したということは上述の通りであるが、大きく変わったのは言語の扱いである。第一回のワークショップでは、博士課程在籍中の大学院生による研究発表と質疑応答からなる第一部において一貫して日本語を使用言語とし、より大きな教室に移動して行った特別講演と討論からなる第二部では英語を使用言語とした。これに対し、2018年、2019年のワークショップでは、発表要旨程度の日本語資料を提供したものの、口頭では一貫して英語を使用した。そして本企画の集大成となる本論文集では日本語と英語の二言語併用を試みるという方針に至った。

言語使用に関するこの方針の変更は、「グローバル化」が度々言及される現代における国際的学術交流の複雑化と、それが要求する研究姿勢への対応の結果であると言える。本企画は、いくつかの段階において神戸大学大学院人文学研究科の教員からの助言および同研究科の「グローバル人材育成事業」をはじめとする公的研究費を通じた支援に恵まれた一方、ワークショップを計画し、研究活動を行う上での判断は大学院生の実行委員の自由により決定された。ところが、「グローバル化」の正体に対する理解が必ずしも共有されない状況にあって、その自由をどのように行使すれば良いかは自明なことではない。本論文集の巻頭に、日本語と英語の両方による総論を設けることは、この困難を浮き彫りにし、「グローバル化」をめぐる議論に寄与すべく企図したものであるが、なぜこの対策に至ったのか、言語使用の問題に焦点を当てつつ、日本社会の近年の「グローバル化」をめぐる実態と議論、そして近年の他の「グローバルな」あるいは「学際的」共同研究の試みと関連付けて述べていきたい。

「グローバル化」時代における言語使用の問題

日本のTOEFLランキングが国の「グローバル化」対策の指標とされるよう

in the field of humanities at a Japanese institution and also caught in the whirl of discussion about "globalization" in the context of society and education. However, our attempts were always accompanied by difficulties. And these difficulties, before everything, were deeply concerned with the question of how to deal with language—or, how to use different languages for different purposes.

As stated above, the basic format was maintained throughout all of these workshops, but the way we used language drastically changed. In the first workshop, the Japanese language was consistently used in the first section in which Ph.D. students gave presentations with question and answer sessions, while the English language was used in the second section which consisted of the key note lecture and discussion, held in a larger lecture room. On the other hand, in the workshops in 2018 and 2019, we consistently used English, except for printouts that included abstracts in Japanese. And in this collection of papers, which is the final goal of this project, we have adopted a bilingual style using both Japanese and English.

This change in language use is the consequence of the increased complication of the current state of international academic exchange and the attitude of researchers it requires. In conducting this project we received advice from teachers of the Graduate School of Humanities at Kobe University, and also official financial support including from its Global Human Resources Development Program, but otherwise the workshops were mostly planned and organized in line with the freely made decisions of the Ph.D. students. However, under circumstances in which the definition of "globalization" is not necessarily agreed, it is not always clear how to use such freedom. We set up this introductory chapter with the aim to throw into relief this difficulty and contribute to the controversial debate on "globalization". In the following section, we would like to explain how we have reached the present format, concentrating on the problem of language use, while also referring to the present condition and discussion of "globalization" and "internationalization" in Japanese society, and other recent "global" or "interdisciplinary" collaborative research.

The problem of language use in the age of "globalization"

The controversy surrounding "globalization" is inseparably connected with the use of English and English language education, as indicated by the fact that the ranking of the Japanese in the Test of English as a Foreign Language (TOEFL)

に（鳥飼 2018, 46-47）[1]、「グローバル化」をめぐる議論と英語使用および英語教育は深くつながっている。小説家の水村美苗が2008年に発表した評論『日本語が亡びるとき――英語の世紀の中で』が刊行後すぐにベストセラーとなったように、英語の問題に対する日本社会の関心は深いものである。英語が他の言語に抜きん出て最強の世界的共通語としての地位を固めてきたという水村の認識は広く認められるであろう（水村 2008、特に第三章を参照）。しかし、日本の全構成員を日本語と英語のバイリンガルとして育成しようとする言語政策が植民地的な社会構造に発展するものだとして警鐘を鳴らす水村は（水村 2017、26-33）、それでも英語が世界共通語として機能する限り英語で発信する必要性を説いている[2]。日本の英語教育をめぐる近年の議論においても、高い英語能力を一律に求めることが容易に経済的な格差を助長する危険性は問題視されているが[3]、日本の文部科学大臣はそれでも2019年の時点で「グローバル化が進展する中で、英語によるコミュニケーション能力を身に付けることは大変重要なことです」と念を押したのである（文部科学省 2020）。「グローバル化」の進展は自明ではないとしても（あるいは自明ではないからこそ）、現在も日本における英語教育と英語使用をめぐる議論が白熱しており、そのような環境でどのように言語を扱うかというのは難しい問題である。

その問題を複雑にしている一つの要因は、水村も指摘するとおり、英語がヨーロッパの他の言語（あるいは「西洋語」）と有している近縁性にある（水村 2008, 182）。1947年から1952年までの占領期間を含み、英語を事実上の公用語とするアメリカが極めて深い関わりを日本と持った20世紀を経て、現代日

[1] 鳥飼は2011年に日本政府によって設置された「グローバル人材育成推進会議」が発表した「グローバル人材育成戦略」における英語バイアスを指摘している。

[2] 水村は日本の少数な一部（1パーセント未満）が英語を通して世界に発信すれば十分であると主張しているが、その少数なエリートがどのように構成（選出）されれば良いかについては、自然淘汰に任せている感が強い。『日本語が亡びるとき』前掲書、347-363頁を参照。

[3] 具体的には、「聞く」と「読む」技能だけでなく、「書く」と「話す」技能をも測定する民間試験を日本の大学入学共通テストへ導入する案が社会格差と経済格差との関連で問題視され、見送られるという事態が2019年に起こった。NHK NEWS WEB「英語民間試験 導入延期の経緯と今後は」2019年11月19日を参照
［www3.nhk.or.jp/news/html/20191119/k10012181981000.html］（2020年7月31日にアクセス）。

scores is used as a criterion of "globalization" by the Japanese Government (Torikai 2018, 46-47)[1]. Japanese society has shown a great interest in the issue of English language, as shown by the success of *When the Japanese Language Falls: In the Age of English*, a book-length essay by novelist Minae Mizumura, which became a bestseller upon publication in 2008. Mizumura's recognition of English as by far the most powerful language in the world is probably widely acknowledged (See Mizumura 2008, especially Chapter 3). Mizumura, who warns against a language policy which aims to make all Japanese people bilingual in English and Japanese on the ground that it could result in a colonial social structure (Mizumura 2017, 26-33), still insists on the necessity of contributing to the discourse in English, at least while it functions as a common language[2]. In recent discussions on English language education in Japan, requiring all students to acquire high levels of proficiency in English is regarded as problematic, particularly as it can easily escalate economic disparity[3], but the Japanese Minister of Education, Culture, Sports, Science and Technology again insisted in 2019 that English communication skills are very important in this globalizing world (The Japanese Minister of Education, Culture, Sports, Science and Technology, 2020). Supposing (or precisely because) the progress of globalization is not self-evident, there is still a dispute over English education and use of English language in Japan today, and it is not easy to find a definite answer as to how to deal with language under the current circumstances.

One factor which makes the problem complicated is, as Mizumura points out, the (linguistic) proximity English shares with other European (or "Western") languages (Mizumura 2008, 182). It is likely that the modern Japanese language has been shaped by the strong influence of English throughout the 20th century,

[1] Torikai points out the bias towards English inherent in the "Global Human Resources Development Program" announced by The Council on Promotion of Human Resource for Globalization Development set up by the Japanese Government in 2011.

[2] Mizumura argues that if a few, selected number of Japanese (less than one percent) were able to express themselves to the world in English, it would be sufficient. However, she appears to leave the problem of how members of such an elite minority group should be constituted (or chosen) to natural selection. See *When the Japanese Language Falls*, pp. 347-363.

[3] In particular, the use of private English tests for Japanese university entrance selection, which test not only listening and reading ability but also writing and speaking ability, was put off in 2019 partly because of fears it risks worsening the problem of social and economic disparity. See NHK NEWS WEB 2019.

本語は英語の影響を強く受けていると思われるが、それでも日本語を母語とする人にとって、英語学習の負担はヨーロッパ出身者のそれと比較にならないほど大きいと考えられる。さらに、この問題と隣接して、今も昔も、地球規模における英語の普及、および英語を媒体とした「異文化コミュニケーション」が、英語その他の「西洋語」を母語とする人による媒介に担保されてきたというジレンマ的側面もある。本企画における英語使用も例外ではない。

ところが、同じように「グローバル化」の一側面として考えることも可能なのだが、日本語も、特に日本国内においては様々な文化的や民族的背景を持つ人々を結ぶ「異文化コミュニケーション」の媒体として機能していることがかつてないほど広く認められるようになってきている。このことも、日本で行われる、日本語に習熟した外国人研究者を含む共同研究における言語使用の問題を自明なものではなくさせてきた重要な要因であると考えられる。

稲賀繁美は国際日本文化研究センターにおいて「非母語としての日本語」(すなわち外国人の日本学研究者が使用する日本語）が学術交流の媒体となる可能性に触れているが（稲賀 2013、42-43)、日本語が様々な出自を持つ者にとって学術交流の媒体となる環境は数少ない国際的研究機関に限定されるものではない。留学生受け入れを年々増やしてきた日本全国の大学など高等教育機関でも日常的に見られるものとなっているはずである。

1983年に当時の日本政府は、国際貢献を果たすという名目で、「21世紀の留学生政策に関する提言」（通称「留学生受け入れ10万人計画」）を発表した。これにより、特にアジア近隣諸国からの留学生は年々増え、10万人に達した2005年を経て、2008年には「留学生30万人計画」が新たに打ち出された[4]。その「30万人計画」は2019年についに達成された（文部科学省 2019)。その留学生の多くは日本語による研究活動に携わっていると思われる。この政策により、当初は見込まれていなかった課題が日本社会全体で浮上していることは言うまでもないが[5]、これが私たちの研究活動が行われた背景である。

日本語が日本人として生まれなかった人をも結びつける媒体となりつつある

[4] 以上は東條加寿子「大学国際化の足跡を辿る――国際化の意義を求めて――」（大阪女学院大学紀要7号、2010年）を参照した。

in which America, for which English is virtually the official language, had an inseparable relationship with Japan, including the days of the occupation from 1947 to 1952. However, those who speak Japanese as their mother tongue probably face a far greater disadvantage in learning English than European people. Similarly, there is a dilemmatic aspect that the current and past global spread of English and "cross-cultural communication" through the mediation of English has been heavily reliant upon the mediation of native speakers of English and other European languages. The use of English in the current project is no exception.

Nevertheless, it is now widely admitted that the Japanese language also functions as a medium of "cross-cultural communication" among people—especially in Japan—with various cultural or ethnic backgrounds as never before (possibly this can be considered as one aspect of "globalization", too). This also seems to be one important factor that has obfuscated the issue of language use in collaborative research in Japan, including that involving foreign researchers who have adept Japanese language skills. Shigemi Inaga suggests that "Japanese as a foreign language" (i.e. Japanese language used by foreign researchers of Japanese studies) can be a medium of academic interaction in the International Research Center for Japanese Studies (Inaga 2013, 42-43). However, this phenomenon is not limited to just a few international research institutes; it must be also becoming more common for people with various backgrounds to use Japanese language as a medium of international academic interaction in higher education institutes such as Japanese universities nationwide, which have accepted increasing numbers of international students.

In 1983, the Japanese Government declared a "Proposal of International Student Policy towards the 21st Century" (known as "The 100,000 International Students Plan"), with an aim to make a contribution to the international community. Consequently, more and more international students, especially from Asia, have visited Japan. When the number reached 100,000 in 2005, "The 300,000 International Students Plan" was newly launched[4], which was recently achieved in 2019 (The Japanese Minister of Education, Culture, Sports, Science and Technology, 2019). Many of these international students are likely to engage

---

[4] The discussion here is based on Kazuko Tojo, "Tracing the Progress of the Globalization of Universities: In Search of the Meaning of Globalization." *Journal of Osaka Jogakuin University*, Vol. 7, 2010.

ことは、1990年の時点でアメリカ出身の作家リービ英雄が早くも指摘したことであるが（リービ 1992、22）、近年になりようやく学術論文でも扱われるようになってきている（オストハイダ 2017)。「世界的共通語」=「リンガフランカ」としての地位を固めてきた英語にしても、主に日本の中で多様な出自を持つ人々の「共通語」となりつつある日本語にしても、複雑な社会的・歴史的背景を負うものとして、両者はどちらも究極的に中立的な媒体たり得ないものである。私たちはこの難問にどのように向き合えば良いだろうか。

上述の通り、今回の企画において、私たちが至った対策は二言語併用の形式であるが、この形式を試みる上で、参考になる先行研究があった。言語使用の問題を前景化させた共同研究、ハルオ・シラネ編『越境する日本文学研究：カノン形成・ジェンダー・メディア』(2009) である。アメリカおよび日本を拠点とする日本学研究者が中心となって2007年6月に東京の明治学院大学で行われた国際シンポジウムでの研究報告に基づく小論文集であるが[6]、日本語のみの「編集後記」を除き、完全なバイリンガル形態を実現させたことは注目に値する。本の「序言」では、日本語英語併記の意図として、「日本文学や日本文化とともに英語を学んだり、教えたりする必要のある人々や、文化横断的で学際的な研究に関心のある人々の役に立つこと」が挙げられている（シラネ 2009、2)。また、編者のシラネはこの試みが「日本研究におけるひとつの先例となることを期待」するとともに、「将来のグローバルな共同研究への道をひらくことを望んでいる」ことも表明している（シラネ 2009、2)。

数少ない二言語併用の実践として、この試みは確かに一つの先例になっているが、「将来のグローバルな共同研究への道」を必ずしも説得的に示せてはいない。「日本文学や日本文化とともに英語を学んだり、教えたりする必要のある人々」という正体不明の想定読者が一方にあり、他方に、「二言語併用での

[5] たとえば、芹澤健介はルポルタージュ『コンビニ外国人』（新潮新書、2018年）において、留学生の増加に付け込み、悪質な営業を行う名目のみの「日本語学校」のことについて述べている。

[6] ハルオ・シラネ編『越境する日本文学研究：カノン形成・ジェンダー・メディア』勉誠出版、2009年。本書は左から右の方向で英語が記載され、右から左の方向で日本語が記載されている。本序論日本語版と英語版ではそれぞれ日本語と英語のページを示している。

in research activities using the Japanese language. It is needless to say this policy raised problems that had never been anticipated in Japanese society as a whole[5], but this is indeed the background in which our collaborative research activity has been conducted.

As early as 1990, Hideo Levy, an American-born writer, pointed out that the Japanese language can serve as a communicative medium for those who were not born Japanese (Levy 1992, 22), and quite recently scholarly works have begun to deal with this issue, too (Ostheider 2017). However, since both languages have complicated social and historical backgrounds, neither English, which has established a firm position as "the common language of the world = a lingua franca" nor Japanese, which is now becoming "a common language" mainly among people of various origins in Japan, can ultimately be a neutral medium. The question remains as to how to face this formidable problem.

As stated above, we finally adopted a bilingual format in this project. In attempting this approach, there was a helpful precedent: *New Horizons in Japanese Literary Studies: Canon Formation, Gender, and Media Edited with Introduction* (2009), edited by Haruo Shirane, a collection of short articles based on an international symposium prepared by scholars (mainly Japan- and U.S.-based) of Japanese studies at Meiji Gakuin University in Tokyo in June 2007[6]. It is worth noting that this anthology achieves a perfect bilingual form except for the editor's postscript, written in Japanese only. According to the preface, the purpose of the bilingual style in English and Japanese is "to serve those who need to study or teach Japanese literature and culture as well as English, or who are interested in trans-cultural studies and interdisciplinary approaches" (Shirane 2009, 4), and the editor Shirane at the same time expresses his hope that this attempt will "set a new precedent in Japanese studies" and "set a precedent for future collaborative, global research" (Shirane 2009, 4).

This attempt is certainly one of the few precedents of the practice of a bilingual

---

[5] For example, in *Convenience Store Foreigners* (Shincho Shinsho, 2018), Kensuke Serizawa refers to nominal "Japanese language schools" which take advantage of the increased number of foreign students and run underhand business.

[6] Haruo Shirane ed. *New Horizons in Japanese Literary Studies: Canon Formation, Gender, and Media*, Bensei Publishing, 2009. In this book, the English pages are read left to right, and the Japanese right to left. Page numbers given in the Japanese and English versions here refer to the Japanese and English pages respectively.

研究」の意義が、「同一の前提を共有しない異なる文化・言語共同体」に属する読者へ伝えようとする翻訳的活動と結びつくものとして、以下のように提示されている。

> 翻訳とは同一の前提を共有しない異なる文化・言語共同体に伝えようと、著者の論旨や研究方法の背後にある前提を説明することでもある。二言語併用での研究を重要なものとし、また将来における大きな刺激となりうるのは、まさにこの文化横断的プロセスであり、それは著者と翻訳者の双方の責務でもある。(シラネ 2009、2)

ここでは、個々の投稿者(あるいは少なくとも個々の投稿論文)は旧来の画一的な「文化・言語共同体」に属する(つまり「同一の前提を共有」する)ものとして提示されている。実際には、編集後記を除く28稿のうち、著者以外の者に翻訳された日本語原文は5稿、英語原文は9稿、そして原著者による両言語での執筆と思われるものは14稿ある。すなわち、この共同研究企画では、他者による翻訳を経ていると思われない論考が全体の半数を占めている[7]。このことは、上記の引用で「二言語併用での研究」に与えられている価値のみならず、「同一の前提」を共有するものとしての単一的「文化・言語共同体」の概念それ自体とも相容れないと思われるが、これについて一切の説明が施されていないことに、むしろ同一の前提が共有されないことを特徴とするグローバル化時代に十分に対応できているとは言いがたい点があるのではないか。

さらに、英語と日本語の使用が完全に対称的な扱いを受けているため、以上に述べた英語と日本語の間の非対称性にも対応できていない面もある。特に、「グローバル化」の主な要請を英語によるコミュニケーション能力の向上と捉えた場合(他の解釈もあってもよい)、その先にある「グローバル共同研究」の在り方は不問のままに終わっている感がある。

もちろん、その問題についての解決策をここで提示することはできない。しかし、本企画における「二言語併用での研究」の試みの背景にある意図を示す

[7] 他の論考と異なり、この14稿に(訳:◯◯)の記述はない。

style, but it does not necessarily succeed in showing persuasively "a precedent for future collaborative, global research." On one hand, the book assumes unclear readers, "those who need to study or teach Japanese literature and culture as well as English, or who are interested in trans-cultural studies and interdisciplinary approaches," but on the other hand, it attributes the significance of "bilingual study" to translative activity which is intended for readers who belong to "another cultural-linguistic community that does not share the same assumptions", as shown in the following quotation:

> Translation involves explaining the assumptions behind the methods and approaches of the authors in an effort to reach out to another cultural-linguistic community that does not share the same assumptions. It is this trans-cultural process, which is both the responsibility of the author and the translator, that makes bilingual study important and that can be of great stimulus in the future. (Shirane 2009, 4)

Here, the individual contributors (or the individual articles, at least) appear to belong to the traditional, uniform "cultural-linguistic community" (that is, one that *does* "share the same assumptions"). Actually, of 28 papers excluding the postscript, 5 Japanese papers and 9 English papers are not translated by the author, but the other 14 papers are presumably both written and translated by the original author; that is to say, half of this collaborative research consists of papers which probably have not in fact passed through the translative activity of others[7]. This seems to be at odds with both the value ascribed to "bilingual study" above and the very concept of a unitary "cultural-linguistic community" that shares "the same assumptions", but since there is no explanation about this matter, it remains doubtful as to whether it sufficiently meets the requirements of the age of globalization, which is characterized by common assumptions not being shared.

Furthermore, since English and Japanese are dealt with in a completely symmetrical way, this attempt fails to address the asymmetry between English and Japanese as discussed above. Especially if we regard the development of communication skills in English as the essence of "globalization" (allowing that there may be other interpretations), the way future "collaborative, global research"

[7] Unlike the other papers, these 14 articles do not contain a note stating: "Translated by XX".

ことで、問題の輪郭をよりよく可視化することはできるであろう。

サイード著『オリエンタリズム』から40年

本論文集企画の母体となった「他者をめぐる人文学研究会」では、西洋の学者による東洋研究を批判的に捉えたエドワード·W·サイードの代表的著作『オリエンタリズム』(1978) を一つの共通の参照項目としてきた。以後の文化研究に多大な影響を与えた『オリエンタリズム』は、一般的に、東西間の政治的力学における不均衡や非対称性、そしてとりわけ「優位」の立場にある（あるいはあった）西洋が学問制度を異文化支配の装置に転じたことを糾弾した書として理解される。しかし、そのような力強い主張を含む著作が実は謙虚な問いで結ばれていることは看過すべきではない。結論部において、サイードは次の根本的な疑問を読者に突きつける。「我々は異文化をいかにして表象することができるのか。異文化とは何なのか」(サイード 1986、329。傍点は原文［今沢訳、以下同様］) という問いである。この問いは、私たちの研究グループがある程度共有するものであったが、その問いを立てる以前に、共同研究を行う「我々」は誰であるのかという問題が立ちはだかって来ざるを得ない。そして、言語使用を問い始めると、日本語の「我々」と、たとえば英語の“we”との間の差異も不可避に視野に入ってくる。

この点に関し、サイードの問題意識の核心に言語使用の問題があったことは改めて注目するに値するだろう。上記の問いに先立って、サイードは次のような問題意識を提示している。

> 問題の核心は、ある事物の真の表象というものが実際に存在しうるものなのかどうか、また、およそあらゆる表象というものは、それが表象であるがゆえに、まず表象するものの使用する言語に、次いでその属する文化・制度・政治的環境に、しっかりとはめこまれているのではないか、という点なのである。(サイード 1986、277)

『オリエンタリズム』の原文は英語であるが、パレスチナ人として生まれ、エジプトのキリスト教系の学校で英語による教育を受けた上でアメリカの大学

should be seems to pass unnoticed.

Of course, it is beyond the reach of our capability to present a definite answer. However, it is possible to better visualize the outline of the issue by explaining our intention behind our own attempt at "bilingual study" in this research project.

(Translated by Mizuki Tsutsui and Thomas Brook)

Forty years since Said's *Orientalism*

In the meetings of the "Others in the Humanities Research Group," the members of which are the Ph.D. students who organized this collection of papers, Edward W. Said's representative work *Orientalism* (1978), which criticizes Oriental studies by Western scholars, has been employed as a common reference point. Exerting an enormous impact on the subsequent cultural studies, *Orientalism* is generally recognized as a volume that does not merely question inequality and asymmetry in East-West political mechanics but also accuses the West, which is (or was) in a "dominant" position, of having transformed academic institutions into a device to rule over other cultures. Nonetheless, it should not be overlooked that a book that includes such a strong assertion is actually wrapped up with a modest question. In the concluding part, Said poses the following radical question to his readers: "How does one *represent* other cultures? What is *another* culture?" (Said 2003, 325; emphasis in original). This is a question that we, the members of the "Others in the Humanities Research Group," have shared to a certain degree, although preceding this question is the unavoidable issue of who "we," those who do the collaborative research, are. Moreover, asking about language use inevitably makes us aware of the difference between "*ware-ware*" in Japanese and, for example, "we" in English.

In this regard, it is notable anew that the issue of language use lay in the core of Said's problem consciousness. Prior to the above-mentioned question, Said presents his own awareness of the problem in the following terms:

> [T]he real issue is whether indeed there can be a true representation of anything, or whether any and all representations, because they *are* representations, are embedded first in the language and then in the culture, institutions, and political ambience of the representer. (Said 2003, 272; emphasis in original.)

Although *Orientalism* was originally written and published in English,

で英文学を専攻したサイードにとって、「我々」は単純に「英語使用者」（の知識人）に還元できるものではなかったはずであり、そしてそのことは彼が『オリエンタリズム』を執筆する上での大きな動機の一つでもあったに違いないだろう。東西間（具体的にイスラム教文明とキリスト教文明の間）の力学に根付いたその属性に関する葛藤と問題意識は安易に普遍化すべきものではないものの、彼が発した問いは世界に複数の言語、国、文化が共存する限り、学問や国境の垣根を越えた学際的ないし国際的共同研究が直面せざるを得ないものであり、そして究極的には解決され得ないものでもあると言って良いだろう。しかし、究極的に解決され得ないものであればこそ、現在の状況に合わせて、常に維持し更新しなければならないものでもあるであろう。

本論文集の形式を決定する上で大きく参考になったもう一つの文献がある。中井亜佐子著『他者の自伝――ポストコロニアル文学を読む』(2007) である。本文中でもサイードについて多くのページを割いている中井は、「あとがき」において、実は当初英語で書くことも検討したということを打ち明けている。結局そうしなかった理由について、著者は次のように述べている。「最終的に日本語で書くことを選んだのは、この本が日本の大学制度のなかで、日本語を媒介にして思考し意志交流した成果だという事実を尊重したかったからである」(中井 2007、347)。本論文集の成立事情も少し異なるものの、「日本の大学制度のなかで」、その制度において日本語と英語の間の境界線が交渉されるのを背景にして、ワークショップという表舞台とその裏舞台としての勉強会や個人間の連絡において（程度の差こそあれ）日本語と英語の両方を媒介にして企画を進めたことは事実である。本論文集における二言語併用はその事実を尊重する上で最も適切な対策と思われたのである。

もっとも、二言語併用をどのように実現するかという問題に対し、本企画を取り巻いている状況に十分に適応できる既存の解決策が見出されなかったため、この試みは高い実験性を持つものとなった。英語だけではなく、日本語も共通語として機能する環境において、こうした問題をめぐり何語で議論するかという二次的な問題も浮上する。二次的とはいえ、その問題が解決されない限り、議論そのものは発達しにくい。前述のとおり、私たちはこの問題に対し世界中どこでも通じるような回答を提供する立場にはいない。しかし、次節でよ

"we" could surely not have simply been reduced to "speakers of English" (or intellectuals comprised of them) for Said, who was born as a Palestinian, educated in English at a Christian school in Egypt, and majored in English literature at a university in the United States; rather, that must have been one of the great motivators for him to write *Orientalism* in the first place. Even though his inner conflict and problem consciousness regarding his personal affiliation, which was rooted in the East-West power balance (that between Islamic and Christian civilizations in particular), should not be generalized readily, it can be noted that the question raised by Said is, as long as multiple languages, countries, and cultures coexist in the world, something that any interdisciplinary or international collaborative research project cannot help facing, and ultimately something that cannot be solved. However, precisely because it cannot be ultimately solved, the question is one that should be maintained and renewed on a continuous basis according to the current situation.

The style of this collection of papers is heavily drawn from other literature as well: particularly Asako Nakai's *Autobiography of the Other: Reading Postcolonial Literature* (2007). Devoting a number of pages to descriptions concerning Said, Nakai discloses in the "Afterword" her initial consideration of writing the volume in English. Nakai explains her final decision of not doing so as follows: "Eventually I have chosen to write in Japanese because I desire to esteem the fact that this volume is the outcome of thoughts and exchanges of views through the mediation of Japanese within the Japanese university system" (Nakai 2007, 347). Although this collection of papers has come into existence in slightly different circumstances, it is true that the project has been conducted "within the Japanese university system", while in the background the boundary between Japanese and English has been negotiated within that system, and through the mediation of (in varying degrees) *both* Japanese and English, both in the workshops as the "front stage" and study meetings and individual communication as the "back stage." The concurrent use of the two languages in this volume can be regarded as the most appropriate measure to esteem that fact.

However, it must be noted that this attempt has been highly experimental as no existing solution could be found that was adaptable enough to the conditions surrounding the project, particularly regarding the question of how we put into practice the concurrent use of the two languages. Under circumstances where not only English but also Japanese functions as a lingua franca, a secondary question

り詳細に記述するように、本企画のメンバーが日本語と英語のそれぞれでの執筆、および日本語の英語への翻訳過程に直接立ち会うことができる作成プロセスを設けることにした。その理由としては、私たち一人ひとりがお互いの模索を参照しつつ、この問題と向き合い、その向き合いの結果を広く公開することができれば、それ自体は当該の問題を考える上で参考になると考えたからである。

現代日本は確かに世界中の他の国と地域と多くの共通点を持っていることは間違いないとしても、近代を通じて、日本がその外側にある「世界」と非常に深いかつときに特異な関わりを持ち続け、その結果として21世紀の現在に至り、世界の中でも極めて複雑な「異文化コミュニケーション」の一つの主要な現場になっているということも認めるべきであろう。現代の日本に住む（特に「日本の大学制度」によって支えられている）私たちに求められているのはおそらく、そうした日本の「特殊性」に酔うことなく、「他者との出会い」が、「ここ」では他所とは異なる形態を取る可能性を十分に考慮した上で[8]、日本の内部にもあり、日本の外部にも広がっている「世界」との関係を真剣に考え続けることではないかと思う。本論文集において、「この言語」（日本語）と「世界の言語」と見なされもする英語を併用することは、そのような作業を行う上での、ほとんど必然的に至った実験であると理解いただければ幸いである。

本書の二部構成について

上述の通り、本論文集は二言語併用の形式を採用しているが、参照したハルオ・シラネ編の論文集と大きく違うのは、それぞれ二言語併用の形態が異なる二部からなる構成を採用した点である。この導入文を含む第一部「総論」は原文が日本語で書かれ、文章が完成した上で作成した英語訳を併載している。対して、第二部「各論」では、第2回以降のワークショップで、そのワークショップの間は一貫した英語空間の中で学術交流を行った事実を配慮して、英語の

[8] この点に関し、東條（前掲）がEUと日本が置かれている状況の違いを踏まえて、EUが促進する言語政策が必ずしも日本で応用できないことを主張していることは重要な視点と思われる。細川英雄、西山教行編『複言語・複文化主義とは何か：ヨーロッパの理念・状況から日本における受容・文脈化へ』（くろしお出版、2010年）も共通した問題意識を示している。

emerges: which language should be used in discussing such issues. Secondary as the question is, unless it can be solved the debate itself is difficult to develop. As noted above, we are not in a place to provide a response to this question that would be applicable anywhere in the world. Instead, as will be described in the next section in more detail, we decided to design a process in which each member of the project could be present at the scenes of writing in both Japanese and English as well as translating Japanese into English. The reason for this method is that we thought it would be relevant to future consideration of this very issue if each individual member were to tackle the problem while seeing each other's own exploration and then we were to publicly present the outcome of our efforts.

Although there are certainly parallels between present-day Japan and other countries and regions, we should also recognize that Japan has throughout the modern era continued to maintain a deep and at times exceptional relationship with the "outside world", and as a result is home to processes of "intercultural communication" which, even considered on a global scale, are of great complexity. As those who are living in Japan today (in particular, those who are supported by the "Japanese university system"), we are presumably required to continue thinking seriously about the relationship between "us" and the "world" that exists both within Japan as well as spreads outside it, without becoming intoxicated by such "specificity" of Japan and yet with due consideration of the possibility that "here" encounters with the other may take on different forms than in other places.[8] It would be much appreciated if the concurrent use of "this language" (Japanese) and English, as one that is sometimes considered the "language of the world", is understood as an almost inevitable experiment in order to perform such a task in this collection of papers.

The dual structure of this collection of papers

As noted above, this collection of papers employs the concurrent use of Japanese and English, which is substantially different from the book edited by Haruo Shirane referred to above in that this collection is divided into two parts,

---

[8] In this regard, it is significant that Tojo (see above) argues that the language policy pursued by the European Union cannot necessarily be applied identically in Japan. A similar problem consciousness is offered in Hosokawa, Hideo, and Noriyuki Nishiyama, eds. *What is plurilingualism/pluriculturalism? From European philosophy/conditions to reception/ contextualization in Japan*, Tokyo: Kuroshio Shuppan, 2010.

みを使用言語とした。

「異文化コミュニケーション」に特化した（不完全な）中立的媒体としての英語を使用した国際的・学際的共同研究の功罪や、その可能性について詳しく論じることは筆者の力量を遥かに超えるが、この共同研究を通じて認めざるを得なくなった一つの問題は、口語の媒体としての英語と論述もしくは記述の媒体としての英語の違いである。ワークショップでは「一貫した英語空間」を設置したとはいえ、そこでは、表情と視線、その他の身振り、ときには参加者の一部のみによって共有される言語を介した臨機応変の補足と通訳も重要な役割を果たした。紙と印字、場合には図形を通じて、たった一人の（共著の場合もあるが）論者が自らの見解を提示する学術論文とは全く違う世界である。前者では、話し手の言葉が文法的に正しいか、十分に「学術的」であるかという問題は二次的な問題となり、非常に限られた空間の中で、論文の潜在的な可能読者数に比べ極めて少数の同席者とともに知的交流を行うことに重みが置かれる。これはおそらく、諸古代文明における学問の古来の姿であろうが、古来の学問は世界全体の規模で、一つの言語によって営まれたものではない。世界中に最も広く浸透している言語である意味で「グローバル」な媒体としての英語を用いるだけで、従来の形での学問、とりわけ人文学的な学問を「グローバル」な規模に適応することが必ずしもできない所以である。

しかし、論述の言語が英語である場合、それが世界中の（少なくとも高等教育を受けた）読者に届くことが容易になることは事実である。実際に、本論文集が日本と日本語の事情に専門的な知識を有しない読者の手にも届くことを大いに期待している。「グローバル」な媒体としての英語の魅力が近代におけるイギリスとアメリカの圧倒的な経済力と地続きであることを配慮しても、この歴史的な瞬間において、それが他の言語と比較にならないほど世界規模に浸透している事実は変わらない。そこには、「グローバル」な媒体としての英語の潜在的可能性があるが、それをどのように発揮する（あるいはしない）かという問題が21世紀の人類にとって決定的な意味を持つものとなるであろう。その問題をめぐる議論は始まったばかりであるが、その議論を行うためにも、今回のワークショップがそうであったように、「グローバル」な媒体としての英語は（先の段落で書いたことと矛盾するようだが）もっぱら単一言語的な状況

each part having a different form of the combined use of the two languages. The first part, "Overview", including this introduction, is originally written in Japanese and presented alongside the English version that was subsequently translated after the completion of the original text. In contrast, the second part "Articles" presents papers written in English only, out of regard for the fact that the academic exchanges were made in a consistently English-speaking environment throughout the workshops, from the second workshop onwards.

It goes far beyond my individual capacity to discuss in detail the merits and possibilities of international/interdisciplinary collaborative research by means of English as a (non-perfect) neutral medium dedicated to "cross-cultural communication." However, what has emerged in the course of this collaborative research is one problem that cannot help but being admitted: the difference between English as a colloquial medium and English as an academic or literary medium. Although throughout the workshops a "consistently English-speaking environment" was indeed prepared, facial expressions, eye contact, other gestures and at times the flexible supplementation and interpretation mediated by languages that were shared by only part of the participants played a significant role as well. That is a completely different world from an academic article in which only one scholar (although there are also cases of joint authorship) offers her/his own viewpoint through paper, typed words, and in some cases pictorial figures. In a workshop, whether a speaker's language is grammatically correct and whether it is fully "academic" are merely secondary problems; instead, a greater emphasis is placed on intellectual exchange in a very limited space with participants and attendees, the number of whom is considerably smaller than that of the potential readership of an academic paper. Possibly this is the traditional form of classical scholarship in ancient civilizations; however, such scholarship was not pursued on a worldwide scale in one language. It is for this reason that scholarship in such a conventional form, that of the humanities above all, cannot necessarily be adapted to "global" dimensions just by employing English as a "global" medium in terms of it being the most widespread language in the world today.

It is nonetheless true that easier delivery of an academic article to readers of the world (at least those with a higher education) can be fulfilled if it is written in English. Actually, it is strongly hoped that this collection of papers will also reach readers who do not have specialized knowledge of Japan and the Japanese language. Considering the fact that the fascination of English as a "global"

に依拠していることを認めることが重要と考えられる。本論文集の第二部を構成する各論を、要旨を除き英語のみとしたのも、そのことに配慮した結果である。

本序論に続く４章は、冒頭で述べたように本企画参加者がそれぞれの専門的領域から「グローバル化」と「他者」の問題を併せて考察した内容からなる。まず、筒井瑞貴と尾田知子はアメリカ文学とイギリス文学の観点から「グローバル化」に対する視点を提示する。筒井は、イギリスを中心に近代における「グローバル化」の歴史を概観した上で、ヴィクトリア朝文学作品において、「世界市民」と自称する悪役がイギリスという「自己」にとっての「他者」を炙り出す存在として登場することを、当時のグローバル化に対する一つの受容の仕方として分析する。尾田は、アメリカの比較文学研究者デイヴィッド・ダムロッシュに至る英語圏（西欧・西洋）における「世界文学」の概念の変遷を概観してから、現代日本を代表する作家でありつつ、世界中の文学市場で広く読まれる村上春樹の作風における、自らの「他者性」を配慮した戦略としての「前翻訳」を取り上げる。

続いて中村紀彦と林玲穂は映画研究と観光学という観点から同問題にアプローチする。中村は、映画というメディアを、仮想的な他者との出会いを通じて「グローカリゼーション」が生じる場として紹介してから、グローカルな状況が他者との統合／分断を同時にかつ逆説的に進行させる様相を、東南アジア映画における「遅さ」の表象を通じて具体的に確認する。最後に林は、世界中に通用する「グローバル」な日本イメージを発信する、グローバル化対策としての観光政策が、他者性（異質なものを認識することではじめてわかる）と世界への発信力を同時に追究するというジレンマ的な側面を抱えている問題を紹介してから、観光者が持つ「他者のまなざし」が働く現場を理論的に考察する。

これらの考察は、本序論と併せて、現代における「他者」と「グローバル化」の問題を浮き彫りにし、その両者が人文学研究に課している課題を提示するものとして構想された。第二部の「各論」については、冒頭で述べた通り「他者」または「他者性」を動きの中に捉えることに重点を置いた意味において、間接的には上述の問題とつながるが、形式的には通常の論文集と異ならず、要旨が巻末に収録されているため、ここでは詳細な説明を割愛する。

最後に、より実験的な方法で成立した本第一部の作成作業について一言述べ

medium is continuous with the overwhelming economic power possessed by the United Kingdom and the United States of America in modern times, it is no less true that, in this historical moment, English is widespread on a global scale in an incomparable manner with other languages. It is in this regard that the potential of English as a "global" medium can be found, while the way in which one exercises that potential (or does not exercise it) will be a critical question for human beings living in the twenty-first century. The debate on the problem having only just begun, for the promotion of the debate it is vital to recognize that English as a "global" medium leans on a nearly completely monolingual condition (although this may seem to contradict with what is stated in the previous paragraph), as was the case with these workshops. As a result of consideration for this matter, the articles constituting the second half of the collection of papers are written only in English except for the abstracts.

The four chapters following this introduction are composed of contents that explore the issue of "globalization" in conjunction with "others" and "otherness" by the Ph.D. students who organized this project from their respective fields of specialization. First, Mizuki Tsutsui and Tomoko Oda offer viewpoints on "globalization" from the perspectives of American literature and British literature. Tsutsui, after conducting an overview of the history of "globalization" in the modern era with a focus on the United Kingdom, demonstrates how villains in Victorian literary works who proclaim themselves to be "world citizens" draw attention to the "others" that threaten the "self" of Britain, and discusses this as an example of how globalization at the time was perceived. Oda then outlines the history of the concept of "world literature" in the English-speaking (Western-European) world leading up to the work of American comparative literature scholar David Damrosch, dealing with "pretranslation" in the fiction of Haruki Murakami, a representative writer of contemporary Japan whose works are read widely throughout the global literary market, as a strategy concerned with his own "otherness".

Then Norihiko Nakamura and Akiho Hayashi take an approach to the same issue from the standpoint of film studies and tourism studies. Nakamura introduces the medium of film as a space in which "glocalization" arises through the encounter with virtual "others," ascertaining in detail the way in which aspects of "glocal" conditions paradoxically promote both the integration and disjunction with others simultaneously, via analysis of the representation of "slowness" in South East

ておきたい。上述の通り、この第一部は元から日本語で執筆されたものである。まず、約半年にわたり、各担当項目の進捗状況を月一回の会議で共有し、全体の方針を調整しつつ、それに沿って文章を完成させた。それから各原稿を英語に翻訳した。翻訳は、当該の執筆者以外の者がその第一稿（下訳）を作成するという方法にこだわった。次に、原著者が自らの原稿を必要に応じて修正し、翻訳担当者がそれを反映させた。その作業を経て、原著者は最後に自らの原稿の英語版を必要に応じて修正し、それから筆者が冠詞など英語文法に関する最小限の訂正を加えてから、原著者が最終稿を提出した。すなわち、ここに収まっている両言語の文章は双方とも原著者に帰されるものとして理解される。この作成方法は、英語使用を主とした第二回以降のすべてのワークショップ準備において、筆者が日本語で書いたワークショップ概要文をイギリス文学専攻の筒井瑞貴が英訳したことを端緒にしている。他者の翻訳を媒介させることにより、原著者が必ずしも意識していなかったニュアンスが浮かび上がることもある。原文を日本語で作成し、英訳を隣のページで示す形式により、自ら英語や日本語で表現することと、他者によって英語に翻訳されることの違いについて、参加者および読者の意識を呼び起こす意図もあった。

この方針を採用する上で、もう一つ参考になった前例は、アメリカの大学で教授を務めつつ、英語と日本語の両方による研究書の刊行を行ってきた酒井直樹の研究活動である。その主著の一つである『日本思想という問題——翻訳と主体』（1997）において、一部の章では、酒井が英語で執筆した原文を、他の研究者が日本語訳を用意した上で、酒井自身が用語など表現の細部を修正したという[9]。もっとも、本企画において類似した試みを行い得たことは、英語の専門的な知識を有する参加者と、英語を母語とする筆者が関係していたことに大きく関わっていることを強調しなければならない。

とはいえ、英語をはじめ、執筆者にとって育ちの言語ではない言語で研究を行う場合、様々な他者の介在は必ずと言って良いほどよく生じることである。以上述べてきた実験的な形式と作成方法に関する説明と、これに続く個別の論

[9] 酒井直樹『日本思想という問題——翻訳と主体』、岩波書店、2012年の「あとがき」において、酒井は「主要用語の選択や読みにくさの責任は酒井にある」と明記している。327頁。

Asian film. Finally Hayashi, after presenting the problem of tourism policy as a means to realize globalization, which is accompanied by the dilemmatic aspect of pursuing otherness (that which can only be revealed by recognizing foreign elements) and worldwide communicability, theoretically speculates the locale in which the "eyes of the others" owned by tourists function.

These discussions, along with this introduction, have been envisaged with the aim of revealing the issue of "others" and "globalization" today and the challenges they present to the humanities. The second part "Articles" is also linked to this issue in that an emphasis is placed on capturing "others" or "otherness" within a specific movement; however, as this section is similar to standard collections of papers and abstracts are included at the back of the book, further details will be omitted here.

Lastly, I would like to say a brief word about the writing of the first part of this collection, which has been come into existence in a more experimental manner. As noted above, it was originally written in Japanese. First of all, over approximately six months the progress of each section assigned to each member was shared in monthly meetings, to adjust the overall direction and complete the manuscripts according to it. Then, each manuscript was translated into English. The translation was worked on via a method in which a translator, who was not the original author of the text, prepared the first draft (rough translation). Next, the author of the original text revised her/his Japanese manuscript as needed, followed by the translator reflecting the revision. Finally, the author of the original text corrected the English version of her/his manuscript and subsequently I (Thomas Brook) made as minimal corrections as possible in terms of English grammar before the author of the original text submitted the final version of the text and translation. Therefore, both the texts in Japanese and English collected in this part should be understood as being attributable to the original authors. This method of writing has its origin in the preparation for all the workshops since the second one, in which I wrote the general outline in Japanese and subsequently Mizuki Tsutsui, Ph.D. student in British literature, translated it into English. The mediation of translation by others occasionally highlights nuances that the author of the original text was not necessarily conscious of. Through the format of presenting the original text created in Japanese and its English translation on the adjacent page, I had the additional intent of awakening the consciousness of both participants in the project and potential readers to the difference between expressing oneself in

考を通じて、そのことと、それから発生する問題と可能性を読者が汲み取り、これからの共同的、あるいは学際的、国際的、はたまた「グローバル」な研究活動を行う際に参考にしてもらえることを、執筆者一同は切に願っている。

実行委員会

- トーマス・ブルック（神戸大学大学院人文学研究科）
- 奥堀　亜紀子（神戸大学 学術博士 学位取得）
- 尾田　知子（神戸大学 学術博士 学位取得）
- 筒井　瑞貴（神戸大学 学術博士 学位取得）
- 中村　紀彦（在野研究者、神戸大学大学院人文学研究科博士課程前期課程修了）
- 林　玲穂（神戸大学院人文学研究科）

English or Japanese and being translated into English.

Another precedent in adopting this principle is the work of Naoki Sakai, who has taught in the United States as a university professor as well as published his studies both in English and Japanese. In a portion of one of his important volumes *Translation & Subjectivity: On "Japan" and Cultural Nationalism* (1997), Sakai first wrote the original text in English, other researchers translated it into Japanese, and again Sakai corrected details such as terminology[9]. Understandably, an emphasis should be placed on the fact that the involvement of both participants with specialized knowledge of English and myself as a native speaker of English made a strong contribution to the executability of an analogous attempt in this project.

Be that as it may, when it comes to conducting research in a language other than that which is native to an author, such as English, the mediation of various kinds of others almost necessarily occurs. All of the authors of this collection of papers sincerely wish that, through the explanation on the experimental style and method of composition of this "Overview" as discussed above and the subsequent individual articles, readers will not only acknowledge the current situation as we perceive it and the problems and possibilities that can be derived from it but also consult this book in doing future collaborative, interdisciplinary, international, or even "global" research.

(Translated by Tomoko Oda and Thomas Brook)

Organizing Committee

- Thomas Brook (Graduate School of Humanities, Kobe University)
- Akiko Okubori (Ph.D. Kobe University)
- Tomoko Oda (Ph.D. Kobe University)
- Mizuki Tsutsui (Ph.D. Kobe University)
- Norihiko Nakamura (Independent scholar, M.A. Graduate School of Humanities, Kobe University)
- Akiho Hayashi (Graduate School of Humanities, Kobe University)

[9] Sakai, Naoki, *Translation & Subjectivity: On "Japan" and Cultural Nationalism*, Tokyo: Iwanami Shoten, 2012. In the "Afterword" of the book, Sakai explicitly states "I myself take responsibility for the choice of important words and any unreadability" (327).

参考文献

稲賀繁美「非母語という疑似餌には何が掛かるか」(郭南燕編『バイリンガルな日本語文学：多言語多文化のあいだ』三元社、2013年)

NHK NEWS WEB「英語民間試験 導入延期の経緯と今後は」2019年11月19日［www3.nhk.or.jp/news/html/20191119/k10012181981000.html］(2020年7月31日にアクセス)

オストハイダ テーヤ「日本の多言語社会とコミュニケーション——意識・政策・実態」(宮崎里司、杉野俊子編『グローバル化と言語政策——サスティナブルな共生社会・言語教育の構築に向けて』明石書店、2017年)

エドワード・W・サイード『オリエンタリズム』今沢紀子訳、平凡社、1986年

酒井直樹『日本思想という問題——翻訳と主体』、岩波書店、2012年

ハルオ・シラネ編『越境する日本文学研究：カノン形成・ジェンダー・メディア』勉誠出版、2009年

芹澤健介『コンビニ外国人』新潮新書、2018年

鳥飼玖美子『英語教育の危機』筑摩書房、2018年

東條加寿子「大学国際化の足跡を辿る——国際化の意義を求めて——」『大阪女学院大学紀要』第7号、2010年

中井亜佐子『他者の自伝——ポストコロニアル文学を読む』研究社、2007年

細川英雄、西山教行編『複言語・複文化主義とは何か：ヨーロッパの理念・状況から日本における受容・文脈化へ』くろしお出版、2010年

水村美苗『日本語が亡びるとき——英語の世紀の中で』、筑摩書房、2008年

水村美苗「中途半端な英語より、一葉を読む豊かさを 言語の植民地化に日本ほど無自覚な国はない」『中央公論』2017年8月号

文部科学省「萩生田光一文部科学大臣記者会見録(令和元年11月1日)」、2020年［www.mext.go.jp/b_menu/daijin/detail/1422393.htm］(2020年4月18日にアクセス)

文部科学省「「外国人留学生在籍状況調査」及び「日本人の海外留学者数」等について(令和2年4月22日)」2019年［www.mext.go.jp/a_menu/koutou/ryugaku/1412692.htm］(2020年7月31日にアクセス)

リービ英雄『日本語の勝利』講談社、1992年

Bibliography

Hosokawa, Hideo, and Nishiyama, Noriyuki eds, 2010. *Fukugengo/fukubunka shugi to wa nanika: Yoroppa no rinen/jokyo kara nihon ni okeru juyo/bunmyakuka he* [What is plurilingualism/pluriculturalism? From European philosophy/conditions to reception/contextualization in Japan], Tokyo: Kuroshio Shuppan.

Inaga, Shigemi, 2013. "Hibogo to iu rua ni nani ga kakaru ka" ["What is Caught on the Lure of a Non-Native Language?"] in Guo, Nanyan ed. *Bairingaru na Nihongo bungaku: tagengo tabunka no aida* [Bilingual Japanese Language Literature: Between Multilanguages and Multicultures], Sangensha.

The Japanese Minister of Education, Culture, Sports, Science and Technology, 2019. "Hagiuda Koichi monbukagaku daijin kishakaiken roku (Reiwa gan'nen 11 gatsu 1 nichi)" [The Record of the Press Conference by Koichi Hagiuda (November 1 2019)]. www.mext.go.jp/b_menu/daijin/detail/1422393.htm (Accessed 18 Aug. 2020)

---2020. "'Gaikokujinryugakusei zaiseki jokyo chosa' oyobi 'Nihonjin no kaigairyugakushasu' to ni tsuite (Reiwa 2 nen 4 gatsu 22 nichi)" [On 'An Investigation of Circumstances of Foreign Students' and 'The Number of Japanese Students Abroad' (April 22, 2020)] www.mext.go.jp/a_menu/koutou/ryugaku/1412692.htm (Accessed July 31, 2020)

Kumiko Torikai. 2018. Eigo kyōiku no kiki [The Crisis of English Language Education], Tokyo: Chikuma Shobo.

Levy, Hideo, 1992. *Nihongo no shori* [The Victory of the Japanese Language], Kodansha, 1992.

Mizumura, Minae, 2008. *Nihongo ga horobiru toki: eigo no seiki no naka de* [When the Japanese Language Falls: In the Age of English], Chikuma Shobo.

---2017. "Chuto hanpa na eigo yori, Ichiyo wo yomu yutakasa wo: gengo no shokuminchika ni Nihon hodo mujikaku na kuni wa nai" [The Richness of Reading Ichiyō, Rather Than Incomplete English Ability: There is No Country like Japan So Apathetic Towards Linguistic Colonization]. *Chuo Koron*, Aug., 2017, pp. 26-33.

Nakai, Asako, 2007. *Tasha no jiden: posutokoroniaru bungaku wo yomu* [Autobiography of the Other: Reading Postcolonial Literature], Tokyo: Kenkyusha.

Ostheider, Teja, 2017. "Nihon no tagengoshakai to komyunikeshon: ishiki/seisaku/jittai" [Japanese Multilingual Society and Communication: Consciousness, Policy and Realities], Miyazaki, Satoshi and Sugino, Toshiko eds. *Gurobaruka to gengo seisaku: sasutinaburu na kyoseishakai/gengo kyoiku no kochiku ni mukete* [Globalization and Linguistic Policies: Toward the Establishment of a Sustainable Co-existence Society and Language Education], Akashi Shoten.

Said, Edward W., 2003. *Orientalism*, Penguin: London.

Sakai, Naoki, 2012. *Nihon shiso to iu mondai: hon'yaku to shutai* [Translation & Subjectivity: On "Japan" and Cultural Nationalism], Tokyo: Iwanami Shoten.

Serizawa, Kensuke, 2018. *Konbini gaikokujin* [Convenience Store Foreigners]. Shincho Shinsho.

Shirane, Haruo ed. 2009. New Horizons in Japanese Literary Studies: Canon Formation, *Gender, and Media*, Bensei Publishing.

Tojo, Kazuko, 2010. "Daigaku kokusaika no ashiato wo tadoru: kokusaika no igi wo motomete" [Tracing the Progress of the Globalization of Universities: In Search of the Meaning of Globalization]. *Journal of Osaka Jogakuin University*, Vol. 7.

図1, 2　2019年7月4日のワークショップ「局地的・地域間の潮流」の様子。
Images 1 and 2: Research presentations at the “Local and Global Currents” workshop, 4th July 2019.

図3　2018年5月24日のワークショップ「ジャンル間における題材の転用」のポスター。

Image 3: Poster from the “Adaptation from One Medium to Another” workshop, 24th May 2018.

図4　2019年7月4日のワークショップ「局地的・地域間の潮流」のポスター。

Image 4: Poster from the “Local and Global Currents” workshop, 4th July 2019.

19世紀イギリスの観点から見たグローバル化

筒井 瑞貴

はじめに　グローバル化の歴史

広義のグローバリゼーションの起源については諸説あるが、A. G. ホプキンズ（Hopkins 2002, 3）は、グローバル化の歴史を四つの段階に分類している。国民国家や工業化以前にあたる「前近代的グローバル化」では、海上交易やキャラバン交易を通じて地域間の結びつきが強められた。アジアや中東など非ヨーロッパ世界が重要な担い手となったことも特徴である。17 世紀から 19 世紀にあたる「プロトグローバル化」の段階では、航海技術の発展を背景として、西ヨーロッパ世界が大西洋から世界各地に進出し、三角貿易を成立させ、複数の大陸にまたがる経済システムが生み出された。19 世紀には、産業革命を経て工場制機械工業がもたらされたイギリスをはじめとするヨーロッパ諸国が、政治的・経済的に他の民族や国家への侵略と支配を企て進出する帝国主義政策を積極的に推し進めるなかで「近代グローバル化」へと移行していった。第二次世界大戦後から今日に至るまでの国際化の流れは「ポストコロニアル・グローバル化」として捉えられ、アメリカとソ連の対立構造からその後の国際秩序のもとで、インターネットなど新たなメディアが登場し、デイヴィッド・ハーヴェイがポストモダニズムを特徴づける概念として提唱した、時間的・空間的な「圧縮」（Harvey 1990, 7）がいっそう顕著になっている。本項ではイギリスを中心に近代のグローバル化の歴史について振り返っていきたい。地域間の交流が加速度的に進行した 19 世紀の国際化の展開を、当時の覇権国家であるイギリスを中心に、この時期のグローバル化のもたらした恩恵と弊害を考察することで、今日の我々を取り巻く世界の状況を再考する格好の端緒となるだろう。

1. 工業化と世界経済

ケヴィン・オルークとジェフリー・ウィリアムソンによると、さまざまな商品の価格が収斂され、標準化されていくという意味でのグローバリゼーション

Globalization from the Perspective of 19th Century Britain

Mizuki Tsutsui

Introduction: The History of Globalization

Although there are several theories regarding the origins of globalization, its history can be divided into the following four stages, as described by A. G. Hopkins (2002,3). In the first stage, "archaic globalization", which predates the nation state and industrialization, maritime and caravan trade led to strengthened inter-regional links. This period was also characterized by the significant role played by Asian, Middle Eastern, and other parts of the non-European world. The second stage, "proto-globalization" refers to the process which took place between the 17th and 19th centuries, whereby advancements in navigation technology allowed Western Europe to extend its influence abroad, establishing triangular trade and contributing to the development of complex economic systems that straddled multiple continents. In the 19th century, the countries of Europe, led by Britain, which via the Industrial Revolution had now switched to factory-based machine industry, began to actively pursue imperialist policies through which they aggressively exercised their influence throughout the world, encroaching upon and subjugating other peoples and nations using both political and economic means. This third stage was the period of "modern globalization". The fourth stage, coinciding with the period of internationalization which commenced with the end of the Second World War and continues into the present, is termed "post-colonial globalization", and is characterized by a process through which, against the backdrop of the American-Soviet conflict and the ensuing international order which took its place, and aided by the rise of the Internet and other new media, both temporal and spatial "compression" is becoming increasingly evident, to use the term coined by David Harvey to characterize postmodernism (Harvey 1990,7). In this chapter, I will conduct an overview of the history of globalization in modernity with a focus on the experience of Britain in the 19th century. By considering both the beneficial and detrimental effects of globalization in the context of the 19th century, a period of internationalization characterized by accelerating inter-regional exchange, during which Britain was the hegemonic power, I hope to provide a useful starting point from which we may re-evaluate

は1820年代に始まったという（O’Rourke and Williamson 2002）。世界経済の一体化が推進されていった大きな要因としては、自由主義経済体制下の貿易と大量の移民があげられている。輸送コストや情報の伝達時間を大幅に短縮した鉄道、蒸気船、電信、海底電信もその原動力となった。他国に先んじて工業化に成功したイギリスは世界金融の中心地となり、さらにはイギリス製の電信、船舶、海上保険（ロイズなど）が他国の取引でも用いられるようになり、世界経済のヘゲモニーを掌握した。

2. 余暇の誕生と交通網の拡大

さらに、工業化により人々の所得水準が上昇し、かつては上流階級においてのみ許されていた「余暇」が多くの階級・階層でも享受されるようになる。イギリスでは鉄道網の発展から余暇を観光で費やす人々が誕生した。トーマス・クックはツーリズムを開拓し、イギリス国内の長距離移動からヨーロッパ大陸、さらにはパレスチナやシリア、エジプトなど中東地域へとツアーを拡大した。鉄道や蒸気船は帝国主義政策の一環として積極的に活用される一方、このように商業目的のツーリズムの手段でもあった（玉木 2018,163）。しかしながら、地球規模の交通網の整備によって「移動」が容易になったのは人や交易品だけではない。1817年にインドのカルカッタ周辺で発生したコレラは、駐留していたイギリス軍の移動に伴って瞬く間に世界的な感染爆発となり、中東から東アジア、ヨーロッパやアフリカに伝播し、多数の死者を出した。

3. ナショナリズムと文明化の使命

ナポレオンのエジプト・シリア遠征を受けて、フランス国内ではアフリカ・中東世界やその文化への関心が高まった。19世紀のヨーロッパ美術や文学など芸術分野においては、アラブ･イスラーム文化がしばしば「未開」や「官能的」といったイメージと共に表象された。エドワード・サイードの指摘するように、こうしたロマン主義的な意識のもとで形成された東方趣味・オリエンタリズムは、図式化された「東洋 / 西洋」あるいは「自文化 / 異文化」という二項対立を生み出し、西欧諸国による支配の「様式」（Said 1978, 3）として利用されたことは否定できない。政治・経済面においても同様に、植民地の搾取は、「文

the situation of the present day world we find ourselves in today.

1. Industrialization and the World Economy

According to Kevin O'Rourke and Jeffrey Williamson, globalization, understood as the convergence in price and standardization of various products, can be traced back to the 1820s. (O'Rourke and Williamson 2002) they argue that this integration of the world economy was largely prompted by trade conducted under liberalist economic policies and a massive growth in immigration. This development was fueled by the emergence of modern inventions such as the railway, steamboat, telegraph and submarine telegraph, which all significantly lessened the cost and time constraints of transporting goods and information. Britain, having claimed victory over competing countries in the race for industrialization, became the center of global commerce. Through the worldwide uptake of the British-engineered telegraph and British ships, and the use of British maritime insurance policies (such as Lloyd's) in foreign transactions, Britain was able to tighten its hegemonic grip on the world economy.

2. The Birth of Leisure and Development of the Transportation Network

In addition, industrialization meant a rise in the standard wage, resulting in "leisure", once the preserve of the privileged upper classes, being made available to many people of varying social classes and strata. Furthermore, the development of the railway network in Britain led an increasing number of people to spend their leisure time as tourists. Thomas Cook, the pioneering tourism agency, carried people across the length and breadth of Britain and ferried them overseas to the European continent and beyond, also conducting tours to Palestine, Syria, Egypt and other destinations in the Middle East. The railway and steamboat were thus not only actively enlisted for the purpose of carrying out imperialist policies, but also became the means of commercial tourism (Tamaki 2018,163). However, it was not only the movement of people and goods that was facilitated by the development of a worldwide transport network. Cholera originated in the surroundings of Calcutta, India, in 1817, and was quickly spread via the British soldiers stationed there to various locations all around the world, where it soon became a pandemic of explosive proportions, claiming the lives of many from the Middle East to East Asia, Europe and Africa.

明化の使命」あるいは「白人の責務」といった理念のもと正当化された。また、アジアに関する国家観として、民主化が進む自由主義的な西欧諸国と対照的な「東洋的専制主義」という認識が構築され、その前近代性・後進性が強調され、帝国主義的な植民地支配が思想的に補強された。

4. 19世紀のグローバル化がもたらしたもの――言語・文化帝国主義

積極的な帝国主義政策により世界の経済システムを牛耳った宗主国の言語は、植民地においても広く普及するようになった。特に19世紀の覇権国家であるイギリスの公用語である英語は、北米のみならず、この時期に相次いで植民地化されていったアフリカ、アジア、オセアニア地域の諸国において広まった。イギリスからの移民によってこれらの地域において英語の母語話者の人口が増加し、さらに現地の支配階級のエリート教育の一環としても組み込まれていった。言語的障壁を超えて他者とのコミュニケーションを可能にする媒体として、英語がもたらした恩恵は計り知れないが、その一方で英語圏の国家が政治・経済のみならず文化という側面においても強力な影響力を獲得する上で大きな要因となったこともまた事実である。その状況は英語が事実上の「国際共通語」となった現在も変わらない。このように世界中の国や民族がある言語によって実質的に支配されている状況を批判的に捉えて「言語帝国主義」と呼ばれることがある。

5. ヴィクトリア朝文学作品にみるグローバル化の受容

19世紀の文学作品には様々な形でグローバル化が描かれている。例えば、ジュール・ヴェルヌの『八十日間世界一周』(1873) では、交通手段の飛躍的な発展により「小さくなった」地球を移動する主人公が描かれる。同時に、一地方・国家の枠組みにとらわれない「世界市民」あるいは「国際人」を自称する人物がヴィクトリア朝の小説にはしばしば見られるようになる。興味深いことに、多くの場合こうした人物は悪役の一つの典型像として登場しており、ここに当時急速に拡大しつつあったグローバル化に対する反動あるいは潜在的な恐怖感を見出すことができるかもしれない。チャールズ・ディケンズの作品では、18世紀を舞台とした『バーナビー・ラッジ』(1841) の中で、盲人の小悪

3. Nationalism and the Civilizing Mission

Following Napoleon's expeditions into Egypt and Syria, France saw a flowering of interest in the world and culture of Africa and the Middle East. This interest reverberated in the artworks and literature of 19th century Europe, in which Arab and Islamic culture was frequently portrayed together with imagery that suggested an underdeveloped civilization and/or appealed to the carnal senses. It is undeniable that this romantic Western-European longing for the East (i.e. Orientalism), as argued by Edward Said, functioned to reproduce the schematic binaries of "East vs. West" and "own vs. other culture", and was strategically deployed by Western-European nations as a "style" (Said 1978, 3) for dominating the "Orient". The same applies to the political and economic aspects of encounters between the West and East, in which the exploitation of colonies was justified through ideals such as "the civilizing mission" and "the white man's burden". Meanwhile, the construct of "oriental despotism" became the standard Western interpretation of the Asian nation, which, in contrast to the liberal and democratizing Western-European nations, was characterized by premodernity and backwardness, providing logical argumentation to support their imperialist colonization policies.

4. Linguistic and Cultural Imperialism as the Heritage of 19th Century Globalization

As Britain tightened its grip upon the world economic system through the active pursuit of imperialist policies, the language of the suzerain spread widely throughout its colonies. English, its official language, particularly during the period of Britain's hegemony in the 19th century, spread far beyond North America into the various colonized regions of Africa, Asia and Oceania. Not only did the population of native English speakers increase in these regions as a result of emigration from Britain, but the language was also incorporated into the education of colonial elites. As a medium which has enabled communication between people of differing backgrounds, overcoming the language barriers that had previously separated them, the benefits bestowed by English and its spread cannot be overstated. However, it is also a fact that the spread of English has also contributed greatly to the English-speaking nations' acquisition of immense global influence, not only in political and economic terms but also with regards to culture. That situation remains the same today, even as English has become the

党スタッグが「おれは世界市民でね。[. . .] おれの振る舞いが無礼に見えたとしても、そのせいなんだ」(Dickens 1986, 422) と発言し、『リトル・ドリット』(1857) では残忍な悪党のリゴーが、「私は国際人だ。これという祖国はない。父親はスイス人――ヴォー州の出だ。母親は血筋はフランス人で、生まれはイギリスだ。私はベルギーで生まれた。世界市民なのだ」(Dickens 2008, 8) と述べている。トマス・ハーディの『熱のない人』(1881) でも、私生児で陰謀家のウィリアム・デアが似たようなバックグラウンドを持っている。「おれは世界市民なんだ。どの国にも愛国心を持ついわれはないし、どの国王や女王にもひれ伏しはしない。国境のない国に属している者こそが、本当の紳士なんだ」(Hardy 1907, 161)

このような類型の悪役でおそらく最も有名で印象深いのは、ウィルキー・コリンズの『白衣の女』(1860) に登場するフォスコ伯爵だろう。前述の3人と同様に「世界市民」と自らを称するフォスコは、「私ほどの歳になると、どの美徳が正しく、どの美徳が間違っているのか、困惑してしまいます。イギリスにはイギリスの美徳がある。中国には中国の美徳がある」(Collins 1985, 256-257) と、イギリス的価値観を相対化してみせる。これに対して善良で聡明なマリアン・ハルカムが反論する際に引き合いに出すのは、前項で述べた「東洋的専制主義」の論理そのものである。「お説はもっともですが、イギリスにはあって、中国には欠けている確かな美徳が一つあります。中国の権力者は、いわれのない口実の下に、無辜の民を殺しております。私たちの国イギリスは、その類の罪とは無縁です――そのような恐ろしい罪は犯しません。見境のない流血沙汰を心の底から忌み嫌っているのです」(Collins 1985, 257) フォスコは彼女の意見を認めながらも、「ジョン・ブル (引用者注: 典型的イギリス人の名)」は「隣人の欠点を見つけるのは誰よりも早いが、自分自身の欠点を見つけるのは誰よりも遅い」(Collins 1985, 257-258) と、重ねてその自文化中心主義的な価値観に疑義を呈している。

フォスコ伯爵のような「世界市民」の登場人物たちが標榜する言説から浮かび上がってくるのは、自文化の常識や道徳律に拘束されることのないイギリス国民にとっての「他者」の存在と、それに対して抱かれた潜在的な恐怖だろう。物理的な移動や情報の伝達手段の飛躍的な向上により、国家や共同体の価値観

de-facto language of choice for international communication. This state of affairs, in which countries and peoples all over the world are in effect dominated by a specific language, is sometimes critically referred to as "linguistic imperialism".

5. Reading Responses to Globalization in Victorian Fiction

Globalization is depicted in various forms throughout 19th century works of fiction. The protagonists of Jules Verne's *Around the World in Eighty Days* (1873), for example, are described travelling around a world which had "become small" due to massive strides in locomotion. Similarly, Victorian-era novels are notable for the frequent appearance of a self-professed "citizen of the world" or "metropolitan": a character who is unbound by the constraints of a single region or nation. Interestingly, in many cases such characters feature as a stereotypical villain, which could be read as a backlash against, if not a subconscious fear of the rapid spread of globalization as it was recognized at the time.

Looking at the works of Charles Dickens, for example, in *Barnaby Rudge* (1841), which is set in the 18th century, we find the cunning blind man Stagg, who announces: "I am a citizen of the world, [...] and if I seem to conduct myself with freedom, it is therefore" (Dickens 1986, 422). Likewise, *Little Dorrit* (1857) features a cold-hearted villain called Rigaud, who proclaims: "I am a cosmopolitan gentleman. I own no particular country. My father was Swiss—Canton de Vaud. My mother was French by blood, English by birth. I myself was born in Belgium. I am a citizen of the world" (Dickens 2008, 8). Thomas Hardy's *A Laodicean* (1881) also features a character with a similar background—the bastard conspirator William Dare, who says: "I am a citizen of the world. I owe no country patriotism, and no king or queen obedience. A man whose country has no boundary is your only true gentleman" (Hardy 1907, 161).

Among these stereotypical villains, Count Fosco of Wilkie Collins' *The Woman in White* (1860) is surely one of the most famous and memorable of them all. Like the three characters mentioned above, Fosco also refers to himself as a "citizen of the world", but he also goes further, relativizing British values as follows: "I am puzzled, in my old age, to say which is the right sort [of virtue] and which is the wrong. Here, in England, there is one virtue. And there, in China, there is another virtue." (Collins 1985, 256-257) In response to this, the good-natured and intelligent Marian Halcombe counters with the exact same kind of logic introduced above: "oriental despotism". She says to him: "Accepting

を揺るがしうる異質な「他者」との接触は避けられないものとなった。その脅威を封じ込めるべく、悪徳、未開、幼稚、前近代的といった劣等性を喚起するイメージが用いられたのはすでに見た通りである。特定の地域や社会集団に帰属することを拒否する「世界市民」は、こうした二項対立的な思考的枠組みをも放棄しているがゆえに、イギリスという「自己」の孕む様々な矛盾や欺瞞を容赦なく明るみに出す。グローバル化とは「他者」との交流の拡大のプロセスであるが、その中で同時に「自己」そのものと対峙し問い直すことを促さずにはおかない。政治、経済、文化など多面的な次元で急速に展開し、世界の「一体化」を推し進めながらも、支配・被支配の枠組みの中で構築された歪な19世紀のグローバリズムのもたらした功罪を考察することは、現代の世界をめぐる諸問題と向き合ううえで有益な視座を与えてくれるだろう。

your illustration, surely we have one unquestionable virtue in England which is wanting in China. The Chinese authorities kill thousands of innocent people on the most frivolous pretexts. We in England are free from all guilt of that kind—we commit no such dreadful crime—we abhor reckless bloodshed with all our hearts." (Collins 1985, 257) Fosco accepts Halcombe's view, but he also notes: "John Bull [the typical Englishman] does abhor the crimes of John Chinaman. He is the quickest old gentleman at finding out faults that are his neighbours', and the slowest old gentleman at finding out the faults that are his own," (Collins 1985, 257-258) further undermining the ethnocentrism of her argument.

The discourse espoused by Count Fosco and other self-professed "citizens of the world" in Victorian fiction makes it possible to infer the awareness and subconscious fear that was aroused by the existence of "others" who were not bound by British cultural norms and moral codes. The massive strides achieved in physical transportation and communication technology had made it impossible to avoid encounters with the "other", people whose very existence threatened to disturb the previously established value systems of the state and community. That images which implied various forms of inferiority, such as immorality, savagery, infantility and premodernity were used to contain this threat is a fact that hardly needs repeating. The "citizen of the world" in Victorian fiction, who not only refuses to belong to any specific region or social group, but has also discarded such a binary framework, remorselessly exposes the various contradictions and duplicities embodied by Britain's "self". Globalization is a process by which encounters with the "other" are multiplied, but it is also one that compels a confrontation with and re-examination of the "self". The distorted guise of 19th century globalism, which, while rapidly progressing on political, economic, and cultural fronts to further realize the "oneness" of the world, was constructed within a framework of domination and subjugation, provides much food for thought. To consider both the good and the bad which it unleashed is surely meaningful groundwork which can help us to face up to the various problems concerning the contemporary world.

(Translated by Thomas Brook and Mizuki Tsutsui)

参考文献

Collins, Wilkie. (1860) 1985. *The Woman in White*. Harmondsworth: Penguin.

Dickens, Charles. (1841) 1986. *Barnaby Rudge*. Harmondsworth: Penguin.

---. (1857) 2008. *Little Dorrit*. Oxford: Oxford University Press.

Hardy, Thomas. (1881) 1907. *A Laodicean: A Story of To-day*. London: Macmillan.

Harvey, David. (1989) 1990. *The Condition of Postmodernity: An Enquiry into the Origins of Cultural Change*. Oxford: Blackwell.

Hopkins, A. G., editor. 2002. *Globalization in World History*. New York: Norton.

O' Rourke, Kevin H., and Jeffrey G. Williamson. 1999. *Globalization and History: The Evolution of a Nineteenth-Century Atlantic Economy*. Cambridge: MIT Press.

Said, Edward. 1978. *Orientalism*. New York: Pantheon Books.

玉木俊明. 2018.『ヨーロッパ 繁栄の19世紀史: 消費社会・植民地・グローバリゼーション』東京: 筑摩書房.

Bibliography

Collins, Wilkie. (1860) 1985. *The Woman in White*. Harmondsworth: Penguin.

Dickens, Charles. (1841) 1986. *Barnaby Rudge*. Harmondsworth: Penguin.

---. (1857) 2008. *Little Dorrit*. Oxford: Oxford University Press.

Hardy, Thomas. (1881) 1907. *A Laodicean: A Story of To-day*. London: Macmillan.

Harvey, David. (1989) 1990. *The Condition of Postmodernity: An Enquiry into the Origins of Cultural Change*. Oxford: Blackwell.

Hopkins, A. G., editor. 2002. *Globalization in World History*. London: Pimlico.

O'Rourke, Kevin H., and Jeffrey G. Williamson. 1999. *Globalization and History: The Evolution of a Nineteenth-Century Atlantic Economy*. Cambridge: MIT Press.

Said, Edward. 1978. *Orientalism*. New York: Pantheon Books.

Tamaki, Toshiaki. 2018. *Yōroppa han'ei no 19 seiki shi: shōhi shakai/shokuminchi/gurōbarizeishon* [Europe—A History of its 19th Century Prosperity: Consumer Society, Colonies and Globalization]. Chikuma Shobō.

「グローバル化」の時代における「世界文学」

尾田 知子

第一部　概観

1．英語圏（西欧・西洋）の「世界文学」概念の変遷

「世界文学」という語は長年、世界各国の文学の集積を指して使用されてきた。しかし、英語圏において「世界各国の文学」としてリストに挙げられてきたのは、主としてヨーロッパ圏の正典と呼ばれる文学作品であった。日本で出版されている「世界文学全集」等のシリーズの大半も、欧米をはじめとする海外の文学中心のラインナップであり、日本文学を含む欧米圏以外の文学作品はごく少数しか収録されていないことが多い。「世界文学」はきわめてヨーロッパ（すなわち白人）中心に展開されてきたと言っても過言ではない。

その傾向に一定の変革をもたらしたのが、ゲーテ（1749-1832）の「世界文学」の概念である。彼は、国民・民族固有の特性を描いた「国民文学」を深化させることで、時代や民族といった制約から脱却し、その枠組みを越えたところに誕生する「世界文学」を志向した（三浦 2013, 217）。元はスエズ運河やライン川とドナウ川の連結への期待から、世界規模での人的交流を思い描き着想された（日地谷 1996, 113）ゲーテの「世界文学」の概念は、結果として「全世界の文学の総量」という従来の意味を問い直し、ヨーロッパ以外の国の文学にも光を当てた。

いわばゲーテ自身にとっての「他者」を世界に向けて伝達する文学的試みとも呼ぶべき「世界文学」は、「世界文学」概念の変遷史において重要な転換点と言えよう。

2．デイヴィッド・ダムロッシュの「世界文学」と翻訳の役割

「他者」への眼差しを包含したゲーテの「世界文学」の流れを汲みつつ、「グローバル化」の時代における「世界文学」の位置づけを大きく変えたと言えるのが、比較文学者デイヴィッド・ダムロッシュである。著書『世界文学とは何

“World Literature” in the Age of “Globalization”

Tomoko Oda

Part 1: Overview

1. The History of the Term “World Literature” in the Anglophone (Western European) World

The term “world literature” has long been used to refer to an amalgamation of the literature of all the various countries of the world. However, in the English-speaking world, this “literature of all the various countries of the world” has traditionally referred primarily to those works considered to be the literary canon of Europe. This is reflected in Japanese publications such as the *Collection of World Literature (Sekai bungaku zenshū)* series, in which the majority of volumes are concerned mainly with European, American, and other foreign works of literature, with works outside of the European-American canon, including works of Japanese literature, often not even receiving a mention. It is no exaggeration to say that the term “world literature” has therefore in practice been developed along distinctly Euro-centric (i.e. Caucasian-centric) lines.

The first major change to this model was enacted by Goethe (1749-1832) and his notion of *Weltliteratur*. Goethe believed that by nurturing the development of national literatures, which were concerned with the unique qualities of specific nations and/or peoples, it would be possible to eventually break free from the constraints of era and ethnicity, and it was in this context that the *Weltliteratur* he pursued came into being (Miura 2013, 217). Goethe’s *Weltliteratur* vision, supposedly inspired by the hope he invested in the development of the Suez Canal and Rhine-Danube Canal, was based upon the intermingling of people from all around the world on a global scale (Hijiya 1996, 113). It resulted in the heretofore notion of “world literature” as “the amalgamation of the world’s literature” being brought into question and cast a new light on the literatures of non-European countries.

Goethe’s notion of *Weltliteratur*, which could be characterized as a literary project embarked upon by the author to communicate his respective “others” to the rest of the world, marks an important turning point in the history of the

か？』（2011）でダムロッシュは、「世界文学とは、把握しがたい無数の正典のことではなく、流通や読みのモードだ」（17）と説いている。ここで彼は、存在論的な「正典の集積」から方法論的な「流通や読みのモード」へと「世界文学」の定義を転換させている。

さらに、「流通や読みのモード」としての「世界文学」においては、原語テクストの精読だけでなく、様々な言語に翻訳されたテクストを使用しての文学研究も可能となる。ダムロッシュによって提唱される「世界文学」は、時代や民族などの制約から文学作品を解き放ち、様々なバックグラウンドを持つ世界各国の読者一人ひとりに、「世界文学」という多種多様な読み方の可能性を拓いた。この点で、ダムロッシュの「世界文学」は、原語テクストはもちろん、翻訳テクストを通じて文学のより豊かな受容を可能にするものであり、「グローバル化」の時代における文学研究をさらに多様化・活性化させる「ブースター」的概念であると言えよう。

第二部　専門的な視点

「流通と読みのモード」としての「世界文学」：村上春樹作品の英訳テクストの場合

翻訳を通して国境を越え流通するダムロッシュの「世界文学」のうち、日本人作家による作品の最たる一例として、村上春樹（b. 1949）の小説が挙げられることは論をまたない。日本だけでなく欧米諸国でも人気を博す一因は、ニューヨークを海外出版の拠点としたことであろう。作品は世界各国の言語に翻訳され、次々にベストセラーとなっている。

「プリ＝トランスレーション（前＝翻訳）」（日地谷＝キルシュネライト 2011, 121）[1]という概念を用いて、村上作品の越境性を裏付けているのが、日本文学研究の大家であるイルメラ・日地谷＝キルシュネライトである。日本における共通知識の説明から物語を始めている森鷗外（1862-1922）の『百物

[1]「プリ=トランスレーション（前=翻訳）」（pretranslation）の日本語訳は湊圭史訳（2011）に従った。以下の他の引用はすべてHijiya-Kirschnereit（2012）からの拙訳による。

concept of "world literature".

2. David Damrosch's "World Literature" and the Role of Translation

The contemporary conception of "world literature" in the current age of globalization surely owes much to the work of David Damrosch, the scholar of comparative literature who has drawn from and developed upon Goethe's notion of *Weltliteratur*, notable for its incorporation of the other's point of view. In *What is World Literature?* (2003), Damrosch puts forward the following thesis: "[W] orld literature is not an infinite, ungraspable canon of works but rather a mode of circulation and of reading" (5). By proposing the methodology of a specific "mode of circulation and of reading" rather than an ontological "collection of canonical works", Damrosch inverted the standard definition of "world literature".

Furthermore, "world literature", when understood as a "mode of circulation and of reading", paves the way for new avenues of literary research, which are not simply concerned with the close reading of an original text but also take into account its translations into various other languages. The notion of "world literature" proposed by Damrosch frees the individual literary text from the constraints of era and ethnicity and provides individual readers, of various backgrounds all over the world, with the opportunity to engage with its highly diverse "mode of reading". In this sense, Damrosch's "world literature" has enriched the potential of literary texts to reach and impact readers, not only in their original form but also through their translations, and it can thus be considered as a kind of "booster" concept, a catalyst for the continuing diversification and energization of literary research in the age of "globalization".

Part 2: A Closer Look

"World Literature" as a "Mode of Circulation and of Reading": Haruki Murakami in English Translation

One of the most representative examples of "world literature" produced by a Japanese author, that is, in Damrosch's terms, as a process of circulation beyond national borders via the medium of translation, is without a doubt the novels of Haruki Murakami (b. 1949). The great popularity enjoyed by Murakami not only in Japan but also throughout Europe and America probably originates in the fact that New York has been the base of operations for the publication of his

語』（1911）や、仏教哲学の詳説を多分に含む三島由紀夫（1925-70）の四部作『豊饒の海』（1965-71）と同様に、村上作品は「日本語というよりもむしろ英語として自然な言い回し、比喩表現、身振り」（Hijiya-Kirschnereit 2012, 173）や徹底的な主語の表出、日本文化に依存した語の最小限の使用によって「前＝翻訳」されている、すなわち、あたかも外国語（とりわけ英語）に翻訳されることを念頭に置いているかのようにテクストが編まれているというのが、日地谷＝キルシュネライトの指摘するところだ。

文学の世界市場における「他者」とも呼ぶべき日本人作家によって編まれた文学テクストの世界的流通を促す「前＝翻訳」の問題点は、「グローバル化」における英語中心主義の問題と密接に関連している。村上の長編小説『ねじまき鳥クロニクル』（1994-95）が、アメリカ人翻訳者によって英訳される際、「アメリカの読者の好みや基準に合わせるため、多くのエピソードや場面が切り詰められ、修正され」（173-74）たが、村上自身もその大幅な改稿に肯定的なスタンスを取っていた。日地谷＝キルシュネライトはそのことに触れ、「グローバル化」におけるコミュニケーションのツールとしての英語使用は不可避としながらも、アメリカ／英語中心主義を支持するかのような村上の姿勢を批判している（174）。

したがって、「前＝翻訳」は諸刃の剣とも呼ぶべき現象である。一方では、文学の世界市場を通じて、作品が広く受容され、議論されることに寄与する。しかし他方では、自作品の翻訳の主要な読者層として、英米の英語話者を念頭に置いた文学者によるテクストは、ダムロッシュも指摘するアメリカ中心の出版市場のヘゲモニー構造（ダムロッシュ 2011, 36）に荷担することとなる。英語圏（村上の場合は特にアメリカ）中心の英語話者を念頭に置くことで、前翻訳が「他者」、つまり英語圏の英語話者以外の読者を遮断してしまうことも多分にありうる。

しかしながら、自作品の英訳出版に対する村上の「自由放任主義」とも言うべき姿勢は、翻訳者への全幅の信頼と、翻訳作品を原文テクストから独立した作品として尊重する態度の証左でもある。一時は原文に対する従属的な位置づけに甘んじていた翻訳テクストを通じて、世界規模での流通が可能になっていることから、「前＝翻訳」された村上作品はダムロッシュの「世界文学」のヴ

works abroad. Murakami's novels have been translated into many languages and published in various countries throughout the world, frequently becoming bestsellers.

Veteran scholar of Japanese literature, Irmela Hijiya-Kirschnereit has enlisted the notion of "pretranslation" to describe the border-crossing nature of Murakami's work. Like *A Hundred Tales* (1911) by Ogai Mori (1862-1922), which opens with an explanation of what in Japan is common knowledge, and *The Sea of Fertility* (1965-71) by Yukio Mishima (1925-70), which contains numerous explanations regarding Buddhist philosophy; Murakami's works, according to Hijiya-Kirschnereit, have been "pretranslated". In Murakami's case, this is achieved by the use of "expressions, figures of speech, and gestures that seem more English than Japanese" (Hijiya-Kirschnereit 2012, 173), the comprehensive use of the grammatical subject, and the absolute minimal use of words that are culturally specific to Japan, all of which suggest that they have been written with a strong awareness that they will be translated into a foreign language (specifically English).

The problematics of "pretranslation" as a process that facilitates the worldwide circulation of the literary texts written by a Japanese author, who could be called an "other" on the global literary market, are closely linked with the problematics of the English-centrism of "globalization". When Murakami's novel *The Wind-up Bird Chronicle* (1994-95) was translated into English by an American translator, "the shortening and straightening out of a number of episodes and scenes in order to adapt the work to American readers' tastes and standards" (ibid. 173-4) was undertaken, and Murakami himself approved of this heavy-handed approach. Hijiya-Kirschnereit, although noting the unavoidability of using English as a communication tool in the context of "globalization", criticizes Murakami's stance towards the English translations of his work as being an implicit display of support for American/English-centrism (ibid. 174).

Therefore, the phenomenon of "pretranslation" should be considered something of a double-edged sword. On one hand, it contributes to a literary work's potential to be widely read and discussed by facilitating its circulation on the global literary market. On the other hand, a text that is written by a writer conscious of its future translation, and who chiefly has Anglo-American English-speaking readers in mind, is inevitably complicit with the ethnocentric hegemonic structure of the American publishing marketplace as indicated by Damrosch (2003, 18). By giving

ァリエーションであるといえよう。「世界文学」としての村上作品は、原文だけでなく翻訳テクストを通じて、世界中の多様な読者（英語圏諸国の英語話者に対して「他者」とみなされてきた様々な言語的バックグラウンドを持つ人々を含む）を獲得し、「グローバル化」社会そのものを体現するかのように、広く受容されているのである。

参考文献

デイヴィッド・ダムロッシュ『世界文学とは何か？』秋草俊一郎他訳（国書刊行会、2011年）

Hijiya-Kirschnereit Irmela (2012) Pretranslation in modern Japanese literature and what it tells us about “world literature.” *Translation and translation studies in the Japanese context*, pp. 167–82. Sato-Rossberg N, Wakabayashi J, eds. London: Continuum.

日地谷＝キルシュネライト　イルメラ「日本文学は世界文学たりうるか？」『日本研究・京都会議』III, 1996年, 112–16頁.

日地谷=キルシュネライト　イルメラ「「世界文学」に応ずる日本文学—プリ=トランスレーションなどの戦術について」湊圭史訳『トランスレーション・スタディーズ』佐藤=ロスベアグ・ナナ編, 2011年, 119–34頁.

三浦國泰「今日の視点から見たゲーテの「世界文学」概念—世界文学の新たなパラダイムを求めて—」成蹊大学文学部紀要, 第48号, 2013年, 217–31頁.

Anglophone readers (in Murakami's case specifically American readers) pride of place, pretranslation easily runs the risk of cutting off "others", that is, readers other than the English speakers of the Anglophone world.

However, the above problematics notwithstanding, Murakami's almost "laissez-faire" attitude towards the publication of English translations of his work is also evidence of the unlimited trust that he places in his translators and his respect for the translated work as a unique quantity, which exists independently of the original text. In the sense that his works are able to circulate on a global scale via the translated text, something which has traditionally submitted to a subordinate status with regard to the original, Murakami's "pretranslated" works could be considered a variation of Damrosch's "world literature". Murakami's works, as an example of "world literature", not only in their original form but also through the medium of translation, have succeeded in capturing a great variety of readers (including readers of diverse linguistic backgrounds, who have long been perceived as "others" by the English speakers of the Anglophone world), and, as though they were the very manifestation of "globalization" itself, continue to enjoy a wide reception all throughout the world.

(Translated by Thomas Brook and Tomoko Oda)

Bibliography

Damrosch, David (2003) *What is World Literature?* Princeton University Press.

Hijiya-Kirschnereit Irmela (2012) Pretranslation in modern Japanese literature and what it tells us about "world literature." *Translation and translation studies in the Japanese context*, pp. 167-82. Sato-Rossberg N, Wakabayashi J, eds. London: Continuum.

--- (1996) "Nihon bungaku wa sekai bungaku tariuru ka?" [Can Japanese literature become world literature?] *Nihon kenkyū: Kyoto kaigi*, Vol. 3, pp. 112-6.

Miura, Kuniyasu (2013) "Kyō no shiten kara mita Gēte no 'sekai bungaku' gainen—sekai bungaku no arata na paradaimu wo motomete—" [Goethe's notion of 'world literature' from a contemporary perspective—seeking a new paradigm for world literature.] *Seijō daigaku bungakubu kiyō*, Vol. 48, pp. 217-31.

映画と／におけるグローカリゼーション

中村 紀彦

第一部　グローカリゼーションとはなんだったのか

映画はつねに「他者」であり続け、つねに「他者」を独自の方法で捉え続けてきた。そして映画は、グローバリゼーションの移動システムと流通のネットワークと手を取りあい、同時にローカルな受容や生産と戦略的に手を結んできた。そのことを「グローカリゼーション」の観点から確認するのが本稿のひとまずの目的だ。

そもそも、グローカリゼーションとはなんだったのか。この概念は、1980年代に日本企業が海外進出の際に使用したケースが発端となっている。グローバルな流通の状況下で、日本の自社製品を現地（ローカル）の嗜好や文化のニーズに適応させた製品を販売し、浸透させていった。グローバルな商品にするために、ローカルな「味付け」を加えたのだ。この経済用語としてのグローカリゼーションは、1991年に社会学者ローランド・ロバートソンによって学術的理解と価値を与えられた（ロバートソン 1997）。彼は「土着化（vernacularize）」という言葉に触発されて練り直し、この概念をグローバルとローカルの相互浸透であると簡潔に述べたのだ。ただし、社会人類学者の上杉富之によれば、現在はこうした使用方法は政治学や経済学で支配的ではあるが、社会学および人類学領域では若干異なるという（上杉 2014、7）。そこで上杉は、ロバートソンの定義を踏まえながらつぎのように再定義している。

> グローカリゼーションとは、グローバリゼーションないしグローバル化した要素の影響を受けて、グローバリゼーションと同時ないしそれに連続して起こるローカリゼーションを含んだ一連の現象ないし過程のことであり、特に 1）グローバリゼーションとローカリゼーションが同時ないし連続して起こること（同時進行性）と、2）グローバリゼーションとローカリゼーションが相互に作用・影響を及ぼすこと（相互作用性）に注目し、強調する概念である。（上杉 2014、7）

Glocalization and/in Cinema

Norihiko Nakamura

Part 1: What is Glocalization Anyway?

The medium of cinema, since its conception, has always coexisted with the "other" and interpreted the "other" in its own distinct way. Cinema has also strategically joined hands with both the high mobility and circulation network of globalization and local systems of distribution and production. My aim in this chapter is to consider this aspect of the cinema from the perspective of "glocalization".

First, it's necessary to return to the question of what glocalization actually is. The term originated in the 1980s, when it was used to refer to the entry of Japanese industries into foreign markets. Under the conditions of the global circulation of goods, Japanese in-house manufactured products were tailored to the specific tastes and cultural needs of overseas (local) markets, throughout which they then took root. In order to design a global product, local "flavour" was added. In 1991, sociologist Roland Robertson granted academic recognition and value to the term (Robertson 1992), which had previously only been used in the context of business. Taking inspiration from the word "vernacularize", he reinvented "glocalization" to mean, concisely, the interpenetration of the global and local. However, according to social anthropologist Tomiyuki Uesugi, while such an interpretation is now dominant in the fields of politics and economics, use of the term in sociology and anthropology carries a slightly different nuance (Uesugi 2014, 7). Building upon Robertson's definition, Uesugi provides his own as follows:

> Glocalization refers to a series of phenomena or processes which exhibit aspects of localization and are either influenced by globalization or globalized elements and/or occur simultaneously or sequentially with them; the notion draws attention to and emphasizes, in particular, 1) the co-occurrence or continuity between globalization and localization (*simultaneity*) and 2) the interaction and influence that is mutually exerted between globalization and localization (*mutual interaction*). (Uesugi 2014, 7)

上杉によると、グローカリゼーションは、グローバリゼーションとローカリゼーションの相互作用性だけでなく、同時進行性もまた具えているというのだ。

こうしたグローカリゼーションの具体例として、バンコクのショッピングモール「ターミナル21」を挙げておこう。この巨大な商業施設は、名称の通り国際空港をコンセプトにしている。ここに来ればだれもが世界を一挙に堪能できる。地下にはカリブとパリ、1階は東京、2階はロンドン、そして最上階にはハリウッドと称される映画館がある。海外のブロックバスター映画を堪能し、腹ごしらえにタイのローカルフードなどに舌鼓を打ち、東京の商店街を模したブースで買い物をする。階層ごとに異なる国や諸文化を過剰に意識した装飾が施されている。ここは、ひとつの場所にローカルな事象が折りたたまれたフィクショナルな空間であり、同時にパスポートなしで旅行者やバンコクの住人たちを招き入れる過剰にグローバルな「国際空港」だ。これはグローカリゼーションの端的な例であり、グローバル／ローカルの同時進行と相互浸透が共犯して存続することの証左でもあるだろう。

このようにタイの「ターミナル21」を引き合いに出す理由は、グローバリゼーションの事例はとりわけ欧米中心主義的であり、一方でローカルな事例は、際立ってローカルなものがグローバルの時流に沿って評価された例として検証されることが多く、それらのあいだにあるグラデーション（グローカリゼーション）に注目することが重要だと強調したかったからだ。では、グローバル／ローカルの二項対立を問題視し、そのあいだのグラデーションを見極める態度はどのようにして可能か。

第二部　映画とグローカリゼーション

興味深いことに、そもそも映画というメディアは、つねにすでにグローバルとローカルのせめぎ合う磁場のもとでしか存在しえなかった。19世紀終盤、リュミエール兄弟によってシネマトグラフによる映画上映が実現した。かれらは工場を出入りする労働者たちを捉え、列車の到着を映し出した。映画は、はじめからグローバルなひととモノの流動を象徴し、その動向の加速と拡大を予告してきたのである。

According to Uesugi, glocalization does not only concern the mutual interaction between globalization and localization but is also characterized by simultaneity.

The "Terminal 21" shopping mall in Bangkok serves as a concrete example of this kind of glocalization. As the name suggests, this mega-sized shopping complex is designed with the concept of an international airport. Visitors are given the opportunity to sample the entire world in a single swoop. In the basement is the Caribbean and Paris, on the first floor Tokyo, on the second floor London and on the top floor of the building is a cinema bearing the name Hollywood. Visitors can enjoy an international blockbuster and then fill their bellies with the finger-licking delights of local Thai food before doing their shopping in booths that are modelled on Tokyo's commercial strip. Each floor is characterized by ornamentation that is excessively conscious of various different countries and cultures. Here is a fictional space in which various local things have been folded up on top of one another to fit into a single building; while simultaneously an over-the-top global "international airport" that tourists and Bangkok citizens alike are free to enter without even having to present their passport. This is an extreme example of glocalization, and it could also be considered as proof that the simultaneous progression and interpenetration of the global and local exist in a state of complicity and mutual dependence.

The reason I mention Thailand's "Terminal 21" here is to emphasize the importance of the gradation (glocalization) which is found between the local and the global, as analyses of globalization tend to be particularly Euro-America-centric, and many enquiries into local phenomena tend to focus primarily on the way in which the local adjusts to the temporal flow of the global. So, how can we then overcome the binary opposition of global/local and bring the gradation in between into focus?

Part 2: Cinema and Glocalization

An interesting facet of the medium of cinema is that it has always already found its only raison d'être within the field of tension generated by the competing global and local. The projection of film was first realized at the end of the 19th century with the Lumière brothers' invention of the Cinématographe. The Lumière brothers captured workers leaving and entering their factory; they filmed the arrival of trains. From its conception, cinema has always symbolized the fluid

その一方で、リュミエール兄弟は世界中へキャメラマンを派遣し、各地のローカルな現象や儀礼や人々の生活をキャメラマンに撮影させたことで知られている。兄弟が生み出したのは「ネットワーク」である。撮影フィルムを世界中で上映する環境を生み出したのだ[1]。かれらの映画は辺境の他者と文化を映し出し、時には移民たちの郷愁をかき立てた。つまり映画は、スクリーンや劇場という装置によって、「他者と出会う」という体験をほかのメディアよりも際立たせた。映画を取り巻くグローカルな状況とは、映画が国境や人種や時空間さえも越境し、このように「他者」と出会うメディアとして、あるいはつねに「他者」として存在するメディアとしてあり続けたからに他ならない。

映画がまずもってグローカリゼーションの産物であることは、さまざまなかたちで強調されてきた。たとえば「古典的ハリウッド映画」の時期は、アメリカ映画の諸形式が世界各国に伝達・浸透した事実を象徴している。映画の普遍性が、まさにグローバルな状況において仮想的に確立されてしまった。そして、映画の普遍性＝古典的ハリウッド映画の諸形式こそ、特定のナショナル・アイデンティティや国家を標榜するナショナル・シネマの存在を強化し続けてきたのだ。非欧米圏や周縁とみなされた国々へと越境した「普遍性」は、各国の映画産業で異物としての「他者」とみなされることはほとんどなかった。ナショナル・シネマやローカルな映画作品は、この「普遍性」を大いに消化吸収して強度を高め、グローバルな経済状況との親和性を獲得して流通していったのだ。その結果、逆説的に、現在はハリウッド映画が世界そのものを象徴する時代ではなくなった。いまやハリウッド映画は、ローカルのヴァリエーションに過ぎないのだ[2]。

映画研究者の川口恵子がいうように、グローバル化の促進による映画製作の

[1] たとえば日本国内では、フランス文学研究者の蓮實重彦らを中心に、リュミエール兄弟が派遣したキャメラマンの一人であるガブリエル・ヴェールの調査が独自に進んでいる。彼は日本をはじめとする世界中を飛び回り、各地のローカルな事象や文化を撮影した。その撮影された映像は世界各地で作品として受容された。蓮實重彦編『リュミエール元年——ガブリエル・ヴェールと映画の歴史』（筑摩書房、1995年）に詳しい。

[2] 日本におけるこうした映画動向の成果は、御園生涼子『映画と国民国家——1930年代松竹メロドラマ』（東京大学出版会、2012年）や藤木秀明『映画観客とは何者か——メディアと社会主体の近現代史』（名古屋大学出版会、2019年）が詳しい。

movement of people and things on a global scale and foretold the acceleration and expansion of that process.

On the other hand, the Lumière brothers are also known for having dispatched cameramen around the world to capture the sights of local phenomena, rituals, and day-to-day life. The brothers gave birth to a "network", that is, they created an environment in which the films they produced would be projected at locations worldwide[1]. Their films showed audiences their distant "others" and their cultures, and sometimes they appealed to the nostalgia of immigrants for their homelands. Through the projection of film onto the screens of theaters, cinema, more than any other media, brought "the encounter with the other" into focus. This is because of none other than the global conditions surrounding the cinema that allowed it to overcome the borders and boundaries of nation, race, and even time and space, and the fact that it has always existed as a media in which encounters with the "other" take place, or rather that has always existed as an "other" itself.

The idea that cinema is essentially a product of glocalization is something that has already been asserted in various forms. For instance, the fact that a period of cinema history is classified as "The Classical Hollywood Cinema" is symbolic of the fact that the various forms of American cinema were transmitted to and adopted in other countries all around the world. Through this process, conditions that could only be described as "global" saw the "universality" of cinema being propped up as an imaginary construct. And then, it is none other than this supposed universality of cinema (i.e. the forms of the classical Hollywood cinema) that has provided the means for national cinemas, which claim to represent a certain national identity or nation state, to assert their own presence. The "universality" of Hollywood cinema, which crossed over into non-European regions and countries that were otherwise considered peripheral, was hardly ever marked out as an alien "other" within their national film industries. National cinema and other locally produced film were able to digest and consume that "universality" and further

[1] For example, research on Gabriel Veyre, one of the cameramen dispatched by the Lumière brothers, has been advanced specifically within Japan mainly through the efforts of Shigehiko Hasumi, scholar of French literature. Veyre flew to Japan and various other locations around the world, capturing the local things and culture of his destinations on film. His films were then projected and appreciated as artworks in France and other countries worldwide. See Hasumi, Shigehiko. *Lumière gannen: Gabriel Veyre to eiga no rekishi* [The Lumière Era Begins: Gabriel Veyre and the History of Cinema], Chikuma Shobo, 1995.

トランスナショナル化や国民国家の浸食は、ナショナル・シネマを用済みにすることはない。むしろグローバル化の促進によって、ナショナルな傾向が映画作品のブランディングにおいて有効となった。なおかつ、ナショナルな傾向を作家性にうまく還元する映画作家（オーストラリア出身のジェーン・カンピオンなど）の登場や、たとえばＪホラーという比較的新しいジャンルも端的な例となるように、映画ジャンルそれ自体の活性化に落とし込まれることも珍しくない（川口 2005)。特定の映画作品におけるきわめて具体的にローカルな物語や社会問題、あるいは土着の文化なるものは、特定の国内の消費を超えたグローバルな受容——国際映画祭などでの評価や各国での興行——を想定したものがほとんどといってよいだろう。

第三部　映画におけるグローカリゼーションの定点観測——ツァイ・ミンリャン『行者』——

ツァイ・ミンリャン監督『行者』（*Walker*, 2012）は、複雑な歴史的・政治的文脈をもつ台湾におけるグローバル／ローカルのせめぎ合いから生まれたシリーズ作品だ。本作の登場人物はひとりの僧侶である。かれは市街地をきわめてゆっくりと歩く。その歩みの驚嘆すべき遅さは、数分間で２メートルほどの狭い路地を渡り切るほどの速度だ。僧侶の周囲を忙しなく歩く現代人やテクノロジーは、明らかにグローバルな速度を具えている。だとすると、この僧侶の歩みはローカルな速度なのだろうか？ しかし、かれの手にはファストフード（ハンバーガー）とコンビニの袋が握りしめられており、その矛盾が際立っている。本作は、グローバル（速さ）／ローカル（遅さ）という容易な二分法を受け付けていない。本作が示唆するのは、グローカリゼーションが人間の身体を統御すると同時に引き裂くものであるということだ。僧侶の身体とアイデンティティは、身体運動の遅さ（歩み）とグローバルな経済状況の速さ（ファストフード、コンビニ）とに引き裂かれている。

この『行者』はシリーズ化され、2014 年の『西遊』（*Journey to the West*）には、この僧侶がフランスに到着している（彼の歩く速度では到底辿りつけない距離だ)。僧侶はまた、フランスの街並みを驚くべき遅さで歩き続ける。手にはもはやファストフードやコンビニの袋を持ってはいない。なによりも彼を不思

intensify it, acquiring qualities compatible with the global economy through which they were able to circulate widely. As a result, paradoxically, the present age is no longer one in which Hollywood cinema is seen as a global symbol. Rather, Hollywood cinema today is no more than a single local variation[2].

As scholar of cinema Keiko Kawaguchi argues, the transnationalization of film production and erosion of the nation state brought about by globalization have not finished national cinema off. Conversely, globalization has created conditions in which a national orientation has become an effective form of cinema branding. Furthermore, as seen in the emergence of auteurs who adeptly convert a national orientation into their distinctive style (such as the Australia-educated Jane Campion) and comparatively new genres such as J-horror (Japanese horror), as a particularly unambiguous example, in which a national orientation is turned into the means to energize an entire genre, examples of this kind of branding are widespread (Kawaguchi 2005). It is probably fair to say that the presence of a particularly concrete locally based story or social issue, or instance of vernacular culture in a certain film has been put there with an awareness of not only domestic distribution within the country of production but also reception on a global scale—the way it would be received at international film festivals, for example, or how it would be promoted overseas.

Part 3: Fixed Point Observation of the Glocalization of Cinema—Tsai Ming-Liang's *Walker*

Tsai Ming-Liang's *Walker* (2012) is the first in a series of films born out of the conflict between the global and local in Taiwan, known for its historically and politically complex context. Its only character is a single monk, who walks through the city at a snail-like pace. So slow is his movement that in the space of a few minutes he is just about able to cross an alleyway approximately two meters wide. The world around him—the hustle and bustle of modern-day city-dwellers and new technology—is clearly moving at a global speed. Is it then the case that

---

[2] Detailed analyses of such development of film domestically within Japan can be found in Misonou, Ryoko, *Eiga to kokuminkokka: 1930 nendai shōchiku merodorama* [Cinema and the nation-state : Shochiku melodrama films of the 1930s], Tokyo University Press, 2012 and Fujiki, Hideaki, *Eiga kankyaku to wa nanimono ka: media to shakai shutai no kingendaishi* [What is the Cinema Audience: A Modern and Contemporary History of Media and Social Subjects], Nagoya University Press, 2019.

議そうに見つめているのが、画面内の通行人＝「他者」である。好奇の目で僧侶を凝視する通行人たちの目にオリエンタリズムを指摘するのは容易い。だが、ここでの僧侶は、そうした眼差しの理不尽さを暴露しているのではない。僧侶は、端的にフランスの時間＝普遍性と彼固有の時間との差異を遅々として動かない身体運動によって浮かび上がらせた。つまりここでの普遍性とは、僧侶にとっての「他者」そのものである。僧侶は、さまざまな普遍性を、違和感のある「他者」として書き換えているのだ。

これまで、古典的ハリウッド映画という普遍的なシステムは、周縁の映画産業で柔軟に受け入れられて吸収されてきた。しかしいまや、その普遍性がローカルな映画の特異な表現によって逆説的に異物となっている。グローカリゼーションにおいて浸透してきた普遍性なるものが、あるヴァナキュラーな身体感覚や時間感覚によって突如「他者」となる契機を秘めていること、こうした点をツァイ・ミンリャン監督の『行者』シリーズは教えてくれる。このように、グローカリゼーションは、映画というメディアで特有の状況を引き起こしているように思われる。わたしたちが「他者」と出会う装置としての映画は、いまその役割を背負い過ぎているくらいだ。

this monk is walking at a local speed? In one of his hands he holds an item of fast-food (a hamburger) and from his other dangles a bag of shopping from a convenience store; the irony of which is obvious. This is not a film that panders to a simplistic binary opposition between the global (fastness) and local (slowness). Rather, it suggests that glocalization is a process that simultaneously both controls the human body and tears it in two. The monk's body and his identity are torn between the slowness of his movement (his pace) and speed of the global economy (fast food and convenience stores).

In the follow up work *Journey to the West* (2014), we find the same monk is now in Paris (to which at the pace he walks he would never have conceivably actually been able to reach). Again, he continues to walk through the French streets at an almost unbelievable slowness. On this occasion he is holding onto neither a hamburger nor a bag of shopping. Rather, more than anything else we are struck by the gaze of the pedestrians (his "others") captured by the camera, who stare at him perplexedly. It would be easy to point at the pedestrians' curious gaze as being a case of orientalism. However, the monk, in this instance, is not simply exposing the exaggerated gaze of those around him. Rather, through his incredibly measured physical movement, he draws attention to the disparity between French time (universality) and his own individual time. In other words, universality in this case is none other than the monk's very own "other". He rewrites various kinds of universality as a kind of uneasy "otherness".

Until recently, the classical Hollywood cinema has been flexibly taken in and absorbed as a universal system by other film industries situated peripheral to it. However now that universality is being transformed into something that is paradoxically alien by novel and distinctive modes of expression in local cinema. Tsai Ming-Liang's *Walker* series shows us that the so-called universality that has spread throughout the world through glocalization carries within it the potential to be suddenly transformed into something "other" by vernacular senses of physicality and time. Glocalization, thus, appears to be heralding a new era directly through the medium of cinema. Cinema, as a contraption through which we can encounter the "other", may in fact be carrying more than its share of that burden right now.

(Translated by Thomas Brook and Norihiko Nakamura)

参考文献

上杉富之「グローバル研究を超えて――グローカル研究の構想と今日的意義について――」、『グローカル研究』第1号、成城大学グローカル研究センター、2014年

川口恵子「ナショナル・シネマの研究動向」、『比較文学・文化論集』第22号、2005年、41-69頁

蓮實重彦編『リュミエール元年――ガブリエル・ヴェールと映画の歴史』、筑摩書房、1995年

ローランド・ロバートソン『グローバリゼーション――地球文化の社会理論』、阿部美哉訳、東京大学出版会、1997年

Bibliography

Hasumi, Shigehiko. *Lumière gannen: Gabriel Veyre to eiga no rekishi* [The Lumière Era Begins: Gabriel Veyre and the History of Cinema], Chikuma Shobo, 1995.

Kawaguchi, Keiko, "Nashonaru shinema no kenkyū dōkō" [Research trends on national cinema], *Hikaku bungaku/bunka ronshū* [Proceedings of comparative literature & culture], vol. 22, 2005, pp. 41-69.

Robertson, Roland. *Globalization: Social Theory and Global Culture*, Sage, 1992.

Uesugi, Tomiyuki. "Gurōbaru kenkyū wo koete: gurōkaru kenkyū no kōsō to konnichi teki igi ni tsuite" [Overcoming Global Research: Concerning the Conception and Contemporary Value of Glocal Research], Gurōkaru kenkyū [Journal of glocal studies], vol. 1, Seijo University Center for Glocal Studies, 2014.

グローバル化時代における他者としての観光客—観光のイメージをめぐって

林　玲穂

1．グローバルな行為としての観光

一般的に観光における「グローバル」は、日本国土交通省が「観光グローバル戦略」を掲げ、世界中から人々が何度でも訪れたくなるような魅力あふれる「世界に開かれた観光大国」となることを提唱しているように[1]、外国人観光客の誘致と深い関わりをもっている。その背景には、国境を越えた人やものの往来、文化の交流といった、境界を越えて多彩に混ざり合うという意味が内包されており、観光はこうした多様性を希求するという点で、まさにグローバル化時代における「グローバル」それ自体を具現化した行為だといえる。

また、その一方で、観光行為には同質化、均一化という概念も含まれている。例えば、観光地に設置する観光案内を英語で表記することも、ひとつのグローバルな現象、或いはグローバル化の現象であると捉えられよう。世界共通語といわれる英語を使用することで、言語間の境界線が取り除かれたフラットな状態が目指されている。このようなフラット化は言語の場合のみならず、世界中に似通ったショッピングモールやホテルなどを建設することにも当てはまる。これは「快適」で「安心」できるサービスを提供するといった点でグローバル化による均一化の現象だといえるだろう。以上から、グローバル及びグローバル化は、個々の多様性を追究しながらも、「同質化」や「均一化」といった性質を有しているといえる。

「多様性」と「同質化」という一見相反する価値観をもつグローバル化は、観光者が行先を決定する際に思い浮かべる観光地のイメージ（とその表象）にも影響を及ぼす。具体的には、差異化を図るためのその土地ならではのイメージが、多様性つまりグローバル性そのものに還元されているということである。それは、「技術大国」、「忍者と侍の国」といったイメージによって、むしろそ

[1] 平成15年小泉内閣が提唱する「ビジット・ジャパン・キャンペーン」の前年に打ち出された観光政策である。国土交通省2002。

Tourists as Others in the Era of Globalization: Aspects of Tourism Images

Akiho Hayashi

1. Tourism as a Global Practice

In general, "global" in the context of tourism is often associated with the promotion of inbound international tourism, as seen in the "Tourism Global Strategy" put forward by the Japanese Ministry of Land, Infrastructure, Transport and Tourism (MLIT) in 2002[1], which advocated Japan becoming a "tourism-based country open to the world", an attractive destination to which overseas visitors would want to return to repeatedly. Behind this conception is the idea of people and objects moving freely across national borders, partaking in cultural exchange and overcoming barriers to mix together in a rich flux; in its pursuit of this kind of diversity, tourism could be considered an activity that embodies the very "global" of the globalization era.

On the other hand, tourism also contains nuances of homogenization and uniformization. For example, we can interpret the display of English information at tourist spots as a global, or globalization-related phenomenon. Here, the use of English as a globally shared language is used to create a flat environment in which the barriers between individual languages have been taken away. This kind of flattening out is not limited to language use but can also be observed in the construction of almost identical shopping malls and hotels all throughout the world. In the sense that such cases involve providing a service that can be enjoyed "safely" and "at ease", they can be considered examples of uniformization caused by globalization. Given the above, the "global" and "globalization" are phenomena that embody characteristics of "homogenization" and "uniformization" while concurrently pursuing individual diversity.

Globalization, with its embodiment of the seemingly contradictory values of "diversity" and "homogenization", also exerts an influence on the image held by a potential tourist (and its representation) when they are deciding where to visit.

[1] This tourism policy was followed in 2003 by the Koizumi government's "Visit Japan Campaign". Ministry of land, Infrastructure, Transport and Tourism, *Global tourism strategy*, 2002.

のようなイメージに合わせた観光コンテンツをつくりだすといったような、或いは、イメージが先行し、固有性そのものがみえにくくなってしまうようなジレンマ的な側面を指し示している。

そこで、本稿ではグローバルという懸念がもつ多様性と同質化（均一化）の両義性に注目し、観光との関係性について「観光イメージ」の視点からアプローチを試みている。今後ますます世界規模で観光者が移動していくと予想されるなか、イメージの問題に言及していくことでいまいちど観光そのものの本質を考察することを目指している。

2. 観光イメージとは何か

そもそも「イメージ」とは何か。ジョン・バージャー（John Berger）は、イメージについて、世界にたいする私たちのものの見方を具体化したもの、「外観（appearances）」だと説明する。その際、私たちのものの見方が「何を知っていて、何を信じているのかに深く影響される」（バージャー 1986、9）としながら、イメージがつくり直され、再生産される性質を本質的に有しているとした。バージャーの定義に従うならば、イメージとは、単に見たものを記録したものなのではなく、時代や場所、見る主体によって「どのように見えたか／見られるのか」を示す「ものの見方の結果」であるといえる。その結果が「外観」なのである。バージャーによる外観という表現は、外側から対象を見る主体の存在が不可欠であることを示していると同時に、見る主体によってものの見方が変化するというイメージの性質を表している。

同様に、観光イメージにおいても、観光者に「どう見えたか／見られるのか」が重要となってくる。こうした観光者のものの見方に注目したのがイギリスの観光学者のジョン・アーリ（John Urry）であり、彼はヨーナス・ラースン（Jonas Larsen）との共著『観光のまなざし』において、「観光のまなざし（tourist gaze）」が次のような性質をもっていると述べる。

> ある特定の景色へのまなざしは、その個人の体験や思い出によって決まり、その枠組みは規範や様式で決まり、また、流布しているあれこれの場所についてのイメージとテクストにもよる。こういう「枠組み」は決定的な動機、

Here I am specifically thinking of the way in which an image unique to a certain location, used to enact differentiation, is reduced to diversity i.e. the global itself. This is evident in the way in which images such as "technological superpower" and "land of ninjas and samurai" result in tourism content being created in line with those very images, or alternatively, the dilemma through which an image takes precedent, obscuring actual specificity.

Therefore, in this chapter, I will take a closer look at the contradictory characteristics of diversity and homogenization (uniformization) embodied by the global and attempt to approach its relationship with tourism from the perspective of "tourism images". By considering the problem of images I aim to re-evaluate the essence of tourism itself, at a time in which the movement of tourists on a global scale can be predicted to accelerate into the future.

2. Tourism Images

What is an "image", anyway? John Berger describes images in terms of "appearances", that is, as the physical embodiment of the way that we see the world around us. According to Berger, not only is our way of seeing "affected by what we know or what we believe" (Berger 2008, 8), but also, images are essentially characterized by their being made anew and reproduced. If we follow Berger's definition, then images are not simply a recording of that what has been seen, but can in fact be considered "the result of our way of seeing things", i.e. they reveal "how something is seen/has been seen" by a particular seeing subject or, for example, at a particular time or place. That result is an "appearance". Berger's use of the word "appearance" demonstrates both the necessity of the seeing subject located external to the object being seen and the nature of images themselves, whereby the way of seeing something is variable, dependent on the seeing subject.

Similarly, the question of "how one sees/one is seen by" is also pertinent when considering tourists and tourism images. The question of how tourists see things is one taken up by British practitioner of Tourism studies, John Urry, who in his work *The Tourist Gaze*, co-authored with Jonas Larson, describes the character of "the tourist gaze" in the following way:

> Gazing at particular sights is conditioned by personal experiences and memories and framed by rules and styles, as well as by circulating images and texts of

技法、文化的なメガネとなって観光者が、具体的なモノや実態的な場所を「面白い、いい感じ、美しい」と見るより先に、先行してそう見えるようにしてしまっているのだ。(アーリとラースン 2014、3)

すなわち、イメージとテクストとなる観光写真やガイドブック、テレビなど様々なメディアから得た観光地のイメージを観光者は現地で再確認しているのである。これは、先ほど引用したバージャーの「何を知っていて、何を信じているのかに深く影響される」私たちのものの見方が、実際にどのようなものなのかを示している。しかしながら、アーリらは、そのような観光のまなざしの限界を突きつけながらも、観光者は、例えば写真を撮影することで自ら観光地の魅力を発見し、もともと持っていたイメージを更新する（再生産する）ということを主張している。再生産されたイメージが、また別の誰かのイメージとテクストになっていることから、観光のイメージは絶えず再生産される観光者のものの見方の集積であると考えられるだろう。

では、こうした観光者のまなざしがグローバル化時代において、具体的にどのように観光イメージを形成しているのかについて次節からは一枚の観光ポスターを基点に両者の関係性について考察を進めていきたい。

3. 観光者のまなざしと場所の固有性

図1は、日本を海外に紹介するための観光ポスター「Beautiful Japan（駕籠に乗れる美人）」（吉田初三郎）である。富士山と満開の桜を背景に、手前には駕籠に乗った芸者が大きく描かれており、まさに「日本らしさ」が詰まった一枚であるといえる。このポスターが仮に空港や地域の観光案内所に掛けられていたとしてもおそらく違和感はないだろう。このポスターは『美しき日本　大正昭和の旅展』に収録されており、今からおよそ90年前の1930年に制作されたものである。当時の日本には、外国人旅行者（とりわけ当時海外旅行が盛んだった欧米諸国からの）を呼び込み、自国の文化や風光美を知ってもらうことで、近代先進国家としての国威を世界にアピールしようとするねらいがあった。したがって、大正・昭和初期の日本では自らのイメージをどのようにかたちづくるのかが重要な課題だったといえる。実際に完成した観光ポスター「Beautiful

this and other places. Such 'frames' are critical resources, techniques, cultural lenses that potentially enable tourists to see the physical forms and material spaces before their eyes as 'interesting, good or beautiful'.
(Urry and Larsen 2011)

In other words, when tourists visit a specific location, they are in fact recognizing images of that destination (i.e. tourism images) which they have already gleaned from "images and texts" such as tourist snaps, guidebooks, television and other media. This description again concerns the nature of our way of seeing things, which, according to Berger as above, "is affected by what we know or what we believe". However, while Urry and his co-author confront their readers with the limitations of the tourist gaze, they also emphasize the way in which tourists, by taking their own photographs for example, make individual discoveries within the tourist destination and actively update (reproduce) the images that they had previously held. Because such reproduced images then become the "images and texts" that are seen and read by other potential tourists, tourism images can be thought of as the constantly reproduced accumulation of tourists' way of seeing things.

In the following section, I will ask how this "tourist gaze" actually contributes to the formation of tourism images in the era of globalization, considering the relationship between the two by taking a single tourism poster as my point of departure.

3. The Tourist Gaze and Local Specificity

Figure 1 is a tourism poster introducing Japan to potential visitors from abroad, titled "Beautiful Japan: The Beauty on a palanguin" (designed by Hatsusaburo Yoshida). With a background which is composed of Mount Fuji and cherry blossoms in full bloom, and in the foreground a geisha riding a carriage, we could say that the poster is absolutely full to the brim with "Japaneseness". Few would be surprised to see it displayed in an airport or the information centre of a rural tourist spot. In fact, this poster was included in the collection "Beautiful Japan: Tourism in the 1910s-30s", and actually dates from 1930, approximately 90 years ago. Japan, at the time, had the aim of impressing the rest of the world with its national vigour as a modern developed country, which it hoped to achieve by attracting foreign tourists (particularly from Europe and America, where tourism

Japan」は、外国人旅行者、学者、ジャーナリストたちが抱いていた「日本のイメージを裏切らず」（東京都江戸東京博物館 2005、31）描いたものだという。

さらに、近年、海外で出版された日本のガイドブック『Lonely Planet Japan 14』(2015) の表紙や日本政府観光局（JNTO）が制作した動画「JAPAN-Where tradition meets the future」(2016) をこのポスターと比較してみると、桜や芸者といったモチーフが時代を越えて繰り返し使用されており、観光コンテンツが多様化してもなお、昭和初期のイメージが今日の観光イメージに多大な影響を及ぼしていることが読み取れる。観光ポスターやガイドブック以外にも、2020 年の東京オリンピックを招致する際のエンブレムは桜の花のリースであったし、2019 年のラグビーワールドカップのトーナメントマークに富士山が描かれていたことは記憶に新しい。たしかに桜や富士山は日本のシンボルであるが、それらは、私たちの日常のなかではなく、むしろ外国人のまなざしを意識したときに現れやすいものなのではないだろうか。

このようなモチーフを、ただそこに描かれたものではなく、誰かのまなざしが捉えたあらゆる対象から取捨選択され、キャンバスという枠内に描かれた題材であるとするならば、日本国内の様々な固有性の中から桜や富士山、芸者などが世界共通のイメージとして見出され続けていることは明らかである。ここから、日本らしさという固有のイメージは外部からのまなざしである観光者のまなざしを通して構成されているといえる。

今回取り上げた例から分かるように、「外国人旅行者にどう見られるのか」が日本らしさの一つの基準となっていた。繰り返しになるが、イメージは、単なる表象、或いは記録ではなく、主体のものの見方から現れた外観である。外観とは、「外側から見る」主体の存在が不可欠なのであり、日本のイメージには外国人旅行者というまなざしの存在が日本らしさをかたちづくる上で大きな役割を果たしているといえる。また、「日本らしさ」や「日本のイメージ」といった場所の固有性は、前節でも触れたように「まなざしの集積」によって生じている。すなわち、「固有性」とは、歴史や伝統や文化、或いは昔からその場所に住んでいた人々の記憶といったような潜在的なものである一方、その固有性そのものが「外観」として現われるのは、外からのまなざしとの交流によってなのである。場所の固有性は、観光者という外からの訪問者、つまり「他

was booming), who would visit Japan to learn about its culture and natural beauty. Therefore, the question of how it crafted its own image was of great importance to the Japan of the 1910s to 1930s, i.e. during the Taisho and early Showa eras. Indeed, the tourism poster "Beautiful Japan" is said to have depicted "faithfully the image of Japan" (Edo Tōkyō Hakubutsukan 2005, 31) that was held by foreign tourists, scholars and journalists at the time.

Here, I would like to draw some comparisons between Yoshida's poster and some more recent items: the cover of *Lonely Planet Japan 14* (2015), a guidebook for Japan published overseas; and a video produced by the Japan National Tourism Organization titled "JAPAN-Where tradition meets the future" (2016). Motifs such as cherry blossoms and geisha consistently feature prominently in these productions, crossing the boundaries of era and suggesting that even as tourism content is diversified, the images of early Showa continue to exert a strong influence on today's tourism images. It is not only tourism posters and guidebooks: the use of a cherry blossom wreath in the emblem used for Tokyo's bid to host the 2020 Olympics and the use of Mount Fuji in the tournament logo for the 2019 Rugby World Cup are still in recent memory. Cherry blossoms and Mount Fuji are indeed symbols of Japan, but they are probably more likely to spring to mind when we think of the gaze of foreigners than during our ordinary day-to-day lives.

If we recognize that such motifs are not simply there, but rather the subject matter that has been chosen specifically among all the myriad of images perceived by a certain someone and then placed onto a canvas, then it becomes clear that out of all the local specificity within Japan, cherry blossoms, Mount Fuji and geisha have continued to be sought out as images that can be understood throughout the world. From such a standpoint, we can say that the fixed image of Japaneseness is one that has been formed through the tourist gaze, i.e. a gaze directed from the outside looking in.

In the case illustrated above, for example, "the way of being seen by foreign tourists" has acted as a certain measure of what Japaneseness is. As I wrote above, images are not simply representations or recordings, but appearances that have resulted from a certain subject's way of seeing. Appearances are wholly dependent upon the existence of the externally-situated seeing subject to which they "appear", and therefore we can say that the existence of the foreign tourist's gaze has played a significant role in the crafting of the Japaneseness depicted in images of

者」の存在によって見出され続けている。

4.「他者」とは誰か

「はじめに」でも触れたように、観光イメージには、個々の差異化を図るためにグローバル性そのものに還元されてしまうという側面があった。観光者のまなざしが常に画期的な観光イメージを創造するわけでなく、観光イメージが誰かによってあらかじめ作り上げられたもの、本来の場所の固有性から離れてしまっていること、またそのような観光イメージが観光者の経験それ自体を希薄化してしまうのではないかという見方[2]もある。世界中を移動する観光者がまなざしを向けるのは、固有性を誇張することで理解しやすくなり、目を引きやすくなったイメージにすぎないのかもしれない。

しかしながら、実際に今日書店に平積みされている旅関連の雑誌のなかやInstagramなどに投稿された数多くの観光写真を覗けば、そこには他者の視点が捉えた場所のイメージで溢れている。観光のイメージとなる場所の固有性が、先述したように観光者との交流のなかで形成されていることから、「固有性」とは、そこにもともと備わっている確立した概念でありながらも、変動的な開かれた概念であることは明らかである。ここから、観光のジレンマ的な側面を観光イメージから見直したとき、固有性を見出す「他者の視点」そのものに注目する必要性を提示できる。つまり、「他者」とは誰かという問題に目を向けなければならない。

例えば、自由で非日常的な時間を手に入れるための観光は、仕事の責任など日常から一時的に開放され、何にも属さない他者として振舞うことである。また、国境を越えたり、生活圏を離れたりすることで「言葉の壁や文化の違い」といった見えない境界を越えることも他者になることである。読めない文字や聞き取れない言葉、カルチャーショックなどといったような壁や違いを認識せざるを得ないとき、私たちは必然的に他者になってしまう。もちろん、一国に

[2] ダニエル・ブーアスティンは、「旅行の結果、われわれはいちじるしく視野が広くなり、他国民に対する理解も深まったようには見えない。（中略）経験は希薄化され、あらかじめ作りあげられたものになってしまった」（ブーアスティン 1964、91）とし、観光が「あらかじめ作られた経験」にすぎないとした上で、その現象を「疑似イベント」と称している。

Japan. Additionally, as I wrote in the previous section, local specificity such as "Japaneseness" and "images of Japan" are also the product of an "accumulation of gazes". That is to say, "specificity" is indeed a subconscious quality, consisting of things such as history and tradition and culture, or alternatively the memories of people who have lived in that certain place since long ago, but it is in the process of interaction with an external gaze that that specificity itself takes the form of an "appearance". Local specificity continues to be sought out via the gaze of tourists, i.e. visitors from the outside, that is, the existence of the "other".

4. Defining the "Other"

As I touched upon in the introduction, tourism images are liable to be reduced into an aspect of the global itself via an attempt to realize individual differentiation. The tourist gaze does not always create an innovative tourist image. According to some, tourist images are always created in advance by somebody else: they exist separate from the original specificity of a certain place and run the risk of diluting the actual experience of tourists[2]. Maybe it is true that the gaze of tourists, as they move around the world, tends to focus on eye-catching images that boast of their own uniqueness and are easily understood.

However, if one is to actually look at the ream of tourism photos either within today's travel magazines or uploaded onto services such as Instagram, they will be met by a deluge of images of specific places as they have been perceived by outside visitors to that particular location. As described above, the specificity of a certain place, as it is represented in the form of tourism images, is formed via a process of interaction with tourists. From this phenomenon, it is clear that "specificity", while indeed being an established concept, referring to something originally present in a certain place, is also a variable, open concept. Reconsidering the dilemma-like aspect of tourism from the perspective of tourism images in this way, it becomes necessary to take a closer look at the "gaze of the other", which seeks out local specificity. That is, it becomes necessary to confront the question of who the "other" actually is.

For example, tourism, as a means to enjoy one's time in a free and extraordinary

[2] Daniel Boorstin asserts that, "Our travels have not, it seems, made us noticeably more cosmopolitan or more understanding of other peoples. [...] Rather, the travel experience [...] has become diluted, contrived, prefabricated." (Boorstin 2012, 79) After arguing that tourism is no more than a "prefabricated experience", Boorstin calls the phenomenon a "pseudo-event".

とっての外国人に限らず、自国を旅行する場合であったとしても（各地域によって文化や風習が異なるように)、観光者は誰もが訪れた先では現地の人々にとって「他者」に属している。また、観光者という他者は、他者であるがゆえに差異を敏感に感じ取り、現地の人々のあいだでは日常的で、当たり前であるものごとに関しても新しい発見をするまなざしを所有しているといえる。このようなまなざしの性質は、もともとその場所に住んでいた人々には見えなかった別の魅力を発見するものであり、それが場所のイメージを更新している。すなわち、「開かれた観光大国」になるとは、こうした一時的に滞在する観光者としての「他者」によって場所の固有性及び観光のイメージが形成していく場となることであり、また、このような開かれた状態を形成することが観光の本質であるといえる。

グローバル化時代において、あらゆる民族間の多様な個性を知ることや理解することが求められるようになった。観光も「平和へのパスポート」と称され、グローバル化時代を表す象徴的な現象となっている。しかし、その一方で、「グローバル」という言葉のなかにそれぞれの個性が一括りにされ、「自分とは異なる他者」を浮き彫りにさせてもいる。他者をどのように理解するのか、どのように受け入れるのか、などといった問題はグローバル化時代と言われる今日においても度々俎上にのせられている。しかしながら、自分とは異なる存在に目を向けるとき、自分自身も「他者」という個々の存在であること、また「他者」になりうるという事実がみえにくくなっているとも考えられる。少なくとも、観光において、私たちは誰もが観光者という「他者」になるのである。

manner, involves being temporarily liberated from one's professional responsibilities and day-to-day existence to play the role of an other, who belongs to nothing and nowhere. Similarly, the overcoming of invisible "language barriers" and "cultural differences" via the crossing of national boundaries and the departure from one's ordinary sphere of activity involves becoming an other. When we are confronted with writing we are unable to read and spoken language we are unable to comprehend; when we are forced to recognize walls and differences as in the case of culture shock, we all, inevitably, become an other.

Of course, this does not apply when visiting a country to which we are foreign. Even when travelling within our own countries (just as there are differences between the culture and customs of specific regions), tourists always and without exception belong to the category of "other" in respect to the people who live in that particular place. Additionally, the tourist, as an other, because they are an other, is sensitive to difference, and through their gaze is able to make new discoveries, extending to those things that to the people who live in that place are simply part of unremarkable everyday life. This characteristic of the tourist gaze is able to discover alternative sources of wonder that are invisible to the people originally living in a certain place, and therefore can update the local images. To become a "tourism-based country open to the world", then, means to become a place of which the local specificity and tourism images are formed with the help of such tourists, as "others", who visit and stay temporarily, and the making of such "opened" situations could indeed be considered the very essence of tourism.

In this age of globalization, we are expected to know or understand about the diverse variety that exists among every kind of ethnic group. Tourism is touted as a "passport to peace" and has become a symbolic phenomenon seen to represent the era of globalization. However, on the other hand, tourism also has the effect of clumping all kinds of specificity together within the single word "global" and reinforcing the idea of the "other who is different from the self". Questions relating to the other, such as how the other should be understood and how we should approach or incorporate the other are frequently put upon the table in this present-day so-called age of globalization. However, it is possible that when we cast our gaze upon an existence we consider to be different from ourselves, we are obstructing our ability to recognize both our own distinct "otherness" as individual entities and our own potential to become an "other" ourselves. At the very least, in the case of tourism, we all, each and every one of us, whenever we become a

参考文献

ダニエルJ・ブーアスティン『幻影（イメジ）の時代――マスコミが製造する事実』星野郁美・後藤和彦訳、東京創元社、1964年。

ジョン・バージャー『イメージ 視覚とメディア』、伊藤俊治訳、PARCO出版、1986年。

Lonely Planet, *Lonely Planet Japan 14*, 2015.

ジョン・アーリ、ヨーナス・ラースン『観光のまなざし〔増補改訂版〕』、加太宏邦訳、法政大学出版局、2014年。

国土交通省『グローバル観光戦略』(2002)、https://www.mlit.go.jp/kisha/kisha02/01/011224_3/011224_3.pdf (最終閲覧日2021年1月26日)

財団法人東京都歴史文化財団　東京都江戸東京博物館『美しき日本　大正昭和の旅展』、毎日新聞社、2005年。

日本政府観光局（JNTO）「JAPAN-Where tradition meets the future」(2016)、https://www.youtube.com/watch?v=WLIv7HnZ_fE（最終閲覧日2020年8月1日）

図1　ポスター Beautiful Japan（駕籠に乗れる美人）
吉田初三郎画 1930 江戸東京博物館所蔵。
Poster: Beautiful Japan: The Beauty on a palaguin［sic］
Yoshida Hatsusaburo 1930 Edo-Tokyo Museum.

tourist, also become an “other”.

(Translated by Thomas Brook and Akiho Hayashi)

Bibliography

Boorstin, Daniel J., The Image: A Guide to Pseudo-Events in America, New York: Macmillan, [1962] 2012.

Lonely Planet, *Lonely Planet Japan14*, 2015.

Berger, John, *Ways of Seeing*, London: Penguin Books, [1972] 2008.

Urry, John and Larsen, Jonas, *The Tourist Gaze 3.0*, SAGE Publications. Kindle [2002] 2011.

Edo Tōkyō Hakubutsukan; Tōkyō-to Rekishi Bunka Zaidan, *Utsukushiki Nihon Taisho Showa no ryoten* [Beautiful Japan: Tourism in the 1910s-30s], Tokyo: Mainichi Shimbunsha, 2005.

Ministry of Land, Infrastructure, Transport and Tourism, *Global tourism strategy*, 2002. https://www.mlit.go.jp/kisha/kisha02/01/011224_3/011224_3.pdf Accessed 2021/01/26

JNTO, “JAPAN-Where tradition meets the future” (2016), https://www.youtube.com/watch?v=WLIv7HnZ_fE (Accessed 2021/01/26)

第二部

他者性のアダプテーション、媒介、
及び伝達をめぐる考察

PART 2

PERSPECTIVES ON THE ADAPTATION, MEDIATION AND COMMUNICATION OF OTHERNESS

1
Adaptation of Otherness

The Experimental Self: On the Manifestation of Difference in the Early Careers of Tawada Yoko and Levy Hideo

Thomas Brook

1. Introduction: On the "Radical Potential" of "Border-Crossing Writers"

A focus on difference, asymmetry, and other forms of alterity is a common feature of both critical and academic writing on the recent phenomenon of "border-crossing writers" *(ekkyō sakka)*: a Japanese term which, in common practice, usually refers to "either ethnically non-Japanese authors writing in Japanese in Japan or ethnically Japanese authors writing in Japanese and foreign languages either in Japan or elsewhere" (Sakamoto 2006, 137). Although this focus has been criticized as the "fetishization of nationality and native-language" of the writers concerned (Sierks 2015, 1), it is at least partly justified by a need to distinguish these writers from those who, during modernity, were forced to take up the Japanese language as colonial subjects of Japan, and whose connection to the Japanese language is understood more directly as part of the suffered legacy of colonialism.

Furthermore, such alterity is rarely hidden by the authors themselves but rather features prominently, at least on a thematical level, in their frequently autobiographical works. In particular, the two authors I will consider in this paper, Levy Hideo (1950-) and Tawada Yoko (1960-)—the two leading "border-crossing writers" both in terms of name-value and critical appraisal—have both presented themselves as existing or at least working within the intermediary space between distinct cultures or languages. Subsequently, a number of scholars have attempted to sublimate this difference, or alterity (i.e. externality with regards to the established model of national literatures) into, for example, "the potential for a radical critique of the inside/outside boundary" upon which the modern nation state and its associated linguistically homogenous community is grounded (Sakamoto 2006, 154). That is, such writers are seen to open up the possibility of imagining new realities that are capable of overcoming national boundaries, such as, namely, the conception of the "global citizen" (Miyata 2015, 9), or, alternatively, a "Japanophone literature" (*Nihongo bungaku*) that is at least partially disassociated from the ethnic and geographic borders of the Japanese nation (Scott 2008).

A focus on difference or otherness is thus justified, but it is also problematic, not least because it takes the authors' otherness or foreignness as a starting point. If such a "radical potential" is to be tapped, it is necessary to reconsider the issue of "difference" not just between these newly emergent writers and established models of literature, but also the specific way difference emerges in their work. The aim of this paper is to shine a light on the way both Levy and Tawada, in their early work, seem to actively expose and create various forms of difference and asymmetry that are related to, but cannot be completely reduced to, their essential "otherness" as "foreigners". Considering the issue of authorial intent, I will ask to what degree such manifestation of difference can be attributed to the individual authors, and what such a performance may be intended to achieve.

A key feature of this analysis will be the notion of "self-translation", conventionally understood as the process by which the author of a literary text in one language (language A) then translates that text into another language (language B) (Grutman 2009). In this paper, however, the notion of "self-translation" will be interpreted more broadly to mean the process by which a writer incorporates their own, ostensibly foreign "self" into the linguistic/literary culture they are participating in, in the case of both Levy and Tawada as residents in the country understood as the originary and authentic home of that culture.

2. "Self-Translation" Reconsidered

There is a further notion of "self-translation" used much more commonly in discussions of Levy and Tawada, which involves the influence of the writer's linguistic repertoire external to the language they are writing in, most directly their mother tongue. To quote Suga, "exophonic writing [i.e. literature written in a language not native to the writer], imaginably, involves a constant process of self-translation" (Suga 2007, 27). Masumoto, quoting this statement, then draws from Tawada's own descriptions of her writing process to delineate a kind of "self-translation" in which "inner speech" (Vygotsky) is translated into "external speech" in the form of the written text (Masumoto 2020, 7-9). Although this schematic could be applied to any writer with any linguistic background, it is undeniable that in prior research, such a notion of "self-translation" used in the context of "border-crossing" or "exophonic" writers has tended to involve a focus on the interference or influence of the writer's "foreign" mother tongue. Levy, conversely, although he has frequently alluded to the translative aspect of his writing in Japanese (Levy 2010, 45), has stressed that such an influence of other languages, and in particular his mother tongue of English, while undoubtedly affecting his Japanese prose, is not a conscious part of his writing, somewhat provocatively suggesting that his writing process is "not that different from that of so-called Japanese for whom Japanese is their mother tongue" (Levy 2013, 193). This assertion is an invitation to think of "(self-)translation" in broader terms.

I will return to Levy's cross-genre writing below, but first, I would like to propose a more general idea of "self-translation" as the writing of "I" into a context where it is ostensibly "foreign". In using this term, I mean to emphasize the agency of writers in presenting their "foreign bodies" to their readerships. It is continuous with a term coined by Nakai to describe a feature of postcolonial literature: "autobiography of the Other" (*tasha no jiden*). This term, which has already been applied to Levy's work by Miyata (44), indicates the critical awareness of writers who broadly fit into the category of "postcolonial" that, regardless of their intent, their works will be read autobiographically. That is to say, even if they are set in a completely fictional universe, readers, due to their knowledge of the author's alterity (such as via their evidently "foreign" name), will attempt to read the author through the text (Nakai 2007, 6-7). While Nakai's term refers principally to the critically tuned consciousness of writers, my conception of "self-translation" as used here places an emphasis on the choices made by writers when presenting their "self" through an ostensibly "foreign" language, or in an ostensibly "foreign" context, as is the case with Levy's Japanese writings and Tawada's Japanese poetry that was published in a bilingual format in Germany. It is now to those specific texts I will turn.

3. Tawada Yoko's violent exposition of the self in *Only There Where You Are There is Nothing*

First, I will consider the explicit manifestation of difference in Tawada's debut poetry collection, *Only There Where You Are There is Nothing (Nur da wo du bist da ist nichts/Anata no iru tokoro dake nani mo nai*, 1987; abbreviated to *Only Where You Are* below). The book was published in Tübingen, Germany by independent publisher Claudia Gehrke, now long-term collaborator of Tawada. It is a bilingual text that can be read either from left to right in German, or right to left in Japanese, with the text in the two languages printed on alternate pages, numbered double to accommodate this, and occasionally but not always mirroring each other. It consists of 20 individual poems, two of which include variations in the form of a semi-transparent plastic insert, and ten of which were previously published in a Japan-themed publication of essays and art titled *Konkursbuch 16/17: Japan - Ein Lesebuch* (1986; also published by Claudia Gehrke), a single short prose piece, and a short foreword. The plastic insert is only in German, and the foreword only in Japanese, and this itself is one way in which difference or asymmetry manifests within the text: difference between not only the Japanese and German scripts, but also the content in a way that is conspicuous even to the potential monolingual reader. Below I will quote from the fifth, "unchanged new edition" ("Unveränderte Neuausgabe") from 2015, where in fact the foreword has actually been scrambled to make it almost illegible. The other "differences" I discuss below, however, were also present in the third edition of 1997.

Masumoto, quoted above, has shown how the poems of this work create a narrative from which Tawada's conception of writing as a form of "self-translation", i.e. the verbalization of her "inner speech" into her alienated mother tongue of Japanese, can be inferred. Here, in contrast, I would like to focus on the various ways in which difference is manifested within the book and particularly between the Japanese and German text, and demonstrate how this exposition of difference is also related to the writer's "self" as a young Japanese woman resident in Germany.

Unlike her subsequent German publications, her official website or many of the academic books published on the topic of her literature, which feature vivid photographs of the author's visage, *Only Where You Ar*e does not contain a picture of the writer. She appears, or is presented to the (in particular non-Japanese) reader, through the elegant vertically handwritten Japanese title on the left-opening side of the cover, the Japanese text within, and the note beneath the title on the inside title page that reads: "Translated from the Japanese by Peter Pörtner" ("Aus dem Japanischen von Peter Pörtner"). It is notable that in the initial 1986 publication of ten poems, the translation is credited to both Pörtner and Tawada ("Übersetzt von Peter Pörtner und Yoko Tawada") without reference to the original language, although given the subject of the publication this is self-explanatory. Thus, the "Japaneseness" of the author and her distance from the German translation, and by extension Germany itself, is accentuated in the later standalone publication. Although the Japanese is presented explicitly as the "original", in this paper I will refer to the German titles first, reflecting the fact the book has only been published in Germany.

Turning to the translation itself, Masumoto mentions, drawing from interviews Tawada has given in Japanese, the way in which Tawada granted Pörtner a large degree of freedom in translating the poems from Japanese to German in order to domesticize them for a German-reading audience. The example Masumoto refers to is a poem titled "The Plan" (Der Plan/Keikaku), in which "miso soup" and "tatami" in the original are converted into the more culturally neutral "soup" (*Suppe*) and "carpet" (*Teppich*) in translation. This enables an allegorical reading in German not tainted by Japanese connotations: the soup spilled onto the carpet, in Masumoto's reading, represents the stain of language, and "[w]hether it is Japanese or German is irrelevant here, because this is the mother tongue par excellence" (Masumoto 2020, 12).

However, there are several cases of difference between the two versions of a poem that cannot be attributable so easily to the accommodation of a different audience. Perhaps the most striking of these appears in a poem titled "Shocking quarrel and revolution" (Erschreckendes Liebesgeflüster und Revolution/

Osoroshī chiwa to kakumei), in which a line which in the German translation roughly reads "I wanted to smear dog poo over my coming-of-age ceremony dress" (Tawada 2015, 85/44) corresponds to a Japanese "original" in which this desire is a reality (82/47). The difference in Japanese rests on a single character/syllable, "*nuritakutta*" (to completely smear over, past tense) being translated here as if it were written "*nuritakatta*" (to want to smear over, past tense), the "*ku*" (く) seemingly being read as "*ka*" (か). How this impacts the meaning of the poem is not of primary importance here; rather this difference, pertaining to elementary grammar (if not vocabulary) is an invitation for readers, who are able, to compare or read the two versions together. The authorial intent behind this "error" is playfully hinted at by the fact that the object changed by this alteration, "excrement" (糞), is a compound character made up of the elements meaning "rice" (米) and "different" (異), i.e. "different rice".

Such an approach to reading between or across two versions of a poem reveals additional layers of meaning in the poem "Incident" (Vorfall/Jiken), which contains a similar apparent corruption of the "original" text. For this poem, I present my own attempt to render it into English, in which I have tried to preserve the violent energy of the original.

Incident

bang in the middle
of the middle school school ground
an ant nest resembling a shiso bush
starts to jitter eagerly
and the colour of the sand grows damp
it could have stopped but it keeps swelling up
until lo and behold a white whale
bursts up to the surface
pornography in the blaze of dawn
I see it I see it I see it all
the schoolgirls and the schoolboys both clamp on
to breasts that could only be the breasts of a whale

to drink the salty milk
armpit hairs violining Bach's body odour
while in a place hidden out of sight
the dinner ladies start to kick about a football
it hadn't been allowed for years!
performance rankings flicker in the sky
and the washing machine jolts into full throttle

(Tawada 2015, 79/50-76/53)

The above is a translation of the original Japanese poem, but I have referred to the German version as far as I am able and in particular draw from it in the use of punctuation (brackets and an exclamation mark, although placed differently) that is not present in the unpunctuated original. I have however preserved the "error" of the original, which corresponds to "shiso bush" in the third line of my translation. In the Japanese version this is "*o-shiso*" (おしそ), a neologism consisting of the honorific particle "*o*" and "*shiso*" ("the honourable *shiso*"), the green- or red-leaf plant frequently served alongside sushi and used to colour and flavour pickled plum (*umeboshi*), which thus has distinctly "Japanese" connotations. "*O-shiso*", however, unlike "*o-sushi*" (お寿司), does not exist in the common Japanese vernacular. The poem indeed makes more sense if it is read as "*o-heso*" (おへそ), the second character spun 150 or so degrees clockwise, a very common term for the navel or belly button. Pörtner, accordingly, renders this as "navel" (*Nabel*) in his translation.

Read as "navel", the poem reads as a critique of narcissism (navel gazing) and blind, deluded zeal (the belief that one is able to "see all") in the schoolground, or academy (in particular the humanities, which are by definition human-centric), while the female adults who would have in ordinary circumstances been seeing to the students' nutritional needs are swept up into a game of competition sport; the washing machine, seemingly moving by itself, perhaps a metaphor for the washing away of all stains (i.e. difference, be it cultural, linguistic or other forms of specificity) in the pursuit of universal truth, orchestrated by technology that has slipped out of man's grasp. This in itself could be read as a remarkably prescient, not to mention dystopic, commentary on the current state of a "globalizing" world.

However, the poem takes on further layers of meaning when considered across its various versions. Naval-gazing is transformed into Japan-gazing, a connotation accentuated in the German translation where the "blaze of dawn" (*asayake*) is rendered as "*Morgenröt*e" ("morning red"), continuous with the German term for the Orient, "*Morgenland*" ("morning land"). This connotation is pushed further still with the fact that the "white whale" emerging from this activity, whose "salty milk" becomes the new source of nutrition for the schoolchildren, in German turns into "he, the white whale" ("*der* […] *weiße Wal*"), infusing the already sexualized imagery with specifically male and homoerotic qualities. The combination of these details, although they rest upon a "non-native" reading of German (i.e. a heightened consciousness of gendered nouns and word association), by connoting the taboo topic of how cross-cultural contact is connected to the complexities of human sexuality (see Treat 1999), speak directly to the specific subjectivity and insecurities of particularly male Western-European, if not just German, aficionados of Japan. Read in translation, together with the seeming "error" of the "original", the poem can also thus be read as a critique of the boom in Japanese Studies in the late twentieth century.

This function of the poem, although it exists independently within the words that compose it, is exacerbated by its connection with the poet, a young Japanese woman resident in Germany (at least as early as the 1997 edition, Tawada's biography in the front-matter notes she was born 1960 in Tokyo and has lived since 1982 in Hamburg). It is in this sense that I consider it an exemplary case of "self-translation", in which the writer has transposed her own "self" upon the text. This is an extension of her originary "difference" as a Japanese resident of Germany, but importantly, it is not reducible to her originary, essentialized "difference" as a native speaker of Japanese or non-native learner of German. Rather, it plays upon socially and historically determined forms of "difference" such as gender, ethnicity and cultural specificity that connect to the author's own "self" as they exist within language, to create a powerful, if ambiguous, commentary on academism that is still relevant today. This seems less of an attempt to combine "different national elements, that build a dialogue together and harmonize in order to create a new subject" (Barbieri 2016, 222) than an attempt to pull, or wrench, "difference" out into the open in an attempt to interrogate it.

Whether this leads to dialogue, and how that is possible, rests upon how "we" read her, to repeat a common cliché. The poem, however, following the interpretation I offer above, could also prompt "us" to rethink whether "we" should really be in such a hurry to explicate and harmonize, and thereby wash away all the difference (i.e. specificity) contained within it, and the wider world, in the first place.

4. Mediation of the self in Levy Hideo's "At Tiananmen" and "Tiananmen"

In comparison to Tawada's early attempt at "self-translation" as described above, which is violent and explicit, Levy's is arguably more subtle and yet also more "radical". Indeed, Levy's entire literary project could be considered as an elaborate ongoing act of "self-translation".

His debut novel, *A Room Where the Star-Spangled Banner Cannot Be Heard* (*Seijōki no kikoenai heya*, 1992; translation by Christopher D. Scott published 2011), the only of his works to have been translated into English thus far, is the coming-of-age story of Ben Isaac, a 17-year-old American national staying in Japan with his diplomat father, and his attempt to cleave out a new life within Japan and the Japanese language, based upon Levy's own experiences towards the end of the 1960s. The novel, which has been praised by writers including Oe Kenzaburo and Tawada herself (Levy 2011, back cover), is ambiguous towards Ben's attempt to meld into Japanese society through his mastery of the language, observing it from the distance of the present with a detached irony. The humor suggests that Ben's zeal may be misguided, but this suggestion is complicated by the fact his story is told in a Japanese that is anything but "clumsy" (*tsutanai*), to use the word used to describe Ben's fledgling competency in the language (Levy 2011, 82; Levy 2004, 117), and the fact that while in the process of writing the book Levy relocated from the United States to Japan, where he has continued non-stop to produce challenging and critically acclaimed works of fiction, becoming a major presence in the world of contemporary Japanese literature.

Levy's dramatic debut was followed by a semi-hiatus of around four years, in which he mostly wrote essays and took part in interviews, before he published his second novel, the short story "Tiananmen" (Ten'anmon), in 1996. "Tiananmen" is an impressive text in its own right, receiving a nomination for the prestigious Akutagawa Prize the year of its publication, but it also offers an intriguing window into Levy's creative process. This is because the hardback *Tiananmen* (*Ten'anmon*), published later the same year, includes an extended piece of travel writing titled "Border-Crossing Report from Beijing" (Pekin ekkyō ki), which is in fact the first two parts of a three-part contribution to current affairs magazine *Gendai* (since discontinued) published between December 1992 and February 1993 and originally titled "At Tiananmen" (Ten'anmon ni te). Both "At Tiananmen" and "Tiananmen", as per the titles, retell a journey to the Chinese capital interspersed with memories relating to the author or protagonist's relation to mainland China and the Taiwan of the 1950s in which he spent some of his formative years.

In a recent interview, Levy recalls his experience of writing more or less the same content in two different formats:

> To listen to people's words and write this and that about China is the world of non-fiction or journalism. But to hear those words and then create one's own story. To turn it into an I-novel [autobiographical] text. In that sense, of listening, and speaking, I got the feeling that I could attain another audience to listen to my story, and thought then that I could write [i.e. turn this experience into] not just non-fiction, not just journalism, but indeed a novel.
>
> (Levy 2013, 189)

It should be noted that even in its original form, "At Tiananmen" was not simply "about China" but already a personal account of the author's journey there. Nevertheless, Levy's distinction of a novel from non-fiction and journalism provides an opening from which to consider difference between the two iterations of the journey. I will now turn to some of the most striking differences between the two texts.

The most obvious change is a shift in address from the first-person "I" (*boku*) to the more removed third-person "he" (*kare*) and more ambiguous "(one)self" (*jibun*), which in the context could be rendered "he himself". The pioneer of Translation Studies in Japan, Yanabu Akira, has written about the way "he" (*kare*) emerged as a key item of vocabulary in the context of modern Japanese literature's development, with specific reference to the novelist Tayama Katai (1871-1930) and his novel *The Quilt* (*Futon,* 1907), itself considered the progenitor of the Japanese "I-novel". According to Yanabu, "To the extent that *kare* functions like a third-person pronoun, the "I" of the author is mediated by it to become something like a third person – to become an object of scrutiny" (Yanabu 2011, 70; translation by Andre Haag). It might be that Levy is attempting to scrutinize his "self" through the fictionalization of his journey, but I would go further to suggest it is a scrutiny of the way in which his "self" can be mediated through the Japanese language.

This difference is particularly conspicuous in the opening paragraphs of each text, which I will reproduce here. First, the opening to "At Tiananmen":

> "There are Nationalists and Communists, and we are on the side of the Nationalists."
>
> I heard something along those lines from my mother when I was around eight or nine. I, my younger brother, my mother and father; my family living in Taiwan in relation to my father's work, were all white Americans. My father was of Jewish descent, and when he was first employed by the American government, a Christian colleague apparently said to him: "I thought you guys had darker skin"; in 1950s Taiwan, we might not have fit the image of blonde-haired Christians, but we were without a shadow of a doubt "*Měiguórén*" (Americans).
>
> (Levy 1996, 70; emphasis added)

In the above quotation, underlined text refers to pronouns that directly correspond to the original Japanese text (i.e. "I" = "*boku*" or "we" = "*bokura*"), while waved underlined text indicates those which must be inferred, a common feature of Japanese writing. Although it begins with a quote, giving a sense of drama and immediacy, the narrative is quickly brought under control by the narrating "I" (*boku*), the first word of the second paragraph.

The opening to "Tiananmen", in which I have indicated correspondence to the original Japanese text in the same manner, is drastically different:

Every window, every single portside window was illuminated in a red and orange glow. He knew the sun was setting, but still, those words, that song learnt long ago, rang out in his head. *Tài yáng shēng*… Ironic, he thought, but the words kept ringing.

A flock of clouds gathered at the end of the aircraft's wing, and now, just as it seemed as though he might almost be able to make out the profile of that face he'd seen some time and place ago, just as Chairman Mao began to—somewhere from the right hand aisle, a woman's voice stopped him. "*Bóérběn*". It was a fragile, elegant voice.

The world is no longer merely **bourbon** and *baabon*, now there is *bóérběn* too, he mused, and glanced at the voice to see a tall and, to use the English word his father would often say when describing a woman, **willowy** stewardess, floating gracefully down the aisle. Not "*baabon*". No, this was "*bóérběn*". "…*Bóérběn*". Hearing that word, which to his ear sounded not so unalike *Rìběn* [the Chinese pronunciation of 日本 = Japan], emerging from the mouth of a woman slender and **willowy**, elegant yet unmistakably of the mainland, gave him a shock he knew he was not supposed to feel. Yet, he felt.

(Levy 1996, 6-7; emphasis added)[1]

In contrast to the "I" who appears at the beginning of the second line in the non-fiction text, here the protagonist is not referred to at all until the third paragraph, and even then he is only referred to indirectly via the words of "his father" ("*kare no chichi*") and the way the stewardess's words are intelligible "to his ear" ("*kare no mimi*"). Here the "self", rather than being put on open display, has been embedded deep within the narrative, or rather, the body of the text; an effect that would be challenging to reproduce in English.

The non-fiction text, as suggested by the example above, is direct and explanatory, evident in the way it imparts information to readers in the final

[1] The translation and discussion here is based on an earlier paper written in Japanese. See Brook 2014.

sentence through brackets: "[we] were without a shadow of a doubt "*Měiguórén*" (Americans)". The fiction text, in contrast, seems to recreate the consciousness of "he" the protagonist, leaving readers to decode its meaning themselves. "His" consciousness is unmistakably "foreign", implied by the use of the English words "bourbon" and "willowy", emphasized in bold above, which stand out within the Japanese text in the Roman alphabet. However, unlike the explanatory non-fiction text with its admission that "[we] were all white Americans", "his" foreignness is not explicitly defined but rather must be inferred from the context. In this way, to refer back to the interview above, Levy is skilfully able to relate his own "story" (he uses the expressions "*jibun no hanashi*" = "[my] own (spoken) tale" and "*jibun no koto*" = "[my] own particulars/particularity") without it necessarily being a story about "him".

Aoyagi, in one of the first significant studies on Levy's writings, suggests that the autobiographical style particular to Levy and other "border-crossing writers" is characterized by an "objectifying gaze" and a "relational point of view", through which the author attempts to capture the way in which the unprecedented plurality of his or her own "self" (i.e. its irreducibility to a single monolithic culture such as "American" or "Japanese") is or can be perceived via its relation to its "others" in the external world (Aoyagi 2001, 26). However, Aoyagi's focus on the relationship between Levy's protagonists and their various "others" obscures the close connection between the narration and "his" specific subjectivity, to the extent to which one could arguably replace all instances of "he" and "his" with "I" and "my" without fundamentally changing the general feel of the text.[2] It could be described as a first-person narrative written in the third person. Although this could potentially be attributable to Japanese literary convention, it is still worth considering how the "I" and "he" narratives are different, and the significance of their difference being made conspicuous by including them in the same publication.

---

[2] Levy's first collection of essays includes a short piece of travel writing titled "Moscow: A Journey to the Whispering Capital" (Mosukuwa: Sasayaki no miyako he no tabi), in which the first-person pronoun "I" (*boku*) is used (Levy 1992, 159). In the original publication, "I" had been "he" (*kare*) (Levy 1988, 342), which demonstrates Levy's awareness of the two terms' interchangeability and is suggestive about his early experimentation.

As noted above, in the non-fiction text "I" speaks directly to the (presumably Japanese) reader, at one point even asserting his "decision" or "choice" to "settle down within [this island] country [...] and live within its language" (Levy 1996, 114). This voice is however muted in the fiction text. "His" immediate thoughts and feelings are narrated, but not by "he" himself. To this extent, "he", unlike perhaps the writer himself with his multilingual background, really does "live within" the narrative, written in Japanese which, as noted by critics both at the time of publication and by scholars more recently, strictly adheres to the norms of modern Japanese so that it is fully legible to the (imagined) monolingual reader of the language (see Eto et. al. 1996 and Yokota-Murakami 2018, Ch. 6). The creation of this fiction, then, could be interpreted as an attempt by the author to test the "translatability" of his own "self", or subjectivity, into the Japanese language, as if to prove to both himself and his readers that it is robust enough to carry a narrative even when liberated from its obligation to present itself as "I", the "white American", a native speaker of English (the shade of "his" skin is not mentioned once, although there are numerous references to other physical attributes). I would finally like to introduce an interesting, but also troubling, difference between the two texts that is related to this technique.

Towards the end of "Tiananmen", "he" reaches Tiananmen Square and enters the building housing the body of Mao Zedong, leading to a dramatic confrontation: while in the non-fiction text, Levy recounts pausing briefly, in the novel "he" stops in his tracks and has to be hauled out of the room by armed guards. Rather than this dramatization of events, I would like to focus on the preceding narrative. Soon after entering the building, both the narrator "I" and protagonist "he" encounter a woman giving orders, seemingly to instruct visitors where to lay their wreaths. I will reproduce the scenes below with the original Japanese.

"At Tiananmen" (Levy 1996, 92)	"Tiananmen" (Levy 1996, 62-3)
The lady was shouting in a loud voice near the entrance, "*Yī háng, liăng háng*"—"Okay, make one row now, yes, one row, two rows," she said.	"Make *yī háng!* Make *liăng hángs!*" came a bellowing voice, [...] "*Yī háng! Liăng háng!*" One row for Chairman Mao! Two rows for Chairman Mao!
入り口近くのオバさんが大きな声で、 「一行(イーハング)、两行(リャングハング)」—「はい、二列を作るのよ、はい、一列、二列」と言った。	「一列(イーハング)！ 两列(リャングハング)！」という声が轟き、 […] 「イーハング！ リャングハング！」 はい、毛主席のために、一列を作れ、二列を作れ!

Translation into English inevitably results in a loss of meaning, as Japanese conventions allow one to add phonetic readings to Chinese characters, which in this case spell out "*iihangu, ryanguhangu*" in both versions. The difference between the texts is subtle, but important: in the non-fiction text, the woman is quoted "一行两行" whereas in the fiction text, this is transformed into "一列两列". The former can be read roughly as it is phoneticized here ("*yī háng liǎng háng*" is the pinyin reading and corresponds to "*iihangu, ryanguhangu*"), whereas the latter cannot (一列 would be read "*yī liè*"). That is, in the fiction text, the reader is guided from the characters "一列两列" to the similar Japanese of "一列二列", in a narrative that privileges legibility at the expense of authenticity, specifically relating to the foreign language of Chinese.

The fact that this clear mismatching of sound and written character is, as far as I am aware, an isolated incident within Levy's writing means that it merits special attention. It seems relevant that it appears within a context in which the protagonist "he", before Chairman Mao's stony gaze and beneath the unforgiving glare of the sun in Tiananmen Square, had just become aware of the relative insignificance of "his" own life and personal memories, because within the text itself that power dynamic is inverted completely as the "reality" of modern Chinese is sacrificed, albeit in a single, seemingly insignificant quotation, in order to accommodate the legibility of "his" personal story. I attempted to recreate this in my translation by turning "*liǎng háng*" into a plural with "s", but to the casual reader the inauthenticity of the original "Chinese" is far less apparent.

The ambiguity of this "error" in the text, the lack of an obvious clue like the "different rice" in Tawada's poetry, makes it harder to infer the authorial intent behind it. It may indeed just be a byproduct of the author's sincere attempt to "translate" "his" story into "Japanese", although readers are arguably prompted to compare the two versions by "his" (or the narrator's) rumination on the various ways to say "bourbon", whereby he ponders: "Which could be the true name?" (Levy 1996, 49) Regardless of the intent, however, it seems to suggest the dependence of an individual "self" (in this case "he"), especially a "self" that has been separated from the mediating subject "I", upon the unity or oneness (i.e. identity) of the medium (language) used to convey it, while also demonstrating the exclusionary tendency inherent to that oneness, that is to say, its tendency to disregard “other” realities. The book *Tiananmen* does not directly condemn or criticize this tendency, but by presenting it as a form of asymmetry within a single publication, ostensibly written in a single language (i.e. Japanese), it allows readers to confront it themselves and draw their own conclusions, while prompting them to ask themselves questions like: do they know which is the “correct” version, and should they know? Should they care? Who are “they” anyway?

What is significant here is that, just like the difference manifested in Tawada’s poetry, the difference that emerges here is rooted in a singular subjectivity—the writer’s—but at the same time cannot simply be reduced to the writer’s “foreignness”. This active expansion of existing difference, pursual of difference, and exposition of difference may be one of the key commonalities between Levy and Tawada’s early careers, and it indicates their sensitivity towards local specificity at a time when the discourse on “globalization” and its homogenizing effects was still in its infancy.

5. Conclusion

A quarter of a century has passed since the most recent text discussed in this paper, a time in which both Levy and Tawada have led active literary careers as the world around them continues to shift. Both writers have continued in their subsequent works to address issues relating to movement across specific places, languages and cultures in the contemporary, “globalizing” world, while also emphasizing their own external position vis-à-vis the literary cultures they take part in. While their writing could indeed become a basis for imagining a new, transnational way of belonging in the world, a worthwhile question that is being pursued by existing scholarship, such a future-oriented approach risks essentializing their “in-between” positioning, and thus obscuring the question of how “difference” actually manifests in their work. In this paper I have attempted to address this issue by analyzing striking examples of asymmetry that appear within a single publication in both authors’ early careers. I have demonstrated how both Levy and Tawada seem to exploit their own ostensibly “foreign” “self” as a means through which to expose difference as it exists, or can be made to exist, within the world around them, describing this as a process of “self-translation”.

Just as the original text is not physically present in a translation, the authors' foreign "selves" are not physically present in the texts discussed, nor, at least in my reading, do they exist in the form of writing that is noticeably "foreign" itself. However, just as an original text can gain both a sense of mystique and authority through the process of being translated, such a writing strategy also reinforces the presence of the authors, potentially to the extent that all of the "difference" they uncover is then blocked out by their own looming shadows. How they, and other "border-crossing writers", deal with this conundrum is another issue for future research, but surely one that must be dealt with before they are taken as models for a new kind of subjectivity, be it "transnational", "global", or otherwise.

Acknowledgement: All translations, unless otherwise noted, are mine. This work was supported by JSPS KAKENHI Grant Number JP18J20597. It is based upon a presentation I gave at "Aspects of the Media: Local and Global Currents" on 4 July 2019 at Kobe University. I am grateful for the useful comments received at this and previous workshops through which I developed the ideas expressed in this paper.

Bibliography

Aoyagi, Etsuko. 2001. "Fukusūsei no bungaku: ishokugata <kyōkaiji> Rībi Hideo to Mizumura Minae ni miru bungaku no katsubo", in *Gengo bunka ronshū*, 2001-3, 1-29.

Barbieri, Francesco Eugenio. 2016. "Discovering/Uncovering: Yōko Tawada's *Abenteuer der deutschen Grammatik*" in Valtolina, Amelia and Braun, Michael eds. *Am Scheideweg der Sprachen: Die poetischen Migrationen von Yoko Tawada*, 215-222, Tübingen: Stauffenburg Verlag.

Brook, Thomas. 2014. "Hon'yaku kara mita Rībi Hideo to "Ten'anmon"", in *2013-2014 Nihongo Nihonbunka kenshū ryūgakusei hōkokusho,* Kobe University International Student Center, 134-151.

Etō, Jun, Takubo, Hideo, and Tomioka, Kōichirō. 1996. "Sōsaku gappyō -242- "Ten'anmon" Rībi Hideo, "Gūzen no nettowāku" Aono Satoshi, "Yoru no hōshi" Inaba Mayumi", *Gunzō*, 51(2) (February 1996), 371-388.

Grutman, Rainier. 2009. "Self-translation", in Baker, Mona and Saldanha, Gabriela eds. *Routledge Encyclopedia of Translation Studies: Second Edition*. Kindle edition.

Levy, Hideo. 1988. "Shiberia testudō taikenki: "Nazo no Roshia" nado to iu kimari monku de wa hyōgen dekinai", *Ushio*, v. 350 (June 1988), 342-345.

---1992. *Nihongo no shōri*. Tokyo: Kōdansha.

---2004. *Seijōki no kikoenai heya*. Tokyo: Kōdansha.
---2010. *Wareteki Nihongo The World in Japanese*. Tokyo: Chikuma Shobō.
---2011. *A Room Where The Star-Spangled Banner Cannot Be Heard* (trans. Scott, Christopher D.). New York: Columbia University Press.
---2013. "Nihongo de gendai wo hyōgen suru". In Guo, Nanyan ed. *Bairingaru na nihongo bungaku: tagengo tabunka no aida*, 187-195. Tokyo: Sangensha.
Masumoto, Hiroko. 2020. "The Concept of Translation in Yoko Tawada's Early Work". In *Interface: Journal of European Languages and Literatures*, Issue 12 (Summer 2020), 5-28.
Miyata, Fumihisa. 2015. "Representation of Disasters in Contemporary Japanese Culture: Theoretical Discourses of "Border Crossing" and "War Memories"". Ph.D. Thesis (in Japanese), Nihon Daigaku.
Nakai, Asako. 2007. *Tasha no jiden: Posutokoroniaru bungaku wo yomu*. Tokyo: Kenkyusha.
Sakamoto, Rumi. 2006. "Writing as out/insiders: Contemporary Japan's *ekkyō* literature in globalization". In Allen, Matthew and Sakamoto, Rumi eds. *Popular Culture, Globalization and Japan*, 137-157. Oxon: Routledge.
Scott, Christopher D. 2008. "Queer/Nation: From "Nihon bungaku" to "Nihongo bungaku"". *Proceedings of the Association for Japanese Literary Studies, Literature and Literary Theory*, Vol. 9 2008, 117-123.
Sierks, Eric James. 2015. "Transgressing the Boundaries of Reception: Shirin Nezammafi and an *Ekkyō* Feminist Counterpublic". *Asian Languages & Civilizations Graduate Theses & Dissertations. 16*. Masters Thesis, University of Colorado.
Suga, Keijirō. 2007. "Translation, Exophony, Omniphony". In Slaymaker, Doug ed. *Yōko Tawada: Voices from Everywhere*, 21-33. Plymouth: Lexington Books.
Tawada, Yoko. 1997 [1987]. *Nur da wo du bist da ist nichts*. 3rd edition. Tübingen: Konkursbuch Verlag Claudia Gehrke.
---2015. *Nur da wo du bist da ist nichts*. 5th edition. Tübingen: Konkursbuch Verlag Claudia Gehrke.
---1986. "Zehn Gedichte" (trans. Pörtner, Peter and Tawada, Yoko). In Pörtner, Peter ed. *Konkursbuch 16/17: Japan - Ein Lesebuch*, 41-53. Tübingen: Konkursbuch Verlag Claudia Gehrke.
Treat, John Whittier. 1999. *Great Mirrors Shattered: Homosexuality, Orientalism and Japan*. New York: Oxford University Press.
Yanabu, Akira. 2011 [1982]. "*Kare* and *kanojo* – the shifting referents of two translation pronouns" (trans. Haag, Andre). In Levy, Indra ed. *Translation in Modern Japan*, 61-72. Oxon: Routledge.
Yokota-Murakami, Takayuki. 2018. *Mother-Tongue in Modern Japanese Literature and Criticism: Toward a New Polylingual Poetics*. Singapore: Palgrave Macmillan. Kindle edition.

“Semitic-Celtic Oriental” Seymour: “The Orient” as Counter Culture in J.D. Salinger’s Glass Family Saga[1]

Tomoko Oda

Introduction

It has been eleven years since J. D. Salinger (1919-2010) passed away in January 2010. The publication of multiple biographies gives evidence of the enduring popularity his literary works still enjoy. One of these volumes is *Salinger*, which was edited and released by David Shields and Shane Salerno in 2013. Shields and Salerno regard Salinger’s commitment to Vedanta as one of the most crucial turning points in his whole life. Eastern thought, including Vedanta, Zen and Taoism, is one of the significant themes represented by Salinger, which has inspired a number of critics to indicate the relationship between such “Oriental” philosophy and his literature.

Critics have often considered Seymour Glass, the eldest son of the Glass family, a practitioner of Eastern thought. Seymour, one of the most important characters created by Salinger, is well known particularly for his suicide at the end of the short story “A Perfect Day for Bananafish” (1948) collected in *Nine Stories* (1953). Critiques of Seymour’s suicide vary. Some scholars assert that Seymour shot himself to death because of his maladjustment to and despair at the materialistic side of American society, which is symbolized by the bananafish (Alsen 1983, 15; Baskett 1963, 57; Kaufman 1998/2011, 98; Rosen 1977, 36). Others regard Seymour’s death not as the end of his life but as a process of reincarnation as understood in Eastern thought (Lundquist 1979, 108; Shields & Salerno 2013, 314). Another critic indicates both of these aspects (Lane

---

[1] An earlier version of this paper was orally presented at the Others in the Humanities Research Group workshop *Others and Othering in Modernity: Representation of own and other cultures* held at the Graduate School of Humanities, Kobe University, on 1 November 2017. This work was supported by JSPS KAKENHI Grant Number JP19J10995.

1973/2011, 24-26).

Salinger wrote eight stories starring Seymour and his six siblings, which are commonly called the "Glass family saga." The eight stories are "A Perfect Day for Bananafish," "Uncle Wiggily in Connecticut" (1948), "Down at the Dinghy" (1949), "Franny" (1955), "Raise High the Roof Beam, Carpenters" (1955), "Zooey" (1957), "Seymour: An Introduction" (1959), and "Hapworth 16, 1924" (1965) in order of publication. These stories include Seymour's frequent words and deeds that correspond to Eastern thought. This has enabled readers to have an impression of Seymour as being a person surrounded by an "Oriental" ambience.

For example, in "Raise High the Roof Beam, Carpenters," Seymour is likened to the excellent judge of horseflesh in a Taoist narrative from the Liezi book, which is quoted entirely and included as part of the fiction (Salinger 1963/1994, 3-4). For another example, "Seymour: An Introduction" describes Seymour through the repeated use of Eastern words like "mukta," which refers to an "enlightened man" in Sanskrit, and in the context of Eastern thought—compared to an "Oriental" priest, Chuang-tzu (369-286 B.C.), and a master of Japanese archery (Salinger 1963/1994, 68; 119; 130).

On the other hand, Buddy Glass, the second eldest of the Glass siblings and narrator of most of the Glass family saga, implies that not merely Seymour's affinity with Zen but also his Jewish and Irish ethnicity are relevant to this issue by describing Seymour as a "Semitic-Celtic Oriental":

> As for my brother Seymour—ah, well, my brother Seymour. For this Semitic-Celtic Oriental I need a spanking-new paragraph.
>
> (Salinger 1963/1994, 78)

This phrase derives from the Glass siblings' ethnic background. Seymour and Buddy, as well as the other five siblings, are born half-Jewish, half-Irish. Moreover, the phrase associates Glass family with "Orientals," another category that is thrust into the periphery of American society, in which precedence has been taken by WASPs (White Anglo-Saxon Protestants). This tendency of regarding Jewish and Irish origins as "Oriental" has long been in scholarly neglect; despite the fact that Salinger himself was highly conscious of his own half-Jewish, half-

Irish ethnicity.

Through close readings of the Glass family saga—"Raise High the Roof Beam, Carpenters" and "Seymour: An Introduction" above all—I will reconsider representations of "the Orient" from the perspective of ethnicity in order to explore the way in which otherness is represented in Salinger's literary works. Then, by analyzing the links between Jewish, Irish and "Oriental" imagery seen in the depiction of "Semitic-Celtic" Seymour as a passionate devotee of Eastern thought and culture, I will argue that Seymour plays a mediating role of embodying "Oriental" otherness as a countervailing measure against WASP-centrism in America. I will also indicate the extent to which "the Orient" is juxtaposed in the same literary space as multiple kinds of religious imagery of the West and East, comparing the pluralistic use of different religious themes to one of the important features of world literature as explained by Homi K. Bhabha. Finally I will argue that the adoption of such pluralistic religions is in significant harmony with the counter culture against hegemonic culture mainly performed by WASP people in terms of a counter message being conveyed through "Oriental" otherness.

1. Seymour as Salinger's Idealized Self

The title of "Raise High the Roof Beam, Carpenters" derives from a poem by Sappho, a renowned ancient Greek female poet of 630 to 580 B.C. The story is intended to be an epithalamium for the groom Seymour and bride Muriel—a girl who engages in beautifying herself and indulges in a long-distance phone call with her mother, which resultantly forces her to face Seymour's suicide right by his side in "A Perfect Day for Bananafish." In the beginning of "Raise High the Roof Beam, Carpenters," Seymour is reported missing at his wedding ceremony. This unexplained disappearance of Seymour leads Buddy to be in the same boat as the guests invited by Muriel and her parents. Along the way, the Matron of Honor speaks ill of Seymour as being in the rats, which strains Buddy's patience to the breaking point. Then the news of Seymour having come for and run away with Muriel drops into their laps. That event puts an end to the fuss, with which the story comes to an end. "Seymour: An Introduction," on the other hand, consists of essays written seemingly freely by Buddy. At a glance, the story presents a jumble of such unrelated ideas as the genealogy of the Glass family, the physical features and spiritual life of Seymour, and Buddy's own religious philosophy. This story stands out among the Glass family saga for its conspicuous lack of organization and extreme intricateness in style and content. Each of these two stories was first published in separate issues of *The New Yorker*, but in 1963 they were anthologized and entitled *Raise High the Roof Beam, Carpenters, and Seymour: An Introduction*.

A number of critics of Salinger have provided negative assessments of these stories, particularly of "Seymour: An Introduction." Warren French denounces the novella as "self-indulgent *kitsch*" for its describing Seymour as a "superman" so intrusively that the story presents "feelings no one actually feels" (French 1976, 160). Some scholars, in contrast, have given positive evaluations of both of these two writings. Kenneth Slawenski, for example, argues that "Raise High the Roof Beam, Carpenters" delineates "divine beauty alive within us all," which is repeatedly intended and attempted by Salinger (Slawenski 2011, 274). Dipti R. Pattanaik considers the Glass family saga, including "Seymour: An Introduction," as Salinger's attempt to use "rational language" for the expression of "spiritual realization" (Pattanaik 1998, 122). As Myles Weber notes, countless harsh comments right after the publication notwithstanding, these two novellas began to undergo further reassessment in the early part of the twenty-first century, being appraised for Salinger's "stylistic innovations" (Weber 2005, 139).

Buddy plays a prominent part in the narration of most of the Glass family saga. He tells the story of his beloved eldest brother, who shot and killed himself. Further analysis of Seymour's relationship with Buddy reveals the significant similarity between the two, unveiling another important aspect of their brotherhood. Taking into account the commonly accepted theory that Buddy is Salinger's alter ego, I will demonstrate that Seymour can also be associated with Salinger, casting light upon Seymour as Salinger's idealized self.

As is suggested on the cover notes for *Franny and Zooey*, in which "Franny" and "Zooey" are anthologized, Buddy is often considered as Salinger's authorial alter ego, a view which a majority of critics follow in analyzing the Glass family saga (Baskett 1963, 58; Bryan 1962, 226; Weber 2005, 130). At the same time,

Buddy also psychologically overlaps with his older brother Seymour in "Seymour: An Introduction" in an insistent manner. In the following part, Buddy proclaims that he will substitute for Seymour to teach who he was and how he acted to readers, especially younger ones:

> (This last little piece of pedantry, I repeat, is for the young, who write to authors and never get any replies from the beasts. I'm also functioning, partly, on behalf of my title character, who was a teacher, too, poor bastard.)
>
> (Salinger 1963/1994, 75)

Buddy thus develops a deep sense of mission to inherit Seymour's position; and what is more, he reveals his delight of looking like Seymour as follows:

> However, several members of my immediate, if somewhat far-flung, family, who regularly pick over my published prose for small technical errors, have gently pointed out to me (much too damned gently, since they usually come down on me like grammarians) that the young man, the 'Seymour,' who did the walking and talking in that early story, not to mention the shooting, was not Seymour at all but, oddly, someone with a striking resemblance to—alley oop, I'm afraid—myself.
>
> (Salinger 1963/1994, 71-72)

In the Glass family saga, "A Perfect Day for Bananafish," the actual short story penned by Salinger, is presented as one written by Buddy. Here Buddy recalls how other Glass family members reacted to this short story of his. Buddy notes that several of them pointed out a resemblance of Seymour described in his story to Buddy himself. Buddy's feeling of smugness exposed within this comment shows his longing for Seymour, even implying his desire to be like his legendary brother. Another significant example of this longing is seen in the following phrase:

> [. . .] I was always secretly pleased and proud to bear any physical resemblance to Seymour.
>
> (Salinger 1963/1994, 114)

Buddy clearly expresses his pleasure of being physically similar to Seymour. The exceptionally close kinship between these two Glass brothers is thus exhibited in an articulated manner. Psychological and physical overlap between Seymour and Buddy is demonstrated to such an extent that their relationship appears more significant than just a mere blood relation.

From these examinations, we can see that Seymour embodies the idealized self of Buddy-Salinger. This is also suggested by the name of Seymour frequently being abbreviated to "S." in "Raise High the Roof Beam, Carpenters" (Salinger 1963/1994, 43). The abbreviation prompts us to recall Salinger's own initial. We can identify one of the root causes of Salinger creating Seymour as his own ideal image in the author's ethnic/religious background. Salinger was confused about his complicated ethnic and religious identity in relation to his father being of Jewish and his mother of Irish ancestry (Shields & Salerno 2013, 34; 37; 55). As I will argue below, Salinger projects who he is, and who he hopes to be, upon the portrait of Seymour.

2. Seymour/Salinger as Members of a Minority Ethnic Group

Mirroring Salinger's ideal model, Seymour inherits his Jewish-Irish ethnicity. Numerous descriptions of Semitic-Celtic ethnicity in "Raise High the Roof Beam, Carpenters" and "Seymour: An Introduction" are highly worthy of attention. For instance, Minotaur, the monstrous beast in Greek mythology with a bullish head and human body, is invoked to explain the ethnic background of the Glass family as follows:

> First, there is the matter of family pressure. It's doubtless a very common thing, if not much more common than I'd care to hear about, but I have four living, lettered, rather incontinently articulate younger brothers and sisters, of part-Jewish, part-Irish, and conceivably part-Minotaur extraction— [. . .].
>
> (Salinger 1963/1994, 73)

The Glass family's "part-Jewish, part-Irish" ethnicity appears frequently throughout these two stories. We can thus say that Salinger mentions the mixed ethnicity in a highly conscious manner. Earlier studies, however, have paid little attention to the question of how their "Semitic-Celtic" ethnicity is linked with representation of the "Orient" and how this linkage functions. Therefore I will analyze the relationship between the two, which otherwise tends to be overlooked, through the portrayal of Seymour.

While Buddy consistently reveres Seymour when he narrates the stories, he occasionally mentions Seymour being alienated from society. In "Raise High the Roof Beam, Carpenters," for example, Buddy recalls his childhood, in which he and Seymour appeared regularly on the radio program "It's a Wise Child." He mentions his mother having learned that Seymour and Buddy were in danger of becoming estranged from mainstream society as follows:

> [. . .] but my mother had once read a magazine article on the little crosses professional children are obliged to bear—their estrangement from normal, presumably desirable society—and she took an iron stand on the issue, and never, never wavered.
>
> (Salinger 1963/1994, 5)

Inheriting characteristics of burlesque comedians from the Glass clan, Seymour and Buddy have grown up to be regular performers on the radio. According to Buddy, "It's a Wise Child" was a sort of panel show, in which Seymour and Buddy, as "professional children," responded to abstruse questions. Both of these precocious children performed in such a sophisticated manner that it put even an expert to shame. This episode associates Seymour and Buddy with estrangement from society because of their outstanding genius.

Meanwhile, Buddy correlates the alienation of Seymour with his ethnic background. While "Zooey" portrays Bessie Glass, mother of the Glass children, clinging to Catholic ideas as a way to cure the youngest daughter Franny's heartsickness caused by her boyfriend's inconsiderate attitude,[2] most of the other Glass family saga focuses on their Jewish blood. In "Seymour: An Introduction," Buddy recollects another childhood memory of his great-grandfather Zozo's enormous nose when he portrays Seymour's external characteristics in the following way:

> Noses, however, we emphatically had, and they were close to being identical: two great, fleshy, drooping, trompe-like affairs that were different from every other nose in the family except, all too vividly, that of dear old Great-Grandfather Zozo, whose own nose, ballooning out from an early daguerreotype, used to alarm me considerably as a small boy.
>
> (Salinger 1963/1994, 112)

The great grandfather of the Glass siblings, Zozo, has a Jewish origin. Buddy regards Zozo's "ballooning" nose as a cause of "alarm." Considering these aspects, it can be inferred that Buddy implies that Seymour, as well as the other Glass siblings, are fated to be socially alienated owing to their being Jewish American.

Instead of capitulating to his fate of living in the periphery, Seymour attempts to overcome such adverse conditions through adopting "the Orient." We can see this tendency in the way that allusions to his "Semitic-Celtic" ethnicity appear repeatedly in between references to "Oriental" imagery. For instance, the word "cabalist," which refers to a believer in Judaic mysticism Cabala, is juxtaposed with the term Buddha in the following passage from "Seymour: An Introduction":

> He[Seymour] hadn't, I'm afraid, the ears of a buccaneer but the ears of an old cabalist or an old Buddha. Extremely long, fleshy lobes. I remember Father Waker, passing through here a few years ago in a hot black suit, asking me, while I was doing the Times crossword, if I thought S's ears had been Tang dynasty.

---

[2] Bessie sticks to Catholicism as reiterated throughout "Zooey" as follows: "If it was something strictly Catholic, or like that, I[Bessie] might be able to help her[Franny] myself" (Salinger 1961/2010, 71); ""For your information," she[Bessie] said, "I didn't say I was going to phone Philly Byrnes' psychoanalyst, I said I was *think*ing about it. In the *first* place, he isn't just an ordinary psychoanalyst. He happens to be a *very* devout *Cath*olic psychoanalyst, and I thought it *might* be better than sitting around and watching that child[Franny]—"" (Salinger 1961/2010, 80). Despite the prominent position occupied by the Church of Ireland, Salinger associates Irish ethnicity with Catholicism instead, it being the teaching that his mother once followed. David R. Mayer also mentions the general imagination of Irish people and Catholicism as being "synonymous with each other" (Mayer 1985, 8).

(Salinger 1963/1994, 110)

For another instance from the same story, the Old Testament, the only Judaic scripture, and "Eastern philosophy" such as Vedanta and Taoism lay side by side:

> Would it be out of order for me to say that both Seymour's and my roots in Eastern philosophy—if I may hesitantly call them roots—were, are, planted in the New and Old Testaments, Advaita Vedanta, and classical Taoism?
>
> (Salinger 1963/1994, 131)

As Gordon E. Slethaug asserts, Seymour's Jewish-Irish background evokes the religious tradition of Judaism and Catholicism. This religious aspect of Seymour enables him to convincingly bear the "Oriental" mood that results from his serious commitment to Eastern thought (Slethaug 1971/2011, 10). This seems to imply that ethnic issues lie behind Seymour's pursuit of "the Orient." Therefore I argue that the "Oriental" imagery granted to the Glass siblings, particularly Seymour, is employed by Salinger in order to resist the WASP-centered society and culture that have marginalized both him and his alter egos.

3. Salinger's "Religious Pluralism" and its Counter-Cultural Aspect

The equal significance granted to Western thought and Eastern philosophy in Salinger's works has scarcely been the focus of scholarly inquiry. Instead, critics have been engrossed in indicating which is the most significant religious theme among those adopted by Salinger. Eberhard Alsen estimates Vedanta more highly than any of the other Eastern philosophies, although he has conducted meticulous research on the various kinds of thought of both the West and East employed in the Glass family saga (Alsen 1983, 168).

On the other hand, James Lundquist considers not only Zen but also the Christian imagery within Seymour's characterization, noting that "he[Seymour] is a Zen-master, mystic, seer, and Christ-figure himself," regardless of his discussion of Zen Buddhism as the most influential school of thought on Salinger's literary works (Lundquist 1979, 142). Dennis L. O'Connor values such pluralistic use of religions from both the West and East by saying that it is "the very soul of his[Salinger's] writing" (O'Connor 1984/2011, 80). Moreover, O'Connor asserts the importance of multiple religious themes as follows:

> Rather than blurring or collapsing different Oriental and Western traditions, Salinger's religious pluralism finds artistic expression in a respectful and playful interaction of distinct layers of meaning.
>
> (O'Connor 1984/2011, 89)

As O'Connor maintains, the significance of Salinger's adoption of "the Orient" is ascribable to "religious pluralism"—Western and Eastern religious items juxtaposed in order to balance each other out. This balanced arrangement is made with ostensible nonchalance, yet actually with the utmost attention; and thereby this religious juxtaposition parallels counter culture.

Social anthropologist Peter Worsley, in *Knowledges: Culture, Counterculture, Subculture* (1997), defines counter culture as resistance to hegemonic values (Worsley 1997, 265). In the United States, the movement of counter culture reached its height in the late 1960s. American writers and poets, such as Jack Kerouac (1922-69) and Allen Ginsberg (1926-97), who are known as the Beat Generation, played a central part in the movement. As David Weir maintains, these Beat Generation writers aimed at the detachment from middle-class values, which they criticized as materialistic; instead, they devoted themselves to Eastern thought and took an interest in "the Orient" so as to seek spiritual fulfillment (Weir 2011, 241).

As mentioned earlier, Salinger was also fascinated with the teachings of Zen and Vedanta, incorporating Eastern thought and culture into his literary works. He began his literary career in the 1940s and continued to release publications until the 1960s. Despite the overlapping period and theme of writing with the Beat Generation writers, Salinger's literature has not previously been studied in terms of counter culture.

However, Salinger shows an interest in, and even contempt toward, the Beat Generation writers in the following passage from "Seymour: An Introduction":

> In this entre-nous spirit, then, old confidant, before we join the others, the grounded everywhere, including, I'm sure, the middle-aged hot-rodders who insist on zooming us to the moon, the Dharma Bums, the makers of cigarette filters for thinking men, the Beat and the Sloppy and the Petulant, the chosen cultists, all the lofty experts who know so well what we should or shouldn't do with our poor little sex organs, all the bearded, proud, unlettered young men and unskilled guitarists and Zen-killers and incorporated aesthetic Teddy boys who look down their thoroughly unenlightened noses at this splendid planet where (please don't shut me up) Kilroy, Christ, and Shakespeare all stopped—before we join these others, I privately say to you, old friend (unto you, really, I'm afraid), please accept from me this unpretentious bouquet of very early-blooming parentheses: (((()))).
>
> (Salinger 1963/1994, 62)

There are several phrases related to the Beat Generation in the above passage. Such words and phrases as "the Beat" and "the Dharma Bums"—the exact name of Kerouac's novel published one year prior to "Seymour: An Introduction"—obviously speaks of Salinger's strong interest in the Beat Generation, while another group of strongly worded terms like "the Sloppy," "the Petulant" and "Zen-killers," and the twice repeated phrase "before we join the/these others," denote his negative view towards the "Beat" cultural movement. Although Salinger thus attempts to draw a sharp line between himself and the Beat Generation, which has caused him to be excluded from discussions of those writers who wrote about counter culture, that he makes such a distinction exhibits his consciousness of such counter cultural writings on the opposite side of the same coin.

The essence of counter culture indeed appears in Salinger's literary texts, particularly in his juxtaposition of Western and Eastern religious/cultural themes. In "Raise High the Roof Beam, Carpenters," for example, Seymour adores haiku enough to quote, in his diary Buddy happens to find, an English translation of one of the poems by Saigyo (1118-90), one of the most famous Japanese monks/poets. Seymour quotes as follows: "What it is I know not/But with the gratitude/My tears fall" (Salinger 1963/1994, 43). It seems likely that the English translator of this haiku is R. H. Blyth, as Salinger was an ardent reader of his books and makes a long comment on the English translations of Japanese books in the form of a footnote (Salinger 1963/1994, 75). According to Buddy, the narrator, Seymour was able to write haiku in four languages—Japanese as well as English, German, and Italian (Salinger 1963/1994, 80-81). Seymour thus makes adjustments to Japanese haiku with these Western languages, inventing a way to give equal significance to both the West and East. Handling these two, otherwise conflicting, cultures, on the same level functions to challenge the long-established hegemonic cultural structure separating WASP and non-WASP communities in the United States. Through Seymour's enthusiasm for Eastern thought and the way equal validity is given to Western and Eastern cultural items, we can thus see that Salinger's literary texts imply the Jewish-Irish Seymour's counter-cultural intentions to overcome his own ethnic marginality. We can thus see how such otherness of "the Orient" functions to transmit the countervailing messages against American WASP-centric set of values.

These counter-cultural characteristics of "the Orient" given equivalent significance to aspects of the West echo with one of the features of world literature suggested by Homi K. Bhabha. In *The Location of Culture* (1994), Bhabha views world literature as a "category that is concerned with a form of cultural dissensus and alterity" generated by "foreign" philosophical and cultural representations (Bhabha 1994, 17). Seen in the context of Bhabha's argument on multicultural representations, Salinger's Glass family saga functions as a remarkable example of literature presenting "cultural dissensus and alterity" through the image of "Semitic-Celtic" Seymour exercising Eastern thought to bridge the ethnic barrier built between the dominant WASP community and minority ethnic groups. Ihab Hassan asserts that Seymour "mediates" between the closed world of the Glass siblings and the society of the general public outside of their own world (Hassan 1961, 285). I argue such a border-crossing aspect of Seymour's character can also be read from the way he approaches his Jewish-Irish ethnicity, taking it as a means through which he can go beyond the borders between WASP and non-WASP like the Glass family itself.

Conclusion

In the above discussion of "Raise High the Roof Beam, Carpenters" and "Seymour: An Introduction" from the Glass family saga, I have suggested that Seymour appears as an ideal version of Salinger himself. I have also outlined the way Seymour-Salinger struggles with his marginalized position in WASP-dominated society resulting from his own Jewish-Irish origin. Then I have explored how he attempts to depart from such an ethnically minor status by means of devoting himself to Eastern thought and acquiring "Oriental" knowledge, taking advantage of the otherness of "the Orient" to overcome his peripheral position. Through the investigations of the representations of Eastern thought arranged in balance with Western imagery, I have argued that "the Orient" functions as counter culture to overcome the assigned position in American society, to which Seymour and the other Glass siblings are forced to resign themselves to living as an ethnic minority. I have also pointed out the significant resemblance between such counter-cultural features and "world literature" as explained by Bhabha, in which representations of the "foreign" trigger "cultural dissensus and alterity" which are developed through the texts.

From the character of Seymour and the "Oriental" ambience surrounding him in the Glass family saga, we can see clearly Salinger's own experience of being from a minority ethnic group and of his ardent reading of Eastern thought. In a similar fashion to Seymour, Salinger had conflicted feelings about his alterity—his own half-Jewish, half-Irish blood and being placed in the periphery of American society. Hence, "the Orient" as counter culture, which is granted to Seymour as the idealized form of Salinger, mirrors the author's anguish over being a Jewish-Irish American, an "other" in the WASP-centric American society.

Bibliography

Alsen, Eberhard. 1983. *Salinger's Glass Stories as a Composite Novel*. New York: The Whitston Publishing Company.

Baskett, Sam S. 1963. "The Splendid/Squalid World of J. D. Salinger." *Wisconsin Studies in Contemporary Literature* 4(1): 48-61. http://www.jstor.org/stable/1207184.

Bhabha, Homi K. 1994. *The Location of Culture*. London & New York: Routledge.

Bloom, Harold, ed. 2011. *J. D. Salinger's Short Stories*. New York: Infobase Publishing.

Bryan, James E. 1962. "Salinger's Seymour's Suicide." *College English* 24(3): 226-29. http://www.jstor.org/stable/373294.

French, Warren. 1976. *J. D. Salinger*. Boston: Twayne Publishers.

Hassan, Ihab. 1961. *Radical Innocence*. Princeton: Princeton University Press.

Kaufman, Anthony. 1998/2011. "'Along this road goes no one': Salinger's 'Teddy' and the Failure of Love." *Studies in Short Fiction* 35: 129-40. repr. in Bloom: 95-106.

Lane, Gary. 1973/2011. "Seymour's Suicide Again: A New Reading of J. D. Salinger's 'A Perfect Day for Bananafish.'" *Studies in Short Fiction* 10(1): 27-33. repr. in Bloom: 21-27.

Lundquist, James. 1979. *J. D. Salinger*. New York: Frederick Ungar Publishing Company.

Mayer, David R. 1985. "The American Neighborhood Novel." *Nanzan Review of American Studies: a Journal of Center for American Studies* 7: 1-22.

O'Connor, Dennis L. 1984/2011. "J. D. Salinger's Religious Pluralism: The Example of *Raise High the Roof Beam, Carpenters.*" *The Southern Review* 20(2): 316-32. repr. in Bloom: 79-94.

Pattanaik, Dipti R. 1998. "The Holy Refusal: A Vedantic Interpretation of J. D. Salinger's Silence." *MELUS* 23(2): 113-27. http://www.jstor.org/stable/468015.

Rosen, Gerald. 1977. *Zen in the Art of J. D. Salinger*. Berkeley, CA: Creative Arts Book Company.

Salinger, J. D. 1961/2010. *Franny and Zooey*. London: Penguin Books.

Salinger, J. D. 1953/1991. *Nine Stories*. New York: Little, Brown & Company.

Salinger, J. D. 1963/1994. *Raise High the Roof Beam, Carpenters, and Seymour: An Introduction*. London: Penguin Books.

Shields, David and Shane Salerno. 2013. *Salinger*. New York: Simon & Schuster.

Slawenski, Kenneth. 2011. *J. D. Salinger: A Life*. New York: Random House.

Slethaug, Gordon E. 1971/2011. "Seymour: A Clarification." *Renascence* 23(4): 115-28, repr. in Bloom: 5-20.

Weir, David. 2011. *American Orient: Imagining the East from the Colonial Era through the Twentieth Century*. Amherst: University of Massachusetts Press.

Weber, Myles. 2005. "Reading Salinger's Silence." *New England Review* 26(2): 118-41. http://www.jstor.org/stable/40240714.

Worsley, Peter. 1997. *Knowledges: Culture, Counterculture, Subculture*. New York: The New Press.

2
Mediation of Otherness

Nostalgia as a Modern Myth: From Modern Europe to Contemporary Japan

Kantaro Ohashi

0. Introduction

This paper aims to analyze the aesthetic problems surrounding the modern culture of nostalgia in Japan. Nostalgic feelings are generally considered to be linked to our structure of memory and remembering. Human beings possess memory. Once plural short memories have been assembled and fixed, the assembled memory changes to long-term memory and becomes intellectual property like knowledge. In this sense, all human beings have the capacity to memorize. But from another point of view, it is memory that dominates humans. Sometimes it drives us, and sometimes it soaks us within another temporality, as is written, for example, in the novel of Marcel Proust, *A la recherche du temps perdu*. Thus man can by chance be immersed in a deep feeling of nostalgia brought about by his or her memory system, which normally underlies his or her daily consciousness. Memory is not only our mental property, or owned goods in our minds, but also a strange agent that drives us.

'Nostalgia' is a name specially given to one sort of memory act which attaches us and attracts us. The reason why I focus on this idea is that we can notice nostalgic movements in several cultural contexts, especially after the 1990s. To begin, I will show here some examples of the nostalgic movement found in today's Japan.

The first example I take here is a poster of the Liberal Democratic Party of Japan (Jiyuu-Minsyu-Tou) in 2012. Beside the face of former Prime Minister Shinzo Abe, we see the Japanese phrase "Nihon wo torimodosu (Take back

Japan)". This message implies a sense of loss, as if something important has been robbed and is in peril in Japan, and as if the Japanese governor (who is in the picture) is trying to reestablish their country. Behind this phrase, there hide some past figures of strong Japan in and after 1960s; the Olympic Games in Tokyo in 1964, the Japan World Exposition in Osaka in 1970, and the catchphrase "Japan as No.1" from 1979, etc. Governors want to retain the image of "strong" Japan which they once had and now feel to be weakened. The phrase "take back" means here a complicated double movement of progressive political decision-making on one side and a retrospective mental attitude on the other. As we will see afterwards in certain examples, the image of strong Japan depends on the collective memories of the boomer generation born soon after WWII, and who therefore cannot help but experience some accompanying feeling of nostalgia. This is an inclination behind the politico-cultural trends in recent Japan.

The second example I will introduce is more directly linked to the cultural industry. The number of works on nostalgic subjects has become larger and larger in recent Japanese cultural products, for example films and popular songs. Many of them refer to works of the 1960s or later, which has led some scholars to name this phenomenon "Showa-Nostalgia". By my own observation, the inclination toward Showa culture reached its peak approximately during the ten years after the coming of the new millennium, that is to say, from 2000 to 2010. Shinzo Abe's poster bears witness to one of the typical phenomena of this trend. Here is a brief list of mass culture products which reflect the 'nostalgic' feelings of this time. Referring to hit songs of the 60s, or remembering or re-constructing the past atmosphere through images, these nostalgic products of recent years constitute one of the dominant trends in contemporary Japanese culture.

Typical examples of the nostalgic movement in Japanese culture after 2000

2001 音楽「明日があるさ」Remake of Kyu Sakamoto's song(1963) [popular song]

2002 音楽「亜麻色の髪の乙女」Remake of Village Singers' song(1968) [popular song]

2004 テーマパーク『道頓堀極楽商店街』Reproduction of shopping mall in 1950-60's [Theme Park]

2005　映画『Always 三丁目の夕日』“Always Sunset on Third Street” [Film]

2006　小説『永遠の0』(Novel) “Eternal Zero Fighter plane” [Novel]

2006　映画『Always 続·三丁目の夕日』“The Sequel to *Always Sunset on Third Street*” [Film]

2006　映画『フラガール』 About the remote coal mining city in 1960's [Film]

2008　音楽“60s 70s 80s” “60's 70's 80's” by Namie Amuro [popular song]

2011　映画『サウダーヂ』 “Saudade” [Film]

2012　映画『Always 三丁目の夕日 '64』“Always Sunset on Third Street '64” [Film]

2013　映画『永遠の0』“Eternal Zero” [Film]

2014　展覧会「Nostalgia&Fantasia」“Nostalgia&Fantasia” [Art Exhibition]

2020　東京オリンピック Olympic Games in Tokyo (cf. Tokyo Olympic Games in 1964)

2025?　大阪万国博覧会 Japan World Exposition in Osaka (cf. EXPO '70 Osaka in 1970)

Here we choose one typical example among these line-ups: the film series “San-chôme no Yuhi,” directed by Takashi Yamazaki, within which a symbolic role of nostalgia can be recognized, and with its effect, they dramatize the atmosphere of the period of rapid economic growth after WWII in Japan. The Japanese word “San-chôme” signifies a downtown street. People living there are relatively poor, but they don't abandon their dream to prosper, or to contribute to the development of their family, community, and nation. “Yu-hi” signifies the sunset in Japanese. The title connotes that “San-chôme” streets are *always* enveloped in sunset twilight. Their inhabitants are people living in imaginary nostalgia, that is to say, people living only in “our” memory.

It is worth noting that two recent Japanese Prime Ministers, Yoshihiko Noda and Shinzo Abe, not only both appreciated this film but also both made political efforts to re-establish Japan after the big earthquake in 2011. For them, the image of resurrection is superposed to the positive image of the ‘60s, for example, the success of the Tokyo Olympic Games in 1964, achieved after the experience of ruins caused by WWII. Also in the third film of the “San-chôme” series, the Tokyo Olympics are considered as a symbol of Japanese reconstruction after the war. The image of the Olympics of nearly 50 years ago still motivates today's

Japanese cultural scenery. In short, a sense of nostalgia directs the Japanese atmosphere through mass culture products such as films, comics, and artworks. As almost all of these nostalgic products appeal firstly to our sensibility, it would be useful to precisely define the role of this nostalgic movement from the point of view of aesthetics, in order to make clear the characteristics of our contemporary phenomena which work on us like quasi-propaganda media.

It is possible to make an additional remark on this matter: this politico-cultural movement of nostalgia is not limited to Japan, especially in the realm of politics. As we can see in many political and social movements such as the election of Donald Trump, Brexit or any other manifestation of conservative politics in Europe, a conservatism (or radical-conservatism) in which the mental basis is deeply rooted in the mechanism of nostalgia or retrospectiveness becomes more powerful than before. These tendencies testify that nostalgia has now become worldwide or global symptom among westernized modern countries.

My aim is to analyze several aspects of the aesthetics of nostalgia in order to search for the source of its power. In my opinion, feelings of nostalgia not only give us a strong attachment to the past but also work as a form of *mental mobilization*. It makes it possible to gather mentally. Nostalgia may possess the power to collect a certain amount of people, people of a certain generation, through the organization and orientation of collected memory. At the theoretical level, I will make three considerations regarding what makes nostalgia influential. First, I will begin from general analysis of the concept of nostalgia in the context of European modern history. Secondly, I will pose this concept as being essential to modern cultural movements by following the arguments raised in Adorno and Horkheimer's *Dialect of Enlightenment*. Thirdly, I will also refer to analyses of nostalgia by the French philosopher and philologist Barbara Cassin in order to evaluate the utility of this notion. After these steps, I will pick up an example of a modern Japanese novelist's concept of nostalgia, that of Ango Sakaguchi, which suggests the necessity of a radical development of this idea, re-starting from the experience of total destruction after WWII.

1. On the notion of "nostalgia" in the European tradition

The word "nostalgia" is composed of two Greek words, nostos (return to home) and *algia* (pain). Nowadays it signifies a feeling of loss and displacement, but it originally meant a physical pain when the word first appeared: it was a physical disorder that Swiss hired soldiers felt when they were engaged in war in a foreign land for a long time.

So "Nostalgia" appears as a neologism in early modern Europe, and two origins are known today. Sometimes it is attributed to the French doctor Jean-Jacques Harder. He is said to have introduced this symptom in 1678. Another origin, which is better known than the former, is attributed to Johannes Hofer, a Swiss medical student. Hofer proposed the notion in 1688 in his book *De Nostalgia*.

In the European tradition, a work by the French painter Claude Lorrain is considered to be one of the first artworks featuring nostalgic representation. It is entitled "Seaport with the Embarkation of the Queen of Sheba". This painting depicts the port scene in which Queen Sheba embarks on a return journey to her homeland. The color of the sky with a beam of sunlight is said to be an origin of subsequent expressions of nostalgia. At a glance, we cannot tell whether it is sunset or sunrise. This makes us lose our sense of time passing in the ordinary order. According to an expression of Shakespeare, "the time is out of joint" at the nostalgic moment. Does time pass from day to night, or night to day? Does it really pass in the order we tend to think? At the nostalgic moment, time has the possibility of passing from the future to the past. In this way, the sepia-colored sky of Lorrain's painting becomes symbolic in nostalgic description. Being covered by a sepia-colored sky, we cannot tell whether we are in progression or in regression in time. Our sense of time loses its normal order in the nostalgic moment.

2. Nostalgia as a condition of human reason in *Dialect of Enlightenment*

In *Dialect of Enlightenment*, Max Horkheimer and Theodor Adorno (AH) locate the origin of modern development in ancient Greek mythology. For them, the ancient and the modern do not exist as separate historical stages. These two instances are necessarily associated. Modernization necessarily includes mythology as its proper structure. In other words, modernity and its crisis are already inscribed in the structure of ancient mythology.

It is very interesting that AH consider Odysseus's return as essential to modern enlightenment. Homeland is not a mythological allegory prior to modernity, nor is mythology a homeland of modernity at all. The concept of homeland, far from being mythological, furnishes the structural basis of modern subjectivity. Here we can suggest an essential role of nostalgia in the formation of modernity.

In 'Excursus I: Odysseus or Myth and Enlightenment' of *Dialect of Enlightenment*, AH define Odysseus's journey as a "nostalgic stylization":

> The celebration of the wrath of Achilles and the wanderings of Odysseus is already a nostalgic stylization of what can no longer be celebrated ; and the hero of the adventures turns out to be the prototype of the bourgeois individual, whose concept originates in the unwavering self-assertion of which the protagonist driven to wander the earth is the primeval model. (Horkheimer&Adorno 2002: 35) [emphasis added]

Odysseus is considered as the prototype of "the bourgeois individual". He is not a mere mythological figure. Rather, he can be considered to be the first modern citizen and has become already an agent with nostalgia when he appears in *Odysseia*. We can discover in his journey the process of development of the modern individual.

> The hero's peregrinations from Troy to Ithaca trace the path of the self through myths, a self infinitely weak in comparison to the force of nature and still in the process of formation as self-consciousness. (Horkheimer&Adorno 2002: 38)

AH distinguish three stages of modernization in Odysseus's journey. According to them, Odysseus is considered to modernize strange lands one after another by using his reason. Each stage of his journey tells a condition of modern human activity. We can summarize them as follows:

1. Episode of Lotus-eater (Lotopagos): obligation of work for humans
2. Episode of Cyclopes: justification of possession and private property in barbarians' land
3. Episode of Circe: possession of a woman through marriage

Among these steps, a nostalgic feeling (the desire to return) plays an important role in the first episode. Loss of nostalgia becomes loss of the human condition.

> Thence for nine days' space I was borne by direful winds over the teeming deep; but on the tenth we set foot on the land of the Lotus-eaters, who eat a flowery food. There we went on shore and drew water, and straightway my comrades took their meal by the swift ships. But when we had tasted food and drink, I sent forth some of my comrades to go and to learn who the men were, who here ate bread upon the earth; two men I chose, sending with them a third as a herald. So they went straightway and mingled with the Lotus-eaters, and the Lotus-eaters did not plan death for my comrades, but gave them the lotus to taste. And whosoever of them ate of the honey-sweet fruit of the lotus, *had no longer any wish to bring back word or to return* (νόστος), but there they were fain to abide among the Lotus-eaters, feeding on the lotus, and forgetful of their homeward way. These men, therefore, I brought back perforce to the ships, weeping and dragged them beneath the benches and bound them fast in the hollow ships: and I bade the rest of my trusty comrades to embark with speed on the swift ships, lest perchance anyone should eat of the lotus and *forget his homeward way*. (Homer 1919: IX, 309) [emphasis added]

AH interprets this episode of the Lotus-eaters as the lack of consciousness of historical work. Lotus-eaters don't harm human beings directly. When men eat only wild lotus, and become intoxicated by its drug-like effects, they lose the feeling of needing to work for a living. According to AH, Lotus-eaters live in fake-utopia, because utopia must be realized through historical labor for the modernist Odysseus.

This episode of the Lotus-eaters shows another aspect of reason. AH don't indicate explicitly, but it plays an important role in formulating the relationship between reason, mythology, and homeland. The point is that irrational beings like Lotus-eaters don't have a desire to return to their homeland. They don't have nostalgia. On the contrary, beings equipped with reason are always accompanied by the will to return to their homeland. Reason presupposes the existence of a homeland. The act of reasoning requires a nostalgic desire in order to achieve future success. Modern subjectivity is destined to be retrospective in order to continue to live. Work assures the future of modern life, while the fake-utopia life of dreamers has no developmental character towards the formation of subjectivity (and possession of private property).

> The fact that -- despite the fascist lies to the contrary -- the concept of homeland is opposed to myth constitutes *the innermost paradox* of epic. Precipitated in the epic is the memory of an historical age in which nomadism gave way to settlement, the precondition of any homeland. If the fixed order of property implicit in settlement is the source of human alienation, in which all homesickness and longing spring from a lost primal state, at the same time it is toward settlement and fixed property, on which alone the concept of homeland is based, that all longing and homesickness are directed. Novalis's definition according to which all philosophy is homesickness holds good only if this longing is not dissipated in the phantasm of a lost original state, but *homeland, and nature itself, are pictured as something that have had first to be wrested from myth. Homeland is a state of having escaped.* (Horkheimer&Adorno 2002: 60-61) [emphasis added]

Nostalgia is a result of human alienation from the mythical state, but at the same time it functions as a precondition of this alienation itself, that is to say, of modernization and subjectivation. This ambiguity constitutes the essence of what AH call "the innermost paradox". The more we become rational and reasonable, the stronger our sense of nostalgia grows. Nostalgia functions as compensation for the conquest of "barbarians", but this compensation also neutralizes the very violence of conquering. AH says that modern subjectivity neutralizes violence through self-reflection. Here nostalgia appears accompanied by the narrative of escape. We can conclude at present that nostalgia may be the radical negation or transformation of the live memory of violence of civilization in a "tamed and domesticated" (that is, at the same time, cultured and civilized) manner.

3. Nostalgia and language: Barbara Cassin

The notion of nostalgia shows another development. Here I will pick up a further interpretation of nostalgia posed by the French critic Barbara Cassin, which features an emphasis on its fictional character: according to her, nostalgia is not a disease, but a lovable fiction invented by people. Not only does nostalgia rest in the horizon of fictionality for her, but it also has an attractive power that involves us. This notion presupposes the existence of a homeland where people are always welcomed when they come back. In a word, nostalgia implies a welcoming act of hospitality. And in the heart of the idea of "hospitality", Cassin suggests, various beings to be hosted are included: those who welcome guests, and those who are welcomed. The meaning of the word "host" is not limited to welcoming person: the Greek word "xenos" signifies stranger, and the Latin word "hostis" signifies enemy. The idea of hospitality thus includes various standpoints, sometimes opposed ones. In short, hospitality is an idea of total inclusiveness. It is because Cassin says that all beings, as objects of hospitality, feel welcomed by the Universe, even if they are merely located in one small spot in the world, especially in the nostalgic moment in which normal temporality comes to a halt. This is a positive function of nostalgia suggested by Cassin. Everyone feels "at ease" wherever they are in a nostalgic moment.

Cassin says that this feeling derives from the hybridity of the word "nostalgia" itself. In fact, there were many words in 18th century Europe which designated the same symptoms as those of nostalgia: the German word "Heimweh" which means "le mal du pays" (homesick) , the Latin word "philopatridomania" whici is "la folie de l'amour de la patrie" (the madness of love of country) , and the Italian word "pothopatridalgia which signifies "la douleur du désir-passion de la patrie" (the pain of the desire-passion of the fatherland). According to Cassin, it is thought-provoking that the word "nostalgia" remains until now among these expressions. European people could not abandon the connotation of "returning" from this disease. The Greek word "nostos" derives from the verb "neomai", which also means "to save" or "to relieve". This notion retains a conception of homeland as a spot to return where everyone is able to find his or her proper relief.

Moreover, Cassin tries to take up another forgotten aspect of nostalgia: nostalgia toward the mother language. Referring to Hanna Arendt's arguments on *cliché*, Cassin underlines the role of mother language as being inventive, productive, and authentic. On the contrary, the language of cliché, typically found in the speech of Adolf Eichmann, easily falls down to the banality of evil. There is an opposition between mother language and bureaucratic language. We can see here a clear interpretation of Cassin: mother language opposed to fatherland. Mother language would remain as a source of productivity, or creativity, even if one was to become an exile, separated from his or her fatherland. Loss of the fatherland does not necessarily mean loss of the mother language, or loss of home.

> Europe before Hitler? I can't say that I don't have nostalgia of it at all. What remains of it? The language remains. (Hannah Arendt, Dialogue with Günter Gaus [Cassin 2015: 85])

According to Cassin, mother language is the last fortune of exile for Arendt. Of course, it is well known that Arendt tried to establish a public space based on dialogical reason as a philosopher in America, or as an English-speaking Jewish refugee. But Cassin's explanation indicates that a minimal kind of nostalgia remains in her. Cassin concludes, by citing Günther Anders, that nostalgia assures one a "right to return", even if one does not have a proper place to return to, even if the place to return to has totally changed, or been lost, and become another strange place. Nostalgia constitutes an immaterial essence for rootless Europeans.

4. Modern aspects of nostalgia in Japan: Ango Sakaguchi's case

For future consideration, I can indicate another kind of nostalgia found in the Japanese cultural context. One example is from the literary work of novelist Ango Sakaguchi. Another is from the film *Saudade* of Katsuya Tomita (2011). Both of them show interesting similarity relating to the feeling of nostalgia exposed in their work: nostalgia as a deserted or homeless experience. We can recognize in these two cases something that could be called the "nostalgia of ruin", or "nostalgia without a proper homeland".

Ango Sakaguchi (1906-1955) is known as a decadent novelist in the history of modern Japanese literature. One of his famous works is *Hakuchi* (1947), in which he describes the survival of a young woman after the defeat of WWII. In addition to the creation of literary works, he was gifted with a critical mind, and this helped him to become, as Kojin Karatani evaluates, one of the most intellectually engaged novelists of modern Japan. The experience of defeat sharpened his insight on Japan and its culture, and above all, radically changed his initially traditional interpretation of the notion of nostalgia.

"Homeland ("Furusato" in Japanese)" is an essential notion for the literature of Ango, and not a few scholarly enquiries are devoted to this subject. But in so far as I have researched, there are very few that recognize how this notion of homeland constitutes his principal aestheticism after WWII.

In his younger days, Ango had relatively normal feelings about his homeland. In other words, he had a normal, but vivid nostalgia toward his younger days. In the short essay entitled *Furusato ni yosuru sanka* (Hymn for my homeland) (1931), he expresses his honest sensibility colored by energy and emptiness.

> "I was tired of seeking. I sought a long time. My tiredness was thus deep. My fatigue damaged my body so heavily that it was unbearable for me to live. I felt sometime that I couldn't find my body anywhere. I was perplexed, being left behind. [...]
>
> Is there something deserved to seek for?
>
> I sought. But I only felt my body odor radiating from my enthusiasm. I dug my memory. And one day, I found a silhouette folded in the most inner part of my memories. It was a girl. She lived in my homeland. I had a slight memory of talking with her only once or twice. [...]
>
> I returned to my homeland." (Sakaguchi 1931: 35)

His homeland is Niigata, In the north-middle part of the Japanese mainland. But he couldn't find the girl he was looking for when he returned there in summer, although he tried in vain to sketch her concrete figure.

> She? ... indeed, who is she? Each time I probe, her silhouette disappears from my vision, contours always blurred. I shut my eyes rapidly in order to fix her vanishing figure. The darkness only lies. I try to produce her silhouette. (Sakaguchi, 1931: 36)

In *Furusato ni yosuru sanka*, Ango seeks for a nostalgic moment of his younger days but in vain. This vanishing memory is linked with the scenery of his homeland Niigata, which forms a half real and half oneiric vision. Here, Ango's nostalgia is constructed by the aestheticization of his lost memory and a sense of the loss of its object.

But as the war progressed and the moment of defeat approached, Ango's notion of nostalgia began to show a different aspect. We can recognize in its change Ango's radical aestheticism. His new conception of "homeland" is revealed in his essay *Bungaku no furusato* (The homeland of literature) (1941). Though it was written during the war, this essay includes the writer's diverse premonition of losing his "homeland".

Beginning with an analysis of Charles Perrault's fable *Aka-Zukin* (Little Red Riding Hood), Ango abstracts the notion of cruelty that dominates some kinds of literary works. He indicates the absence of morals in literature, but he also acknowledges that it might be a certain realism that literature has to realize.

> In other words, the absence or refusal of morals does not seem to establish literature. But in our life we cannot live without such a cliff, where the absence of morals constitutes morals in itself. (Sakaguchi 1941: 266)

Ango's thought is rather paradoxical. He affirms this absence as necessary to literature and considers it as the homeland of all humans.

> I see here a homeland of literature, or that of humankind. I also think that literature stems from here.
>
> I do not want to say that all literature consists in amorality or in refusal. No, rather I do not evaluate such kinds of stories highly. For, though homeland may be our cradle, the work of adults does not consist in returning to one's homeland....
>
> However, I think, literature does not exist without consciousness of this homeland. Morals and the sociality of literature must be nurtured on the ground of this homeland. I only rely on such literature, and such criticism. This is what I believe. (Sakaguchi 1941: 269-270)

For Ango, amorality, refusal, and abandon constitute the soil of literature. In other words, literature must be built upon the ruins of humanity. Ango does not deny the existence of the homeland or the lure of it. He doesn't deny the ordinary feeling of nostalgia. Nostalgia toward the homeland is a humanistic feeling on the basis of which literature without immorality is created. However, this 'moral' literature doesn't satisfy Ango in that it cannot touch the deepness of human existence and that it risks remaining a fable for children. Mature literature must be more radical, so that it unearths the human condition. This is the true foundation, or existential homeland of literature. Therefore, in its true and radical meaning, the homeland of literature is found in the moment of amorality, in other words, of cruelty. Total destruction becomes a necessary condition of literature. This kind of positive nihilism persists and dominates his literary work until and after the defeat in WWII. It is found especially clearly in *Nihon Bunka Sikan* (My view on Japanese culture) (1943), *Daraku Ron* (Discourse on Decadence) (1946), and *Zoku Daraku Ron* (A Sequel of Discourse on Decadence) (1946) .

This existential homelessness on the edge of literature leads Ango to affirm all the vices of the surviving humans in the ruins after the war. We can refer to one phrase of *Zoku Daraku Ron*.

> We must become naked [as babes] and cast off the taboos that entwine us and

> search for our own true voices. The widows need to fall in love again and descend into Hell. The returning soldiers need to become black marketeers... If we don't rid ourselves of these false robes we will return to the sham country of wartime. This happens by betting our bodies: searching for a surface prettiness will prevent us from reaching the inner reality. There will be nothing pretty and proper about this. It will take an existential gamble, betting with one's blood, with one's flesh, with the most basic of screams. When *Daraku Ron* is called for it must be complete and entire, thorough with no holding back. Only by approaching the gates of Hell will we able to approach Heaven. Only when the nails of all ten toes and all ten fingers are smeared with blood, have been pulled out in the struggle, can we approach heaven. There is no other way. (Sakaguchi 1946: 25)

Denying in *Daraku ron* the Japanese traditional values praised by Bruno Taut (for example values recognized in Katsura Rikyu), Ango tries to find foundation and truth and beauty in the living figure of people. For Ango, only the living body deserves to be supreme. Vices in reality turn into virtues, as long as man lives his hard life with all his effort. This is Ango's aestheticism. Or rather, we can name it anti-aestheticism. Romantic aestheticism based on the traditional nostalgic feeling toward one's homeland is totally changed and denied by Ango. Another nostalgia he does recognize, if it can exist, consists in gazing at human's homelessness and staying there.

5. Conclusion

Before summarizing the arguments raised in this paper, I would like to introduce one further contemporary example of nostalgia in the globalized world, focusing on the film of Katsuya Tomita, *Saudade* (2011).

The story unfolds in Yamanashi prefecture in Japan. Seiji, a worker of a construction site, feels sympathy with his friend Hosaka, who has just come back from Thailand. They pass time together in bars where young Thailand girls work as cocktail waitresses. At the same time, Seiji meets the young Japanese Takeru, who is a member of a hip-hop group. Takeru sings his rage against society, his anger caused by the economic crisis. Takeru and the members of his group meet another hip-hop group of young Brazilians who were born in Japan as second generation immigrants. The two groups have a rap battle, in which the lyrics of both are founded on their own feelings of lost identity...

In this film, all the characters, whether they are Japanese, Thai, or Brazilian, have different problems of identity. As it is rather difficult to explain all of the complicated relationships in this film, I will only submit a rough sketch here. Japanese people who have lost their self-confidence due to the economic crisis. Immigrants who are for example Brazilian or Thai, especially the second generation of them, suffer from another kind of lost identity: They cannot speak their parents' native language, but they have to live in Japan as half-foreigners. All the characters have a feeling of nostalgia, but they do not have their "homeland". They are separated, or abandoned by their origin, uprooted (*déraciné*) and have to drift in tragic Japan. In other words, they live in the *ground zero* of nostalgia: once we had a stable association with nation, land, language, and people, but now, in this new-born ruin, all the previous linkage and bondage has been lost and torn apart. In *Saudade*, people feel the nostalgia of nowhere, of the imaginary place where they are not born, nor grow up, nor visit. Traditional nostalgia never works here as before, and nor are these nostalgic ruins similar to those of Sakaguchi Ango; regeneration from the ruins is never promised now. In this new feeling of nostalgia there can be seen an influence of the globalizing world.

As for the relationships between modern life and nostalgia, another phrase of *Dialectic of Enlightenment* can be referred to here. When culture becomes industry, it also becomes a model which pre-determinates our mental reactions.

> If, before its rationalization, the word had set free not only longing but lies, in its rationalized form *it has become a straightjacket more for longing than for lies*. (Horkheimer&Adorno 2002: 133) [emphasis added]

> [...] the whole inner life [...] bears witness to the attempt to turn oneself into [...] *an apparatus which, even in its unconscious impulses, conforms to the model presented by the culture industry*. The most intimate reactions of human beings have become so entirely reified, even to themselves, that the

idea of anything peculiar to them survives only in extreme abstraction [...]. (Horkheimer&Adorno 2002: 136) [emphasis added]

The first citation explains the influence of modernization over language. Once rationalized, language might become a restriction on our fantasies and control man's longing capacity. Nostalgia, which was once one of twins, has been regulated, controlled, or even abused, by his brother "reason". The second citation describes the workings of this control in detail. The power of the cultural industry reaches us and controls us on an unconscious level through "the model". It might not be an exaggeration to say that the products of the cultural industry make up our unconsciousness. In this sense, the structure of modern nostalgia must be analyzed from the point of view of cultural products such as novels, films, and popular songs.

Reflecting on contemporary examples of modern Japanese nostalgia, there can be recognized some proper tendency among them. We can notice many products which are decorated with "nostalgic gadgets"; artificially emphasized sepia color in things and sceneries, or the slow arpeggio of guitars in the background music, etc.... All are devices invented in order to bring about a nostalgic feeling. We should examine carefully the modalities of these gadgets. This is an urgent problem from the perspective of aesthetics.

In addition, as for the contemporary atmosphere surrounding nostalgia, it must be remembered that not a few politicians choose the word "take back" in asserting their position. Almost all of them use the same phrase. The reason of this global tendency has to be questioned; why does every governor who seems to show a mainly neo-liberal attitude, appeals to nostalgic movements of the mind in cultural and political aspects? Several considerations on the structure of nostalgia tell us that nostalgia exists on the reverse side of rationality. In other words, sometimes nostalgia can be used to conceal a rational process that is going on in the background. To make matters worse, some kind of violence, covered with the appearance of rationality, may possibly progress. Anyway, nostalgia is a signal of developing rationality. The consumption of the nostalgic image is a witness of our ongoing hyper-modernization, and thus it might be a crucial phenomenon that discloses problematics of a Westernized world. Where nostalgia is produced, modernization always proceeds.

Bibliography

Cassin, Barbara. 2015. *La Nostalgie. Quand donc est-on chez soi?*. Pluriel.

Hidaka, Katsuyuki. 2014. *Showa nostalgia towa nanika*. Sekai-shisou-sya.

Homer. 1919. *The Odyssey*. Translated by A. T. Murray, vol.I, Harvard University Press.

Max Horkheimer & Theodore Adorno. 2002. *Dialectic of Enlightenment*. Ed. Ginzelin Schmid Noerr, translated by Edmund Jephcott, Stanford University Press.

Sakaguchi, Ango. 1998. *Sakaguchi Ango zensyu*. 18 vols., Chikuma-shobo.

—1998 (1946). *Zoku daraku ron*. Vol.4, 270-278.

—1999 (1931). *Furusato ni yosuru sanka*. Vol.1, 34-41.

—1999 (1941). *Bungaku no furusato*. Vol.3, 264-270.

Stewart, Susan. 1993. *On Longing*. Duke University Press.

The Image Strategy and Rituals of the Monarchy of Thailand in Thai Cinema: Kings, the Emperor, and 'Ritual Space'

Norihiko Nakamura

1. Introduction

Globalization has long overtaken the world, but nationalism is getting stronger everywhere. In 2019, for example, two new figures ascended to the throne in two countries. I am referring to Thailand and Japan, namely the King of Thailand and the Emperor of Japan. Both countries held grand ceremonies and many people took part in the national celebrations. In other words, it was a year in which many people were reconfirmed as equal members of "a people" under the name of "a nation" and their identities were unified. Throughout these celebrations, Thailand and Japan did not hide their "ritual" aspects.

A nation that values "ritual" can be said to be one that has formed its national identity through national pageants, just as Takashi Fujitani discussed in relation to the Japanese emperor. In addition, national pageants have created a variety of opportunities for the exercise of power as a device for shaping the people as "a people." Fujitani calls the occasion created by national pageants to build national identity "a scene of memory" (Fujitani 1996). From my point of view, the Thai monarchy and Japanese emperor have controlled by the "scene of memory" in their countries by actively using their image. This is the most common factor between the national identities of Thailand and Japan. In other words, the two countries have achieved a sense of national identity through the use of portraits of their kings and emperors. It has underpinned not only national pageants, but also detailed rituals that cover every detail of individual life. Kings and royalty, who are supposed to be the "others," cleverly reach out to us in one way or another, implanting the king as the "others" inside us.

That is why the image of the king or emperor should not be "soiled." At the National Arts Festival "AICHI TRIENNALE 2019: Taming Y/Our Passion," some people were outraged by a video work burning a photo collage of the Emperor Showa, as if they and their "blood" were insulted. The executive committee received a massive volume of criticism and abuse from right-wing groups and social networks. As a result, one of the art festival booths, "After 'Freedom of Expression?'" had to be canceled. The critics of the exhibition acted as if they had been personally slandered. They also railed that the defenders of the art festival would be angry if their family photos were burned. But why are people so angry at the burning of a photograph of a previous Japanese emperor as though their "family" had been insulted? Why was the image of the king or emperor treated as something that should be "guarded" in a ceremonial manner? And why are people motivated to voice strong opinions by the image of a king or an emperor? Is it always difficult to criticize the image of a king or emperor through art and visual works, and if so why? What do the images of kings and emperors convey and what do they hide?

What I would like to disclose here is that my interest is in the image strategy of the king of Thailand and the relationship between the king and cinema. And I want to reveal the strong resistance to the king's image in the video works of contemporary Thai filmmakers. In order to discuss these issues, however, we should at least touch on the present-day use of images of the Thai monarchy. In Thailand, huge portraits of the king and queen are placed all over the country, and small portraits are displayed in each household. Hardly a day goes by that one does not see a portrait of the Thai monarchy members. The people of Thailand are always seen by the king, and the people always see the king and the royal family. In Japan, on the other hand, due to technological progress in photography during the Meiji period, a portrait of the emperor called *goshin-ei* (imperial portrait) was created and came to be displayed in schools, publicly owned facilities, and homes throughout Japan. However, the images of the emperor seen there were strictly kept out of public view. In other words, the people looked at the emperor without looking at him. That is, the public is always being watched by the emperor, but the public cannot see the emperor themselves. The emperor was treated as a synonym of the "sun" and he was not to be looked at with one's own eyes. Photographs of the monarchy of Thailand and Japan are powerful devices that flaunt the presence of the highest powers and create a "ritual space." One functions to enhance the excessive visibility of the Thai monarchy, while the other functions to enhance the invisibility of the Japanese emperor[1].

The political effects exerted by use of the king's portraits continued with the rise of the cinema. The Japanese emperor, who had produced political effects through the suggestion of his own image, was rarely portrayed in films. Surprisingly, the opposite is true in the history of Thai cinema. Although the direct portrayal of the king or royal family in film is currently prohibited by film censorship law, royal families themselves appeared in films during the early stage of Thai cinema. From the point of view of "ritual" the difference in the relationship between the monarchy and cinema in the two countries can be made clear, as I will show below. Moreover, these comparisons will gradually reveal the relationship between the image of the monarchy and "ritual."

Of course, the goal of this paper is not limited to the simple comparative analysis described above. Rather, the aim of this paper is to clarify the differences in the image of the monarchy between the two countries, and to analyze the image of Thai kings by referring to some useful discussion on the image of Japanese emperors. After discussing the relationship between projected images and the king in the history of Thai cinema, this article will then analyze the political and ceremonial spaces in Thailand as revealed by Apichatpong Weerasethakul (1970 -), a contemporary Thai filmmaker. In other words, I would like to discuss the "ritual space" of Thailand itself. It could be said that the unique value of this paper is due to the advancement of such analysis by referring to the discussion on the emperor system in Japan and the image of the emperor.

---

[1] Nevertheless, the division between visibility and invisibility is only an arbitrary comparison. This is because the emperor's invisibility has been massively "consumed" by television images and photographs through post-World War II "symbolization." In other words, the connotations of the "rituals" generated by the image of the king are transformed in various ways depending on the time period, region, history, and culture. In the oral presentation on which this article is based, Dr. Griseldis Kirsch made a useful comment about how the image strategy of the emperor and the king may have focused not only on films but also on television broadcasts. It is true that in Japan there are programs such as the "Imperial Album" that give a glimpse of the imperial family's official duties and daily life, and Thailand also maintains a 24-hour channel that reports on the activities of the king. Although I was not able to deal with this directly in this paper, Dr. Kirsch gave me some suggestions for future research. I appreciate her kindness.

Let me make my interpretation of the word "ritual" clear. Anthropologist Mary Douglas, for example, stated that "ritual is the practice of proclaiming a public definition in a visible way" (Douglas, trans. Asada 2012, 53). If so, rituals refer to situations in which some specific meaning is fixed by the existence of a particular form or to a form in itself. And rituals sometimes enhance the sanctity and authority of a person in power, or guarantee solidarity in a particular community. In this paper, I discuss the space where people are asked to perform such rituals as "ritual space." A prime example of this is seen in the various customs imposed on the Thai people by the Thai king by presenting his image, and the movie theater as a place where his image is projected[2].

The following two people are referred to in relation to the monarchy of Thailand. The first is the former king of Thailand, Bhumibol Adulyadej (ภูมิพลอดุลยเดช, 1946-2016) and the current king of Thailand, Maha Vajiralongkorn (วชิราลงกรณ, 2016-). In terms of the Japanese emperor I will mainly refer to Emperor Meiji and Emperor Showa.

Specifically, I will discuss the ritual spaces that kings and royalty create in Thai movie theaters. Here, the analysis will mainly concern a video work by Thai filmmaker Apichatpong Weerasethakul. Apichatpong received attention as a film director representing Thailand after his *Uncle Boonmee Who Can Recall His Past Lives* (2010) won the top prize at the Cannes Film Festival. On the other hand, he also makes video installations and photographic works for exhibitions in museums and galleries. I think the most important thing in discussing his films and installations is to focus on the practice of projection, which ties these two aspects of his work together.

[2] Tamotsu Aoki, a cultural anthropologist, also pointed out the importance of ceremony for the nation as follows. Aoki said, "It is not only because kings and rulers need a symbolic device to show their authority and power to the whole nation. [...] Rather, the act of conducting a grand ceremony itself shows the existence of the "state" and it is nothing but the "state" itself." Considering this, Thailand itself is a ceremonial space. Above all, the movie theater should be the most specific device to show the "state." Moreover, the existence of films as well as cinemas can easily give the people an image of overthrowing the system by the projection practice by artists such as Apichatpong and other film directors. We should further consider the theater aspect as the most powerful but vulnerable "state" device. Aoki 2006, 203.

2. Creating a Ritual Space: Movie Theaters in Thailand

Now, I will introduce the cinema scene in Apichatpong's *Cemetery of Splendor* (2015). The theme of this film is "sleep." Soldiers who never wake up from their dreams because of "sleeping sickness" lie in a sanatorium. However, in the area where the sanatorium was built, there used to be a royal palace. Even now, the ghosts of kings and soldiers still live under the ground. The reason for the "sleeping sickness" is that the vitality of soldiers on the ground is sucked away by the ghosts. In the middle of the film, Apichatpong inserted a scene where the audience stare at the king on a screen. This iconic scene demonstrates not only his political position, but also his stance on the cinema apparatus and projection practice. The scene begins with a soldier suffering from "sleeping sickness" visiting a movie theater with a middle-aged woman caring for him. The camera sees from behind them a man and woman staring at a horror film trailer projected onto the screen. Suddenly, the screen goes dark, and the sound of the film disappears. Soon, the whole audience stands up, and the camera switches in front of them. They keep staring at the screen, as if they were watching nothing.

Apichatpong is critical of propaganda by the Thai monarchy and royal families. However, Thailand has seen "projection" being used in a unique cultural and political context. Needless to say, it has a close relation with the king and the rest of the royal family. In particular, what is the significance of Apichatpong's strategic use of projected images in his work? What implications do his projection practices have for the projector and screen when he deals with ghosts and the Thai monarchy?

From this point on, I would like to examine the image of the king and focus on the dynamic way in which Thai movie theaters create ritual spaces. Now let us take a closer look at the representation of the king in the films shown at the beginning of screenings. First, let us consider the film used from the time of the former Thai King Bhumibol. The caption at the top says, "Please stand up, and pay respect to the king's anthem." Soon afterwards, images of the king's travels throughout Thailand are presented as animated images. This spectacle, with the king at the center of it, is an appropriate choice of media photographs that are well known to Thai people. Therefore, the Thai people reaffirm the king's achievements in cinemas and reaffirm his authority and dignity. People around the king are lying on the ground and putting their palms together. It shows that there was a touching exchange between the people and the king in various places. In the final shot, the camera proceeds to the palace, framing the king and the royal family.

The image of King Bhumibol effectively brings his authority to the audience. As mentioned above, Thai movie theater attendees have to remain silent and stand up while the film of the King is shown. This ritual space physically forces the audience to express respect for the king and royal family. The king's image strategy is maintained by creating a ritual space that is tightly constructed in Thai movie theaters.

We can now compare the video of King Bhumibol with the latest video of King Vajiralongkorn, the current king of Thailand. This video is characterized by a brief description of King Vajiralongkorn from his childhood to the present. And the fact that all of his images are shown in the form of photographs is the biggest difference from the images used for King Bhumibol. His father, the former king of Thailand, Bhumibol, appears in the video several times. In other words, the story of the succession of the throne from father to son is emphasized. The photograph presented here is of Vajiralongkorn sitting on the side of the official duties of King Bhumibol. This video has an accurate propaganda effect by highlighting the authority of Vajiralongkorn with the majesty of King Bhumibol. In other words, maintaining a ceremonial relationship between the king and the people is what the story of succession to the throne in this film emphasizes.

The images of King Bhumibol were produced with clear political intentions and messages. Therefore, it is very easy for the audience to grasp them. In other words, this propaganda is not actually effective because the images are political in a blatant way. On the other hand, the images of King Vajiralongkorn show the story of his succession to the throne in a roundabout way. For example, there are lots of static images, the relationship between the king and props, and the actual location shooting in the palace. Therefore, it can be regarded as propaganda using deliberately circumvented staging rather than directly showing the authority of the king or royal family. These images form the basis of the audience's "people" and at the same time serve as the "education" of the audience in the necessary rituals.

Thai cinema still function as important "venues" for the education of the people by the king and royal family using projection.

The images of the king of Thailand's admiration suggest how the ritual relations between the king and his people and the ritual spaces repeated and constructed in the history of Thai cinema have been carefully preserved. At the same time, this case illustrates the difficulty of maintaining a formal relationship between the king and his people. As a result, the *Cemetery of Splendor* scene was able to highlight the ceremonial aspect of a Thai movie theater. But it seems to be a strange sight, especially to audiences outside Thailand. As a matter of course, the film has not been shown in its home country. The aim of Apichatpong is not to target the Thai people, but to awaken all those who fall into politically biased and bizarre situations. The next section provides an overview of the important transition in the history of Thai cinema in terms of how this image of the king and royal family became obsessed with film and projection. After that, I will look back on *Cemetery of Splendor*.

3. Cinema is the Monarchy: The King's Film History

There is a difference between film history in Japan and Thailand in terms of how the supreme power was depicted or how the supreme power used films. In Japanese cinema, the emperor was not the subject of films from the very beginning. Makiko Kamiya summarizes these points as follows.

> It is said that in *Komatsunomiya Imperial Prince Akihito's Actual Conditions* (1903), the Imperial Family appeared in films for the first time. This was the filming of the funeral procession. However, it was impossible to film the emperor and the imperial family freely even after the cinema became popular in Japan. ......This indicates why the emperor could not have been the subject of films. (Kamiya 2018, 43)

Filming the emperor and the imperial family has been a taboo since the beginning of Japanese film history.

On the other hand, since its inception, Thai cinema has had a close relationship with the state and the king. Films were introduced to Thailand in June 1897 and the first film was shown in front of the king and the royal family. As pointed out by Inuhiko Yomota, "The reason why the film history of this country is different from that of other countries is that films are produced/financed by royal families and full-length historical films starring the princess herself have been produced" (Yomota 2009, 79). In 1900, King San Fasat Sufakit produced a series of short documentary films, and in 1907, he produced the first narrative film in Thailand (Ishii 2012, 223). Film screening, production and distribution were always under the control of the king and the royal family. According to Patsorn Sungsri, not only were the king and the royal family interested in cinema, but they very well understood that cinema could be used as propaganda to support the monarchy (Sungsri 2004, 103-104).

In 1904, the first permanent movie theater was built in Bangkok by a Japanese entertainer, Tomoyori Watanabe, which dramatically increased the acceptance of cinema. It is ironic that the first film to be shown was a documentary film on the Russo-Japanese War. This is because the cinema captured the imagination of Thai people, not only because it had moving images, but also because it was a propaganda film on the Japanese war. Since then, cinema has been called "Nan Epun" or "Shadow of Japan" in Thailand[3]. Watanabe founded Thailand's first film company, "Royal Japanese Cinematograph." The company had to use the word "Royal" in its name to obtain approval from the King. This was also a strategy used by the king and the royal family. In other words, the aim of the king and the royal family was to separate films from the people by bringing all film-making activities under their control. This control became absolute with the enactment of the "film law," a basic law for film censorship, in 1930. This law prohibits "the direct criticism of the royal family or its political doctrine" (Wongratpanya 1982, 262-263). To this day, censorship of Thai films continues to suppress the political views and free expression of filmmakers[4]. Cinema has become a powerful medium

[3] Nowadays, it is common to refer to cinema with "nan (shadow)" or "papayon." However, in order to separate it from Nan Tarn, a traditional Thai shadow play, the name Nan Epun is still used in some areas. However, the word "nan" is sometimes used to mean "skin" as well. I will examine the relationship between screen and projection in Thailand from the aspect of such a polysemous word in the future.

for displaying the prosperity of the state and the royal family[5]. Thai cinema belongs to the king and the royal family.

King Bhumibol, who ascended the throne in 1946, did so after the tumultuous 1932 fall of Thailand's absolute monarchy. Therefore, it could not be said that he had absolute authority after his enthronement. In this regard, it should be noted that King Bhumibol started a tour of provinces in the 1960s. The people bowed down on the road and welcomed the king's party, and the king listened to the worries of the people living in the countryside. Various photographs were taken of the king's tour around the country. The images used in the video praising the king, which I have just described, were basically pictures taken during a tour to the provinces. The king and the Thai government chose famous images that have been remembered due to their effectiveness as propaganda. This is a persuasive indication that they thoroughly controlled the way the king was "seen."

The king's image was controlled more thoroughly by issuing an official photo when he made a tour of the provinces. According to Chie Sakurada, the photographs used were both of King Bhumibol and his predecessor Rama V (King Chulalongkorn, 1853-1910) (Sakurada 2013, 16). Rama V was a leading figure in Thailand's modernization and is still the most trusted figure among the people. King Bhumibol spread his image as well as his portrait as the symbol that laid the foundation for national unity. In this way, it can be said that King Bhumibol secured his authority and symbolic function.

During the reign of King Bhumibol, it became clear that the Thai monarchy and royal family privatized film. Among examples of this is a project called "The Emperor's Film," which was shown during a series of provincial tours by King

---

[4] The above history of Thai cinema was mainly based on the following documents. Patsorn Sungsri, "Thai Cinema as National Cinema: An Evaluative History," PhD thesis, Murdoch University, 2004. Scot Barmé, "Early Thai Cinema and Filmmaking: 1897-1922," *Film History*, Vol. 11, 1999, pp. 308-318. Adam Knee, "Chiang Mai and the Cinematic Spaces of Thai Identity," *Asian Cinema and the Use of Space: Interdisciplinary Perspectives*, eds., Lilian Chee and Edna Lim, New York: Routledge, 2015, pp. 77-92.

[5] However, there are cases where Thai cinema was used as a diplomatic strategy by the king. For example, *White Elephant* (1941). Rama VIII (father of King Bhumibol), who directed this film, expressed the diplomatic policy that "Thailand will defend neutrality and non-war" in this film, and sent prints all over the world. In any case, Thai cinema is hard to separate from the king. Yomota 2009, 80.

Bhumibol. Images of King Bhumibol's official duties and rituals, or films showing his private appearance, were shown throughout Thailand. Many of those films were directed by King Bhumibol. It is said that a live performance of the "King's Hymn" was held before the screening[6]. All of these events were not national events, but were planned and carried out at the suggestion of King Bhumibol. The purpose of "The Emperor's Film" was to let the people know the rules for the king and royal family, and it was an attempt to place film itself under the king's name. The close relationship between the film and the king suggests that the projection of images at home itself was controlled by the king or royal family.

By the way, if the close relationship between the cinema and the king is recognized, what has been marginalized in the cinema? It is the presence of ghosts in Thailand. Often the ghost is a metaphor for the political context of the moment and the threatening "others." In other words, it can be said that the ghost of "others" has always been caught up in the dynamics of exclusion and inclusion. Through the king's clever strategy, the projection of the image became a conceptual device that both manifested the "others" and exposed and rendered invisible ghosts as separate "other." In the prehistory of Thai cinema, projecting an image was directly connected to the manifestation of ghosts and spirits. For example, Nan Tarun (Or Nan Yang), a Thai shadow play that is said to have been performed since around the 18th century, involved the performance of religious dramas in which the gods of monkeys and the devil Yakusha appeared, as well as ghost stories that consisted of local oral traditions. However, the presence of ghosts was strongly impressed upon the Thai people by the rise of Thai grotesque films that began in the 1930s (O'Hara 2010). As Yomota puts it briefly, the ghosts of horror films have the potential to overturn the values of paternalism and heterocentricity in the way that power and capitalism exist. However, the apparition in Thai cinema was rather used to cover up problems such as the current political instability and poverty in northeast Thailand. Films and projections were not only a device to emphasize the power structure of the king and his people, but also a

[6] For the history of "His Majesty's Films," I consulted the following reference. Sakurada, Chie. *Tai kokuō wo sasaeta hitobito: pumipon kokuō no gyōkō to eiga wo meguru hunntōki*, [*People who supported King Bhumibol Adulyadej on his travels and his struggle to make film*], Hukyōsya, 2017, pp. 43-56.

device to ingeniously forget the king's propaganda itself, along with the mounting social problems in the country.

Thai cinema and their projections are the history of frequent negotiations between the existence of the Thai monarchy and the manifestation of ghosts, and the history of suppressing and exposing the existence of each other. An indirect depiction of this situation is a movie theater scene in *Cemetery of Splendor* by Apichatpong. Apichatpong's critical message to the king and royal family and the manifestation of the ghost in the same piece of work reveal the complex relationship between the "others" who exclude, depend on, and encompass each other. In *Cemetery of Splendor* the ghost was projected on the screen, but the king was not. This film emphasizes that projection can be a method of alternately revealing both ghosts and the Thai monarchy on a single screen at the same time.

What *Cemetery of Splendor* most strongly suggests is the peculiarity that the political and regional context of Thailand is certainly included in the act of projection itself. I can guess at least two of Apichatpong's intentions behind this movie theater scene. The first is to expose the history of Thai cinema in which the king and his ghost have been projected on the same screen. The other is to overthrow the position of the king and ghost in the history of Thai cinema. The political implications of the King's meddling in Thai cinema history and projection have lost their former transparency and are revealed by the manifestation of ghosts. Uncovering these invisible structures is certainly envisioned by the projection practice of Apichatpong's works.

4. The Cremation of the King in *Synchronicity* and *Blue*

In Apichatpong's recent works, he inserts depictions that are often reminiscent of the King Bhumibol who died in 2016. Examples include the video installation *Synchronicity* (2018) by Apichatpong and Tsuyoshi Hisakado, and *Blue* (2018), which is said to be a recompilation of the images projected in this installation. In this section, I will discuss the practice of projecting images in this work and the way the cremation of the king and the screen are arranged in *Blue*, the film based upon this work.

The video installation *Synchronicity* by Apichatpong and Hisakado, a member of Chelfitsch, is a complex work in which several elements are intertwined and operated. First, there is a huge opaque glass screen made by Hisakado. The screen has a huge hole that allows you to see the back of the screen, and part of the projected image leaks behind the screen. Next, a hanging light bulb is seen from the opening of the screen. It blinks at specific intervals, sometimes like a pendulum. There are also a number of light bulbs stacked on the ground behind the screen, which flicker on and off independently of the suspended light bulbs in the exhibition space. A projector and a projected image. A shutter placed in front of the projector blocks the projection image at a specific timing. These movements are controlled by programming.

Let us take a look at the video part of this installation. It is said that unless the body of Thailand is destroyed by fire, evil spirits will reside there and eventually become a ghost. Metaphorical cremation is also conducted within this work. A woman named Jen, who has always been involved with ghosts and spirits in the story world of Apichatpong, appears in this film. Her lying body soon begins to catch fire. The burning of the woman's body would have immediately reminded Thai people of the cremation of the king. In October 2017, one year after the death of the king, a massive cremation was held. When the screen is switched, a background curtain which seems to be the same as that used in traditional Thai musical plays is hung. The curtain is rolled up and down. The curtain seems to depict the royal palace and the scenery of northeast Thailand. There is a frame in front of the curtain that sticks out of the screen for some reason, and there is a light bulb on the top. Flames are already surrounding it, and it shows a situation where everything is about to burn.

The flames surround everything, but the spatial continuity between where Jen sleeps and where the curtain rests is ambiguous. The flames burning on her body give the impression that they are as faint as the image projected and reflected on the glass, and that rather they are burning in front of the camera. The last shot of this movie shows that a transparent glass is placed in front of her lying body caught through the flame. If you look closely, the glass reflects the flame in front of the camera. The flames that had seemed to envelop her so far were a simultaneous image of the flames reflected in the glass. Not only that, but she herself is also finally presented as an image reflected on the glass. Her life/death is even more obscure because of the instability of this reflected image, with subtle movements such as opening and closing her eyes while she is enveloped in flames. This obscurity of life/death may also be a feature of the manifestation of the ghost in Apichatpong. She is now identified with the body of the deceased king.

What happens here is that it represents a tipping point in the history of Thai cinema and projection. In other words, the ghost and the manifestation of the king overlap on the same plane. Let us return to the *Synchronicity* exhibition space. An image projected from a projector in an exhibition space is formed on an opaque glass screen with an opening. The glass screen beautifully overlaps with the background curtain of the story and reflects the flames more clearly. However, in the dark exhibition space where the shutter at the projection aperture of the projector blocks the projection image, the flickering of the light bulb emphasizes the materiality of the glass screen and the strangeness of the opening. The viewer may be prompted to look at the projector. But more than that, they will be prompted to pay attention to the many overlapping and transforming screens and panes of glass in the story, as well as the giant glass screen that clearly reflects the projection. A projector and a built-in shutter are positioned as devices that operate in the conflict between the ghost and the king's appearance on the same screen.

Synchronicity, which revisits the royal mourning, virtually transforms the installation space into a "ritual space." However, "ritual space" here has a different meaning than before. In other words, Thailand, which is subject to performing mourning as a ritual, is turned into a "ritual space." Viewed through *Synchronicity*, the image of the king makes a powerful impression on the audience precisely because of his absence. Following the fall of King Bhumibol in 2016, the image of the king has become even more prevalent in Thailand. However, what this situation suggests is the existence of a kingdom or kingship that has established a political and cultural apparatus with a centrality. An essential element in the operation and maintenance of this apparatus is, of course, the fact that it is a flesh and blood king. A flesh and blood king is endowed with sanctity through the various rituals that convey "death" to him. Thus, the existence of the king, who has gone through the rituals of "death," is embalmed as "others."

5. Conclusion

Using the case of the image of the emperor in Japan as a starting point, this paper has revealed the strategic image strategy of the king of Thailand using cinema and projection. As a discussion throughout this paper, the focus is on the relationship between image and ritual. The analysis of the movie theater scene in Apichatpong's *Cemetery of Splendor* shows how the image of the king of Thailand has been related to cinema and projection. As shown in this film, Apichatpong's projective practice can be used to reconsider the history of Thai cinema's image and rethink the meaning of image projection itself. At the same time, Apichatpong's *Synchronicity* and *Blue* evoke the ritual and ceremonial space of the king's cremation, suggesting that "mourning" itself embalms the king's presence. In the first part of this book, I argued that cinema has always been a device for encountering "others." But the term needs to be modified in a way. This is because cinema that represents "others" always conceals the violence that excludes different "others." Therefore, just as Apichatpong shed light on the political and historical relationship between the king of Thailand and ghosts, we are now called upon to sincerely question what is represented and what is excluded when confronting the images of "others."

References

Aoki, Tamotsu. 2006. *Girei no syōchō sei*, [*Ritual Symbolism*] Iwanami gendai bunko.

Barmé, Scot. 1999. "Early Thai Cinema and Filmmaking: 1897-1922," *Film History*, Vol. 11, pp. 308-318.

Böhler, Natalie. 2012. "Made in Thailand - Thainess, Performance and Narration in Contemporary Thai Cinema," PhD Thesis, Zurich: University of Zurich.

Douglas, Mary and Isherwood, Baron. 2012. *The World of Goods*, [Girei to site no shohi: Zai to shohi no keizai], translated by Asada, Akira and Sawa, Takamitsu. Kōdansya.

Fujitani, Takashi. 1996. *Splendid Monarchy: Power and Pageantry in Modern Japan*, University of California Press: Berkeley.

Iijima, Yoichi. 2003. "Ou no ushinawareta kao" [The Lost Face of the King], eds., Amino, Yoshihiko. *Tennō to ōken wo kangaeru 6: Hyōchō to geinō*, [*Thinking About the Emperor and Kingship 6: Representation and Performance*], Iwanami shoten, pp. 45-68.

Ishii, Yoneo and Yoshikawa, Toshiharu. 1987. *Nichi Tai kōryu 600 nennshi* [*600 Years of Exchange Between Japan and Thailand*], Kōdansya.

Ishii, Yoneo. 2002. "Tai kokuō wo meguru gensetu" [Discourse on the King of Thailand], eds., Amino, Yoshihiko. *Tennō to ōken wo kangaeru 6: Hyōchō to geinō*, [*Thinking About the Emperor and Kingship 5: Royalty and Ritual*], Iwanami shoten, 2002, pp. 297-318.

Ishii, Yoneo. 2012. *Mouhitotsu no ousama to watashi* [*Another "The King and I"*]. Mekon.

Kamiya, Makiko. 2018. "Saisyoki no "kōsitsu eiga" ni kansuru kōsatu: kakusareru/sarasareru "shintai,"" [Reflections on the earliest "Imperial Films": the hidden/exposed "body"], eds., Japan Society of Image Arts and Science, *Eizōgaku*, vol. 100, 2018, pp. 32-52.

Knee, Adam. 2015. "Chiang Mai and the Cinematic Spaces of Thai Identity," *Asian Cinema and the Use of Space: Interdisciplinary Perspectives*, eds., Lilian Chee and Edna Lim, New York: Routledge, 2015, pp. 77-92.

O'Hara, Angela. 2010. "Mysterious Object of Desire: The Haunted Cinema of Apichatpong Weerasethakul," *The Reel Asian Exchange; Transnational Asian Identities in Pan Pacific Cinemas*, eds., Philippa Gates, Lisa Funnell, London: Routledge Advances in Film Studies, pp. 177-190.

Sakurada, Chie. 2013. "Midika na kokuō heno pafōmansu: Tai kokuō pumipon niyoru chihō gyōkō no jittai to sono yakuwari," [The King's Performance as a Familiar Being: The Reality and Role of King Bhumibol Adulyadej's Provincial Trips in Thailand], *AGLOS: Journal of Area-Based Global Studies*, Jyochi University Global Studies, pp. 2-27.

Sakurada, Chie. 2015. "Pumipon zen kokuō ni yoru syoki gyōkō to hōgeihōhō no kakuritu: ikkun banmin no seijikūkan no sōsyutu" [Former King Bhumibol Adulyadej of Thailand establishes the initial outreach and welcome: creating a political space for "one monarch and all the people"], eds., Fuji Xerox corporation's Yotaro Kobayashi Foundation, Kobayashi Fellowship 2015 Research Paper, 2015.

Sakurada, Chie. 2016. "Tai pumipon kokuō no hōgyo to korekara: Towareru kōtaishi no media senryaku," [The Fall of King Bhumibol Adulyadej of Thailand and the Future: The Crown Prince's Media Strategy], *SYNODOS*, October 25, 2016. (https://synodos.jp/international/18328) (Date of last check: October 1, 2020)

Sakurada, Chie. 2017. *Tai kokuō wo sasaeta hitobito: pumipon kokuō no gyōkō to eiga wo meguru huntōki*, [*People who supported King Bhumibol Adulyadej on his travels and his struggle to make film*], Hukyōsya.

Sungsri, Patsorn. 2004. "Thai Cinema as National Cinema: An Evaluative History," PhD thesis, Murdoch University.

Taki, Koji. 2002. *Tennō no shōzō* [*Portrait of the Emperor*], Iwanami Gendai Bunko.

Weerasethakul, Apichatpong. 2015. "Apichatpong Weerasethakul: I won't censor my work for Thailand," *the guardian*. (https://www.theguardian.com/film/2015/oct/16/apichatpong-weerasethakul-cemetery-of-splendour-cannes) (Date of last check: October 1, 2020)

Wongchalard, Natawan. 2015. "Contemporary Thai Action Cinema Genre Spectatorship and National Identity," PhD Thesis, Hyderabad: The English and Foreign Languages University, 2015.

Wongratpanya, Somsak. 1982. "Tai eiga syōsi" [A Brief History of Thai Cinema], translated by Udo, Seiji, Sato Tadao, eds., *Eiga ga ōsama no kuni*, [*Cinema is king in Thailand*], Hanashi no Tokusyū, pp. 248-265.

Yomota, Inuhiko. 2009. *Kaiki Eiga tengoku Asia* [*Asia: Heaven of the Horror Film*], Hakusuisya.

3
Communication of Otherness

Japan's Charm Offensive – NHK World-Japan and Soft Power

Griseldis Kirsch

Introduction: Broadcasting Japan to the world

Cool Japan has been a buzzword since the beginning of the millennium. With anime and manga consumed all over the world and Japanese fashion brands pushing into global markets, everything Japanese is considered 'cool'. While the appropriation of Japanese popular culture across the world has seen a lot of academic recognition, and Japanese soft power has been looked at by various scholars already (see, for example, Iwabuchi 2001, 2002 and 2015; Valaskivi 2013), one of the most prominent outlets of soft power, the satellite station NHK World-Japan, tends to get less attention in spite of its potential reach. On air since 2009, NHK World-Japan provides English-language news and features about Japan, and, to a lesser extent, about the rest of Asia. Its aim is "[…] to allow world viewers to understand Japan better," according to Takashima Hatsuhisa, chairman and CEO of the NHK subsidiary Japan International Broadcasting (JIB) that produces most of the programmes for the satellite-based service (quoted in Kato 2009). NHK World-Japan also live-streams its programmes as well as offers on demand services, making it globally available. In its 2014 annual report, NHK says about its world service,

> "A news/lifestyle channel broadcast fully in English from Japan. Offering the latest news and a wealth of content around the clock, all in HD, the channel serves as your gateway to Japan and the rest of Asia. […] The channel also offers colorful programming on diverse aspects of Japan, from traditional culture to the latest in pop culture. […]" (NHK, "Annual Report 2014/15," 19)[1]

To understand the full implications of why NHK World-Japan is important, it is necessary to look at NHK itself. NHK, which is short for Nippon Hōsō Kyōkai – Japan Broadcasting Corporation, is a public broadcasting corporation and as such, its duty is to its domestic market. In essence, NHK World-Japan is similar to the BBC World Service, a global television outlet under the auspices of a public broadcasting station. But unlike BBC World, which mainly broadcasts news, NHK World-Japan features what the 2014 annual report calls 'colourful programming' more prominently. As of March 2020, NHK World-Japan is available in 380 million households in about 160 countries (NHK, "Corporate Profile 2020/21," 9). Information about ratings, however, is not readily available, making it difficult to assess to what extent these 'colourful' programmes actually reach audiences.

By its mission statement, NHK is a politically impartial, public broadcasting station and as such financed by license fees. Their annual report hints at 'financial independence', stating

> "NHK's mission as a public broadcaster is to deliver impartial, high quality programs. Programs should never be influenced by the government or private organizations. NHK considers it to be the corporation's responsibility to provide a wide range of programs that are balanced, without the influence of ratings or third-party interests." (NHK, "Corporate Profile 2020/21," 3)

However, as in any media system around the world, this only ever represents the ideal. In the case of NHK, the licence fees are set by the Japanese parliament – potentially giving some leverage over NHK via financial pressure (Shimizu 1991).[2] In addition, the Board of Governors of NHK is appointed by the Prime Minister and approved by the Diet. Crucially, however, the license fees are non-enforceable (Okuda 2004): although Article 64 of the Broadcasting Law (*Hōsōhō,* enacted in 1950) states that anyone in possession of receiving equipment must pay a license fee (NHK, "Receiving Fee System"), the law does not mention punitive

[1] Interestingly, this passage never reappears in any future Annual Reports.
[2] Shimizu, "Public Service Broadcasting

measures for non-compliance. In a way, this loophole gives viewers a means of protest. With nearly 100% of its total income coming from license fees (NHK, "Corporate Profile 2020/21," 3), swathes of the audience not paying the licence fee can be financially damaging for the broadcaster. Thus, the NHK is sandwiched between two powerful actors, its audience on one side and the government on the other. Any violation of 'political impartiality' which is set out in Article 4 of the Broadcasting Law (E-Gov, "Hōsōhō") can have dire consequences for the broadcasting station – as exemplified by the 1993 Tsubaki Incident[3] and the sudden replacement of newscasters in 2015.[4] Previous chairmen, such as Shima Keiji, have often pointed at 'indirect influence' from the government, in particular the Prime Minister (Krauss 2000, 81-84; Gatzen 2001, 79-80). The political establishment is thus relatively close to the processes of broadcasting in Japan and for these reasons, NHK has been in the news itself during the tenure of the chairman Momii Katsuto (2013-2017). Momii, a close ally of the then Prime Minister Abe Shinzō, made headlines with statements such as "comfort women were only wrong per today's standards" or "the media should never be too far away from the government" (Kyodo, "Comfort Women"). These quotes illustrate that political impartiality is, like so many other things, in the eye of the beholder.

Into this mixture of government control and free broadcasting, comes NHK World-Japan with its mandate to broadcast news and 'colourful' programs from Japan, Japanese style, to foreign audiences, potentially in the way the government

---

[3] In 1993, the LDP was unable to form a government after losing the majority in the diet. After numerous political scandals, dissatisfaction with the LDP among the electorate had been high. However, the private station TV Asahi had pursued a very open anti-LDP broadcasting policy during the election campaign. Particularly the two anchor-men Kume Hiroshi (*Newsstation*) and Tahara Sōichirō (*Asahi Sunday News Project*) had been very critical of the incumbent Prime Minister Miyazawa Kiichi. While their opinion constituted a matter for freedom of speech, the editor of the political news desk, Tsubaki Sadayoshi, made a statement during a private meeting of the Association of Private Broadcasters, hinting that their 'bashing' of the LDP had had company backing. As this constituted a direct violation of the Broadcasting Law which applies to private stations as well, TV Asahi was threatened with losing its broadcasting licence. See Altman, "Television," for details.

[4] Kuniya Hiroko (*Close-up gendai*, NHK), Furutachi Ichirō (*Hōdō Station*, TV Asahi) and Kishii Shigetada (*News* 23, TBS) – all of who were critical of the Abe administration, were replaced as main hosts of their programmes. See Kyodo, "Censorship," and Kirsch, "Controlling the Media" for details.

desires. In the context of the Cool Japan nation branding strategy, Japan's official 'charm offensive', NHK World-Japan as mouthpiece of Japan becomes a very important object of analysis. Particularly with the so clearly stated aim to make people learn about Japan, looking at the programmes of NHK World-Japan offers an insight into how Japan wishes to be seen throughout the world. While a comprehensive study of all the programmes on NHK World-Japan would be impossible within the scope of this study, I will look at some programmes on NHK World-Japan, in particular those that focus on a representation of Japanese culture. In this paper, I will analyse the shows *cool japan, Japanology Plus* and *BEGIN Japanology*, to answer the question of whether, and to what extent, NHK World-Japan's self-representation challenges stereotypes about Japan, or whether it simply serves to underpin them. Furthermore, I will elaborate on the effectiveness of international broadcasting in regard to soft power. Before that, however, I will look at the concept of soft power and the 'Cool Japan' policy to understand the significance of NHK World-Japan within Cool Japan.

Soft power and Cool Japan

The term soft power was coined by Joseph S. Nye Jr. in his 1990 work *Bound to Lead: The Changing Nature of American Power.* Nye sees soft power in opposition to 'hard power' which refers to economic and military prowess, while soft power is more a 'soft co-opting' to accept the superiority of another country, or to put it in his words: "A country may obtain the outcomes it wants in world politics because other countries – admiring its values, emulating its example, aspiring to its level of prosperity and openness – want to follow it. In this sense, it is also important to set the agenda and attract others in world politics, and not only to force them to change by threatening military force or economic sanctions" (Nye 2005, 5). In other words, if you have values that only you possess, and you can make them desirable to the world, other countries will follow your bidding without force, because they can 'become like you', using the proverbial 'carrot' instead of the 'stick' (Nye 1990, 31).

While there is considerable truth to the fact that some countries simply have more of this soft power than others, political reality means that both hard power and soft power are essential. These ideas about how power could be exercised without force sparked off notions about Japan's 'coolness', first in Douglas McGray's 2002 article 'Japan's Gross National Cool' in which he elaborated upon how Japan continues to accumulate 'cultural capital', wielding enormous power through its video game industry (McGray 2002). Cool Japan has since become the brand image by which Japan is marketing its soft power to the outside world. Looking at the Cool Japan policy as given on the webpage of the Ministry of Economic, Trade and Industry, it is all about cashing in on the increasing love of all things Japanese around the globe, promoting Japanese cuisine, traditional and popular culture (Creative Industries Division, "Cool Japan"; METI, "Cool Japan"), and urging tourists to come to Japan "in search of the real thing" (Creative Industries Division, "Cool Japan", 10). One such achievement is the recognition of traditional Japanese cuisine, *washoku*[5], as a UNESCO Intangible Cultural Heritage, lifting it to the same level as French cuisine. Whether or not the policy has some impact – respectively looking at what has been accomplished since it was drafted and published in 2012 – is certainly impossible to quantify, because, as I elucidated elsewhere (Kirsch 2015), cultural flows are hard to control. Importantly, the way that the Cool Japan policy is defined makes it a government enterprise – yet a large share of Japanese popular culture abroad is being consumed in a way that a government would not condone, namely in pirated versions on the internet, outside of the control of Cool Japan policy, yet feeding directly into it. As Nissim Kadosh Otmazgin puts it, "piracy has diffused culture into the market and has avoided the state's protective shield, and it has been able to facilitate the dissemination of Japan's popular culture both into and within the market" (Otmazgin 2013, 121).

However, every soft power policy assumes, to some extent, a very simple model of stimulus and response, and has the oldest theory of communication (as media were called in the formative years of media studies as a discipline) at its heart. Thus, the debate as to what extent media exposure influences audiences is as old as the mass media themselves. Already in the 1920s, Harold Lasswell postulated in his *Theory of Political Propaganda* that a certain stimulus (media messages)

[5] Washoku as per UNESCO entry is only very narrowly defined, see UNESCO, "Washoku."

invariably leads to a unified response in the audience, that they can be guided to certain beliefs (Lasswell 1927). The media thus came to be predominantly seen as a tool for propaganda, for leading the 'masses' into the most desirable direction. This notion has relevance to this day, even though the fact that there never is a unified response to the same stimulus, due to the polysemic nature of media texts, has long been proven.[6] As propaganda (mis)uses of the media during the Second World War were still stuck in the minds of law makers, most post-war legal frameworks for media are defined in a way as to prevent too strict government control and thus influence on audiences, taking a presumed direct effect for granted. While media may serve the purpose of upholding or legitimizing a certain ideology, "oppositional readings" always remain a possibility (Hall 1992, 138). Yet, by transmitting soft power to the rest of the world, media are reduced to their function as a propaganda tool, because they are the ideal vehicle to make others want to follow you, to paraphrase Nye's assumption. In this respect, piracy of copyrighted works occupies an ambivalent position. On the one hand, the occurrence of piracy shows that some kind of effect (desired or not) seems to have happened, as the copyrighted material was deemed 'worthy enough' to be pirated and be disseminated illegally, while on the other hand, piracy bypasses government control and takes on a life of its own.

Piracy set aside, comparing what Cool Japan is about, namely propagating Japanese popular culture as well as 'traditional' culture to the wider world, this stance corresponds to the image of Japan as a country between 'tradition and modernity' often seen in European media. In that respect, NHK World-Japan could be the most influential mouthpiece of Cool Japan because of its global outreach, and its wide variety of programming which is exactly in line with the official policy, as its 'colourful features' are all about traditional Japanese culture as much as popular culture. Although soft power largely depends on the messages being read in the desired way, in line with propaganda theory, NHK World-Japan does not publish audience data. While this may admittedly be hard to obtain for an internationally broadcast satellite channel, impact can only be measured through

[6] A critical discussion on media effect theories would be beyond the scope of this paper. See, for example, the papers in Gregg and Seigworth 2010; Hall 1992; Fiske 1987.

social media, through followers on Twitter and 'likes' on Facebook. In addition, the 'comments' function on the official YouTube site of NHK World-Japan is disabled (NHK World-Japan, "Official YouTube Channel"), making it hard to gauge audience reception on official channels and almost impossible to quantify the impact of Japan's charm offensive via NHK World-Japan. The number of subscribers for the official channel on YouTube is 719,000 as of 10 November 2020, which is, in comparison to successful YouTubers, a fairly small number (NHK World-Japan, "Official YouTube Channel"). The comparable BBC News YouTube channel has 8.86 million subscribers (BBC News, "Official YouTube Channel"). NHK World-Japan indeed does not have a notable presence on social media, apart from a Facebook page which is regularly updated (NHK World Japan, "Facebook"). It is also active on Twitter, tweeting news items relating to Japan, just like other news providers (NHK World News, "Twitter"). Nonetheless, traditional broadcasting channels remain significant for NHK, in spite of its problems with the quantification of impact – which would be crucial to measure the success of Cool Japan.

Educating the world about Japan? A deeper look at NHK World-Japan

The broadcasting schedule of NHK World-Japan follows a similar routine every day. News and Weather run from the full hour to about ten minutes past, followed by features of varying length filling the rest of the hour until the cycle starts again (NHK World-Japan, "Live & Programs"). As of December 2020, NHK World-Japan lists sixty-two regular shows on their webpage (NHK World-Japan, "Special Programs"), Those programmes introducing Japan often use stereotypical imagery, such as a zen garden for *Core Kyoto* (NHK World-Japan, "Core Kyoto"), or cherry blossoms for the cookery programme *Dining with the Chef*, making them recognisable and quintessentially Japanese (NHK World-Japan, "Dining").

The scope of the programmes as such is to introduce Japanese culture to an interested, non-Japanese audience, very clearly with the business traveller or casual tourist in mind. Shows that have been missed can be watched on the On-Demand site on the webpage – yet not all are available through the service. All the programmes that feature Japan seem to highlight the 'uniqueness of Japanese culture' – putting *nihonjinron*[7] at the heart of the representation, as Japanese culture is presented as impenetrable and hard to understand for non-Japanese. Although *nihonjinron* have by and large vanished from the (academic) discourse on and of Japan, their afterlife, namely the establishment of (auto-) stereotypes of Japan, is well visible within (Japanese) media. If an encounter with the Other is topic of a programme, it very often will only mean that boundaries between Japan and the respective Other are upheld rather than deconstructed. Japan is being sold to the outside world as a quirky place to visit, that will be different from anything else anyone has ever seen. Phrases like, 'this is unique to Japan', 'this is very Japanese' or 'this can only be found in Japan' can be frequently heard throughout a broadcasting day on NHK World-Japan.

The programmes which have been analysed in more detail, *cool japan*, *BEGIN Japanology* and *Japanology Plus*, are exactly in line with these *nihonjinron*. As a show, cool japan uses a format that has been well established in Japan, since it resembles Beat Takeshi's *Koko ga hen da yo, nihonjin* (This is weird, you Japanese) in which foreigners told their host what they thought of Japan, and what 'weird' things have happened to them. Iwabuchi Koichi has worked out that the interviews in *Koko ga hen da yo, nihonjin* are scripted, thus implying intent on the side of the producers to construct, and not to deconstruct, the boundaries between Japan and the Other (Iwabuchi 2010). Kunihiro Yōko and Hagiwara Shigeru have furthermore analysed that the way foreigners are portrayed in this programme is heavily in line with the cultural stereotypes that the Japanese have of them, underlining the difference of those foreigners to 'the Japanese' (Kunihiro and Hagiwara 2004). In that respect, *cool japan* is no different. Hosted by Risa Stegmayer and Shoji Kokami, it is also broadcast in Japan (albeit in Japanese). The discussion on what is 'cool' (which often seems to be synonymous with 'weird') evolves within a panel consisting of foreigners from various countries. As the webpage puts it, "What makes Japan cool? From traditional to on-trend,

[7] Literally translated as 'theories on the Japanese', *nihonjinron* were often pseudo-academic treatises on Japanese culture, always constructing Japan in opposition to the 'West'. The arguments were simple and existed in an 'Us vs. Them' dichotomy, generalising culture and homogenising both Japan and a vaguely-defined 'West'. See Befu 2001 and Kirsch and Martinez 2015 for a critical discussion.

an international panel is immersed in Japanese culture, reporting back on their verdicts!" (NHK World-Japan, "cool japan"). These foreigners will be sent out on a hunt throughout Japan to discover its 'cool', and upon return to the studio, talk about how different their home countries are and how 'unique' Japan is. Like in any Japanese panel show, their faces are superimposed on the screen as the feature runs, allowing audiences to see the reaction of the panel members, thus enabling them to gauge their reaction and relate themselves to their carefully crafted persona.[8]

Features that cool japan has covered since being on air include, for example, 'Bicycles,' 'Advertising,' 'Wabi-sabi,' 'Kimono,' and answers to questions such as, 'Why [are] the Japanese people more stress-tolerant than others,' and 'Why don't Japanese couples kiss?' The show was still running in December 2020 – featuring 'Glasses,' 'Bamboo,' 'Living in the Countryside' and 'Tying' (NHK World-Japan, "cool japan"). This choice of topics highlights clearly that Japan is Othered to the amusement of the audience while upholding the stereotype of national uniqueness. However, it also means that audiences will feel 'superior' to the foreigners – who will, by their journey through Japan, tell the Japanese (and by extension, the global citizens they represent), that there are things that exist only in Japan.

BEGIN Japanology and *Japanology Plus* have slightly different aims. *BEGIN Japanology* was the predecessor of *Japanology Plus* and they are thus very similar shows. NHK World-Japan advertises it as follows: "Fresh insights into Japan. Stories behind Japanese life and culture through the eyes of Peter Barakan, a 45-year resident and watcher of Japan" (NHK World-Japan, "Japanology Plus"). The British host Peter Barakan does not just present *Japanology Plus*, although *BEGIN Japanology* and J*apanology Plus* are probably what made him famous, but he is also in charge of four radio programmes on various stations in the Tokyo area (Barakan, "Barakan Dot Net"). In both television shows, Peter Barakan embarks on a journey of discovery around Japan, explaining how some 'things Japanese', or things commonly associated with Japan have come about, are used,

[8] The para-social relationship between *tarento* (a television personality) and audience is crucial to the understanding of Japanese television. See Kirsch 2014 for a detailed discussion.

or have been used. For *Japanology Plus*, he was initially joined by an American, Matt Alt, who left the show in April 2020 (Alt, "Stepped Away"). Therefore, Peter Barakan has filmed the latest season by himself, bringing *Japanology Plus* closer to its predecessor, *BEGIN Japanology*. Both *BEGIN Japanology* and *Japanology Plus* are educational programmes, not as sensationalising as *cool japan* and the boundaries between Japan (and the Other) are not as clearly established as in *cool japan*. Nonetheless, the main host Peter Barakan is still a foreigner (albeit one with decades spent in Japan and a degree in Japanese) looking at Japanese culture. Although uniqueness is not upheld by direct comparison, it still is underlined by the frequent mentioning of a cultural feature being 'unique' to Japan, almost making it a *nihonjinron* without a properly defined Other. This has been underlined by Matt Alt acting as the interested (yet a little clueless) explorer of Japan, who is happy to be educated by the Japanese about their customs. Both programmes are directed at a foreign audience – and both represent the tourist gaze, the casual visitor's view of Japan.

Between 2014 – when this study commenced – and 2020, when this paper was finished, *Japanology Plus* received its own YouTube channel (Japanology Plus, "Japanology Plus: Official YouTube Channel"), however, fans can only watch parts of the episodes. Full episodes can legally only be found on the webpage of NHK World-Japan. Interestingly, the comments function on the official page is switched on – however, both views and comments are relatively few and far between, with the oldest video, posted in August 2019 scoring a mere 2,654 views and one comment, as of 19 December 2020 (Japanology Plus, "Japanology Plus: Official YouTube Channel"). It seems that NHK has started to take Takashima's statement to educate people about Japan more seriously and is also exploring the avenue of YouTube – previously shunned in favour of the more controlled environment of their own website, but it does not yet seem to be promoted widely.

Conclusion

Matters are thus more complex than the rather optimistic mission statement of Takashima Hatsuhisa, namely to educate people about Japan, would suggest, particularly considering the nature in which most people watch television in the

21st century. NHK World-Japan is still focused on the traditional outlets – satellite broadcasting, with a smattering of online streaming on its own webpage. The full possibilities of social media and YouTube where impact and reception of a particular programme could be more easily measured and thus audience demand met, remain underexplored. It almost feels like NHK World-Japan prefers to talk into the ether, without any real possibility to close the feedback loop.

Whether this may be because the algorithms of YouTube lead viewers to similar programmes outside of the control of NHK World-Japan, or whether it may be because of the pitfalls associated with its presence there (pirated videos are amongst those featured under the suggestions) and trolling, which may make it difficult for a tightly regulated broadcasting station to engage on those sites, it would at least close that crucial feedback loop. Nonetheless, effects can never be pinned down to one factor and are always a combination of many, rendering some assumptions behind what soft power can do over-simplistic. The amount of clicks and comments, however, do at least offer some indication as to what audiences desire. Thus, when people 'watch Japan', it does not mean they will want to go to Japan as an immediate result, or indeed they may not even consciously choose to be educated. From the point of consumption onwards, it becomes hard to work out how they incorporate the information they have gathered through the programmes into their lives – making the actual effect impossible to quantify, in spite of the fact that both soft power policy makers as well as lawmakers of media guidelines in Japan seem to assume precisely this direct stimulus-response model of media effect.

Instead, various factors are at play when it comes to the consumption of media texts. A para-social relationship can be equally as important as an interest in the theme, or the country, and thus the content. Peter Barakan's popularity may attract viewers to *Japanology Plus* just as much as the desire to know more about Japan does. And the casual viewer interested in, for example, ninja, might get interested in a few more items in relation to ninja culture – before moving on to the next show on ninja that will not be provided by NHK and thus outside of their control. In this media-saturated age, the 'next item' is always but one click away. One counter-argument, however, could be that Japan has seen increasing numbers of tourists – one could hold against it by arguing that it would be also oversimplified to put that increase simply down to an increased interest in Cool Japan (Otake, "Visitors", Nihon seifu kankōchō, "Hōnichi"). In addition, the award of the Tokyo Olympics has sparked off further interest in the country, indicating again that more factors are at play than the simple charm offensive being conducted by NHK World-Japan.

When it comes to Cool Japan NHK-style, it remains a celebration of all things Japanese; Japan is constructed as a shiny glittering country with a rich popular culture as well as a several centuries' old tradition of craftsmanship. NHK World-Japan is a product made for foreigners, not Japanese, under the assumption of how a seemingly imagined foreign audience would react to 'Japan' by perhaps also bringing an 'alternative message' out there, one that differs from the quite harsh criticism that some non-Japanese media outlets usually use when dealing with matters relating to Japan. NHK World-Japan remains an assertion of Japanese uniqueness and cultural superiority. It constitutes a veritable charm offensive making use of Japan's image of its own soft power in order to assert Japan's uniqueness to a wide audience at the same time, eternally perpetuating *nihonjinron* on how Japan wants to be seen by an international audience. Japan remains an imaginary space, assembled by audiences in conjunction with NHK World-Japan and its programme makers.

References

Alt, Matt (@Matt_Alt). 2020. "I've stepped away from Japanology Plus to focus on personal projects, [...]." Tweet, 11 April 2020, https://twitter.com/Matt_Alt/status/1248761162998493189.

Altman, Kristin Kyoko. 1996. "Television and Political Turmoil: Japan,'s Summer of 1993." In *Media and Politics in Japan*, edited by Susan J. Pharr and Ellis S. Krauss, 165-186. Honolulu: University of Hawai'i Press.

Barakan, Peter. N.d. "Peter Barakan Dot Net: Official Webpage." Accessed 19 December 2020. http://peterbarakan.net.

Befu, Harumi. 2001. *Hegemony of Homogeneity: An Anthropological Analysis of Nihonjinron*. Melbourne; Portland, OR: Transpacific Press.

British Broadcasting Corporation (BBC). N.d. "BBC News: Official YouTube Channel." Accessed 19 December 2020. https://www.youtube.com/user/bbcnews.

Creative Industries Division, Ministry of Economy, Trade and Industry Japan (METI). N.d. "Cool Japan Strategy." Accessed 19 December 2020.

http://www.meti.go.jp/english/policy/mono_info_service/creative_industries/pdf/120116_01a.pdf.

E-Gov hōrei kenchaku. "Hōsōhō." N.d. Accessed 19 December 2020.
https://elaws.e-gov.go.jp/document?lawid=325AC0000000132.

Fiske, John. 1987. *Television Culture*. London: Routledge.

Gatzen, Barbara. 2001. *Fernsehnachrichten in Japan: Inszenierungsstrategien im interkulturellen Vergleich mit Deutschland*. Tübingen: Gunter Narr.

Gregg, Melissa and Gregory J. Seigworth (eds.). 2010. *The Affect Theory Reader*. Duke University Press.

Hall, Stuart. 1992. "Encoding/Decoding." In Culture, *Media, Language: Working Papers in Cultural Studies*, edited by Stuart Hall, Dorothy Hobson, Andrew Lowe and Paul Willis, 128-138. London: Routledge.

Horton, Donald and R. Richard Wohl. 1956. "Mass Communication and Para-social Interaction: Observations on Intimacy at a Distance." *Psychiatry* 19, no. 3 (1956): 215-229.

Iwabuchi, Koichi. 2010. "'Ordinary Foreigners' Wanted: Multinationalization of Multicultural Questions in a Japanese TV Talk Show." In *Television, Japan and Globalization*, edited by Yoshimoto Mitsuhiro, Eva Tsai and JungBong Choi, 27-50. Ann Arbor: The Center for Japanese Studies, The University of Michigan.

Iwabuchi, Koichi. 2002. *Recentering Globalization: Popular Culture and Japanese Transnationalism*. Duke University Press.

Iwabuchi, Koichi. 2015. *Resilient Borders and Cultural Diversity: Internationalism, Brand Nationalism, and Multiculturalism in Japan*. Lanham, et al.: Lexington Books.

Iwabuchi, Kōichi. 2001. *Toransunashonaru Japan: Ajia o tsunagu popyurā bunka*. Tokyo: Iwanami Shoten.

Japanology Plus. "Bathhouses." Accessed 19 December 2020.
https://www.youtube.com/watch?v=lEDCpohjzZw.

Japanology Plus. "Japanology Plus: Official YouTube Channel." Accessed 19 December 2020. https://www.youtube.com/channel/UC_ot5hhOZFvqqtnJ7dNuZRw/videos.

Kato, Mariko. 2009. "NHK to Launch Global 24-hour News Channel." *Japan Times*, 29 January 2009. http://www.japantimes.co.jp/news/2009/01/29/national/nhk-to-launch-global-24-hour-news-channel/#.VofpGhWLTcc. Accessed 19 December 2020.

Kirsch, Griseldis. 2016. "Controlling the Media in Japan." UoN Blogs, Institute of Asia and Pacific Studies, University of Nottingham. Accessed 19 December 2020.
https://blogs.nottingham.ac.uk/asiapacificstudies/2016/07/11/controlling-the-media-in-japan/.

Kirsch, Griseldis. 2015. "Japan in the Global Context: (Some) Challenges in the 21st Century." *Romanian Economic and Business Review*, 10, no. 4 (Winter 2015): 199-214.
http://www.rebe.rau.ro/REBE_10_4_2015.pdf.

Kirsch, Griseldis. 2014. "Next-Door Divas: Japanese Tarento, Television and Consumption." *Journal of Japanese and Korean Cinema*, 6, no. 1 (2014): 74-88.

Kirsch, Griseldis and Dolores Martinez. 2015. "Japan as an Assemblage." In *Assembling Japan: Modernity, Technology and Global Culture*, edited by Griseldis Kirsch, Dolores Martinez and Merry White, 1-19. Bern: Peter Lang, pp 1-19.

Krauss, Ellis S. 2000. *Broadcasting Politics in Japan: NHK and Television News*. Ithaca, London: Cornell UP.

Kunihiro, Yōko and Shigeru Hagiwara. 2004. *Terebi to gaikoku imēji: media sutereotaipingu kenkyū*. Tokyo: Keisōshobo.

Kyodo. 2014. "New NHK Chief: 'Comfort Women' only Wrong per 'Today's Morality', Programming Must Push Japan's Territorial Stances." *Japan Times*, 24 January 2014. Accessed 19 December 2020. http://www.japantimes.co.jp/news/2014/01/25/national/new-nhk-chief-comfort-women-only-wrong-per-todays-morality-programming-must-push-japans-territorial-stances/#.Vo5W0RWLTcc.

Kyodo. 2014. "Self-Censorship Sensed as Japan's TV Stations Replace Outspoken Anchors." *Japan Times*, 26 January 2016. Accessed 19 December 2020.

http://www.japantimes.co.jp/news/2016/01/26/national/media-national/self-censorship-sensed-japans-tv-stations-replace-outspoken-anchors/?utm_source=Daily+News+Updates&utm_campaign=236bcfa0e5-Tuesday_email_updates27_01_2016&utm_medium=email&utm_term=0_c5a6080d40-236bcfa0e5-332791065#.VqlDjezfXCR.

Lasswell, Harold. 1927. "The Theory of Political Propaganda." *American Political Science Review* 21, no. 3 (1927): 627-631.

McGray, Douglas. 2002. "Japan's Gross National Cool," *Foreign Policy* 130 (2002): 44-54.

Ministry of Economy, Trade and Industry Japan (METI). N.d. "Cool Japan/Creative Industries Policies." Accessed 19 December 2020.

http://www.meti.go.jp/english/policy/mono_info_service/creative_industries/creative_industries.html.

NHK World TV. N.d. "NHK World TV: Official Twitter Account." Accessed 19 December 2020.

https://twitter.com/NHKWORLD_TV.

NHK World-Japan. N.d. "cool japan." Accessed 19 December 2020.

https://www3.nhk.or.jp/nhkworld/en/tv/cooljapan/.

NHK World-Japan. N.d. "Core Kyoto." Accessed 19 December 2020.

https://www3.nhk.or.jp/nhkworld/en/tv/corekyoto/.

NHK World-Japan. N.d. "Dining with the Chef." Accessed 19 December 2020.

https://www3.nhk.or.jp/nhkworld/en/tv/dining/.

NHK World-Japan. N.d. "Live & Programs." Accessed 19 December 2020.

https://www3.nhk.or.jp/nhkworld/en/live/.

NHK World-Japan. N.d. "NHK World-Japan: Official Facebook Page." Accessed 19 December 2020.

https://www.facebook.com/nhkworld/.

NHK World-Japan. N.d. "Official YouTube Channel." Accessed 19 December 2020.

https://www.youtube.com/user/NHKWorld.

NHK World-Japan. N.d. "Special Programs." Accessed 19 December 2020.

https://www3.nhk.or.jp/nhkworld/en/programs/

Nihon seifu kankōchō (JNTO). 2019. "Hōnichi kyakusū (2019 nen, 12 gatsu oyobi nenkan teikichi)." Accessed 19 December 2020.

https://www.jnto.go.jp/jpn/statistics/data_info_listing/pdf/200117_monthly.pdf.
Nippon Hōsō Kyōkai (NHK). 2014. *NHK Annual Report 2014/15*. Tokyo: Nippon Hōsō Kyōkai, 2014.
Nippon Hōsō Kyōkai (NHK). 2020. "NHK Corporate Profile 2020/21." Accessed 19 December 2020. https://www.nhk.or.jp/corporateinfo/english/publication/pdf/corporate_profile.pdf.
Nippon Hōsō Kyōkai (NHK). N.d. "Receiving Fee System." Accessed 19 December 2020. https://www.nhk.or.jp/corporateinfo/english/receivingfee/index.html.
Nye, Joseph S. Jr. 1990. *Bound to Lead: The Changing Nature of American Power*. New York: Basic Books.
Nye, Joseph S. Jr. 2005. *Soft Power: The Means to Success in World Politics*. New York: Public Affairs.
Okuda, Yoshitane. 2004. "Evolution of the Public Nature of NHK's Broadcasting and Its Role in Disaster Reporting." In *Disaster Reporting and the Public Nature of Broadcasting: On the Occasion of the 50th Anniversary of Television Broadcasting in Japan*, edited by NHK Broadcasting Culture Research Institute, 213-260. Tokyo: Japan Broadcasting Corporation (NHK).
Otake, Tomoko. 2016. "Visitors to Japan Surge to Record 19.73 Million, Spend All-time High ¥3.48 Trillion." *Japan Times*, 19 January 2016. Accessed 19 December 2020. http://www.japantimes.co.jp/news/2016/01/19/national/japan-sets-new-inbound-tourism-record-2015-comes-just-short-20-million-target/?utm_source=Daily+News+Updates&utm_campaign=8b698ee997-Tuesday_email_updates20_01_2016&utm_medium=email&utm_term=0_c5a6080d40-8b698ee997-332791065#.Vr9sifKLTcd.
Otmazgin, Nissim Kadosh. 2013. *Regionalizing Culture: The Political Economy of Japanese Popular Culture in Asia*. The University of Hawai'i Press.
Shimizu, Shinichi. 1991. "Public Service Broadcasting in Japan: How NHK Faces the Future." In *Broadcasting Finance in Transition: A Comparative Handbook*, edited by Jay G. Blumler and T. J. Nossiter, 296-311. Oxford: Oxford University Press.
United Nations Educational, Scientific and Cultural Organization (UNESCO). 2013. "Washoku: Traditional Dietary Cultures of the Japanese, Notably for the Celebration of New Year." UNESCO Intangible Cultural Heritage, 2013. Accessed 19 December 2020.
http://www.unesco.org/culture/ich/en/RL/washoku-traditional-dietary-cultures-of-the-japanese-notably-for-the-celebration-of-new-year-00869.
Valaskivi, Katja. 2013. "A Brand New Future? Cool Japan and the Social Imaginary of the Branded Nation." Japan Forum 25, no. 4 (Winter 2013): 485-504.

Listening: The Other in the Dream

Akiko Okubori

Introduction: the other in listening

We have many conversations in our life. For example, a casual conversation with family or a quarrel between lovers, a pleasant chat with a friend, a nervous consultation with a teacher, or an interview concerning a bitter experience. Listening is such an ordinary act that we live without considering the act of listening. However, this act deserves careful attention. This is because listening is the exact start point from where we direct our attention to others. New academic fields are developing in the disaster victim areas of the Great East Japan Earthquake[1]. One of the approaches is *shinsaigaku* (震災学, disaster studies). I would like to focus attention on *reisei no shinsaigaku* (霊性の震災学, disaster studies on spirituality), an approach that has been suggested by Sociologist Kiyoshi Kanebishi. His approach involves firstly listening to others, i.e. survivors of the earthquake, thus placing them in the centre, and then writing the conversation to share it with the reader. How can we listen to the voices of survivors in the disaster victim areas of the Great East Japan Earthquake? The purpose of this study is to examine the relation with the other and the dead through the structure of listening in shinsaigaku and philosophy. I would like to deliberate upon the question of whether finding the connection between two distinct types of listening could help philosophy to commit to the issue of those who passed away after the earthquake.

[1] For example, the religious studies department at Tohoku University founded a "Department of Practical Religious Studies (実践宗教学寄附講座, *Jissen shūkyōgaku kifu kōza*)" after the earthquake. These lectures are given by a "clinical religionist (臨床宗教師, *Rinshōshūkyōshi*)", who goes to the disaster victim areas to listen to survivors' experiences and worries.

1. *Reisei no shinsaigaku*[2]

As the first step in my analysis, I will examine how Kanebishi performed his approach to disaster studies. Within a week of the earthquake, he started a project for recording the earthquake with his students in Sendai. They gathered 500 reports. Tohoku Gakuin University, the university where he was teaching, is familiar to the people of Miyagi prefecture and the people of Tohoku region. Students share bitter experiences with others around, for example relatives, friends, and neighbours, even if they did not go through difficulties themselves. And sharing of the experience expands to the graduate students of various generations and areas. Based on their reports, Kanebishi wrote *3 / 11 Document of Wailing: Great Tsunami・Great Earthquake・Nuclear Power Plant Disaster Experienced by 71 People* (*3.11 Dōkoku no kiroku: 71 nin no taikan shita ōtsunami・genpatsu・kyodai jishin*, 2012). This book was the first publication of his project. The purpose of the book was just to keep a record of the disaster and its aftermath. However, the reaction of survivors led to an unexpected development. Kanebishi turned to the question of the deceased, to which little attention has been given in the literature on the earthquake in general.

In so doing, Kanebishi discovered a so-called "care of keeping the pain." The term "care of keeping the pain" is used to describe a relationship between the dead and the survivors. According to Kanebishi, survivors have paradoxical feelings: they wish to be released from the dead in order to feel relieved, but they feel that they cannot leave the dead in pain. This was the mental state of the survivors after the earthquake. As a result of this research, Kanebishi decided to try a form of care involving keeping the pain and an approach of taking notes on the survivors' records. Based on these records, he published *Memento Mori of the Earthquake: In the Face of the Second Tsunami* (*Shinsai memento mori: daini no tsunami ni*

---

[2] This section is a revised version of a paper that was published in *Journal of Innovative Ethics Special Issue* (See Okubori 2019). The topics and the sentences remain basically the same as the published paper. The purpose of the earlier paper was to discuss the question of death after the Great East Japan Earthquake from the viewpoint of two philosophers after World War II, Vladimir Jankélévitch (1903–1985) and Hajime Tanabe (田辺元: 1885–1962). I explained about disaster studies on spirituality (*reisei no shinsaigaku*) in a section of this paper.

kōshite, 2014). Survivors have reconstructed their relation to the dead by taking notes. Kanebishi thus proposes a disaster study based on spirituality (霊性, *reisei*) in *An Introduction to Shinsaigaku: a plan of society from a view of life and death* (*Shinsaigaku nyūmon: shiseikan kara no shakai kōsō*, 2016).

2. Translating images to words

At the same time, Kanebishi started a field work project with his students. He collected their research and published it in book form. In their field work, they adopt two methods for their research: 1. Have a survivor write a letter to the deceased, 2. Have a survivor talk about a dream where he met the deceased.

2-1. Image of the dead in the dream

Especially in *He Came to My Dream: 3.11 The Future With the Dead* (*Watashi no yume made ai ni kite kureta: 3.11 naki hito tono sorekara,* 2018), Kanebishi aims to share survivor's experiences with readers through listening to their experiences, as can be seen in the following quotation:

> The purpose of this book is to make it easy for people who did not experience the earthquake to share survivor's experiences, through translating one-off phenomena, dreams that are difficult to record, namely images, to 'words' which can be understood by others. (Kanebishi 2018, 258)

The first point that we should discuss is translating images of dreams to words. In this quotation, the dream refers to an image. What is the image in this case? Kanebishi and his students listened to the talk about a dream of the dead in the earthquake and tsunami. The dead that comes to their dream is such an emotional image of the deceased. Kanebishi writes as follows: "I would like you to listen to the voice of the deceased earnestly through dream. I try to listen to the breathing of the deceased and the whisper between survivor and deceased that we lose unconsciously" (264). However, the image of the dream is not real in the present or the past. According to Kanebishi, the deceased invades the present of the survivor and continues relating to the survivor (263). In the dream they have a sort of power to turn the past into the present progressive form (263). From this idea of the dead, we realize that the image of dead in the dream has an atemporal power. We might be facing the atemporal in translating images of dreams to words.

2-2. The appearance that supersedes image and memory

This now raises the question of what the difference between the image of dreams and memory is. Kazuyuki Hosomi made several important statements on the other and memory from the viewpoint of identity. Identity is the "I" who is the successive and the same in our changeable life. Memory helps to keep being "I" and to form one's identity. We recognize a young me as a present me. This is because we have our childhood in mind (Hosomi 1999, 10-11) For a hypothetical example, one evening my father was drunk. He came back home with a shouting voice in the middle of the night. My grandfather took me up to his room. I have such a painful memory, but my grandfather's memory is warm. My identity formed with his memory. For all that, I have lost him since he died. Now I keep my identity without him, and almost do not remember him. However, I have his memory in mind. Hosomi goes deep into the heart of this problem as follows: "We cannot control memory. Proust gives a good account of the structure of memory in *In Search of Lost Time*. Memory is not recalled consciously, all of the sudden memories come back to our mind. Even if we try to recall something into consciousness, needless to say, we cannot know the memory that backs us. Memory is like a shadow picture at best. Therefore, it is just the unknown. However, it is "my" memory not the other's" (11).

Let us now return to the question of the image of a dream. According to Kanebishi, we find it difficult to see the dream and the appearance of the dead in the case of the earthquake as a memory (Kanebishi 2018, 258). This result leads us to the following conclusion: in the case of listening for Kanebishi's project for recording the earthquake, the talker starts to talk with their unforgettable deceased in their dream. They then are translating dreams of the dead to words in front of the listener. The deceased continues growing up in the talker's dream even though he is already dead. Therefore the talker translates his updated version to words. Certainly his update goes to the future, not to the past or his memory. The listener listens not only to the talk from the talker, but to the voice of the deceased as well. The deceased appears not as an image or a memory, but as their dynamic appearance. We finally translate the appearance to words through listening to the content of the talker's dream and making a written record.

3. Clinical philosophy

On the other hand, in *The Power of Listening: Toward Clinical Philosophy* (*Kiku koto no chikara: rinshōtetsugaku shiron*, 1999), Kiyokazu Washida works out a detailed plan for a new philosophy. This philosophy is not based on the philosophical history by the classical philosophers. This is because such traditional methods pressure others to think about philosophical questions, for example through the philosopher himself talking, admonishing, discussing, and emphasizing. Clinical Philosophy starts by listening to the talk of others, placing the others in the centre. On the basis of this structure of 〈talk / listen〉 clinical philosophy creates a new place of philosophy.

Generally, "clinical" is used in the academic fields of medicine and nursing. However, "clinical" for Washida is not limited to the medical field. He refers to "clinical" in the following terms:

> In the case of philosophy, the clinical is the place where social opinion is formed. In other words, it is the place where discourses are formed and flow self-evidently in the place of each emerging issue. (Honma, Nakaoka et al. 2010, xiii)

Traditional philosophy regards the philosophical place as a place of argument about philosophical discourse and theory. However, clinical philosophy according to Washida involves the philosophical discourse that emerges from the bedside of our contemporary society where social opinion is formed. Now his new idea of philosophy is leading to the creation of a multiplicity of meaning by many scholars (xiii-xiv).

3-1. Texture of the voice

Now that we have become familiar with philosophy in the bedside of contemporary society, it will be possible to discuss listening in clinical philosophy[3]. The main point of Washida's idea of listening is the texture of voice. In *The Clinical and Words* (*Rinshō to kotoba*, 2010), he considers the texture of voice in the structure of 〈talk / listen〉. According him, the voice of talk (texture) has a power of voice beyond the meaning of talk (text) (Washida 2010, 223). What is the power of voice? The power of voice is expressed best by Washida when he says the following:

> Threat, temptation, loud laughter, comfort, emotional dependence: the voice has a power beyond meaning. I think that the voice is a face. .... 'the face' is not a shape of the face. When we think of someone's face, the face does not appear minutely. Even if the face of a family member, we cannot replicate the shape of his eyebrow and ears with words. To know 'the face' is not to know well the mould of the face in precise detail. On occasion, 'the face' of someone can be his back shot and the appearance of the palm of his hand. 'The face' of someone is not the shape of his face, but the presence with which he touches me. Therefore, we can say that the voice is his 'face' as well, if his voice sounds when he thinks about someone. '*Kime* (きめ)' spells '*Kime* (肌理)'. The voice is exactly 'the face' of others that touches my skin. (222-223)

In summary, the voice in Washida has not only the enumeration of words as sound, but 'the face' which touches the skin of the listener from the voice of the talker: for example, it is his back shot and the appearance of the palm of his hand. This appearance of talker is the texture of the voice in Washida, which touches the skin (肌) of the listener. Surely, we try to understand our conversation partner when we have a conversation, feeling for a kind of tone of the voice. This 'feeling' can be called listening. Washida's idea of listening, especially the texture of voice, is very

[3] Here I would like to say one more word. Clinical Philosophy was proposed by Kiyokazu Washida in 1999. However, psychiatrist Bin Kimura and anatomist Takeshi Yoro had previously used the term "clinical philosophy". Moreover, now there are many types of philosophy which are going to do fieldwork, including in another philosophical field of Washida's. It would be interesting to follow up this point further, but the systematization of this kind of study is too complicated to be examined in detail here. I limit the discussion here to the consideration of "listening" in Washida.

helpful for the thesis of this paper. This is because we have already considered translating a sort of appearance of the dead that is not the image of memory to words. The appearance of the dead can be explained by the texture of voice. From here, we can now turn back to the initial question of the present study: the relation with the other and the dead in listening.

3-2. Touching a sound and acoustical existence

I will now discuss the appearance of the dead through the texture of voice in detail. The central problem of the texture of voice is "touching a sound" and "acoustical existence." In the beginning, Washida explains touching a sound with a work of Japanese literature, *The Sound in the Kitchen* (*Daidokoro no oto,* 1992) which is written by Aya Kōda. She is a Japanese essayist and novelist. The book is a novel. The heroine of the story is Aki. She lives with her husband Sakichi, who is a chef in Japanese restaurant Nakagawa but is bedridden with a serious illness. One day Sakichi feels a difference in the sound that Aki makes in the kitchen, for example the sound of cutting with a kitchen knife, and the sound of the water. He thinks that she is not in a good condition through her sound. In fact, Sakichi's doctor had told her that his condition will not change for the better. Sakichi noticed her sentimental change, in spite of the distance between the kitchen and living room, furthermore without having a conversation. From this story, Washida considers that we need to avoid assumptions about carrying the voice (Washida 1999, 188-189).

> Carrying the voice or sound and feeling them, strictly speaking, are not the same. They carry us sometimes through "touching." …. Recall Aki and Sakichi. He touched her with feeling her modulation and change of the texture. …. The communion of oneself and others comes calling in the distant contact. (189-190)

To put it another way, after pointing out listening in the relation between Aki and Sakichi, Washida goes on to say: "We would like to think that the sound is a sort of common element, in which we live with others. That kind of element of existence branches to my noise, your noise, his noise and my voice and your voice and his voice. As it were, there is an experience of touching a field of interpenetration in the foundation of listening to the others. We level out the distinction between self and other, inside and outside, active and passive there. The heterogeneity of an other, that has the feeling of another voice and another temperature of the body, emerges from such an experience. We are sent back to the self through touching the voice of an other" (194-195). Washida borrows Maurice Merleau-Ponty's phrase, "acoustical existence," and calls this the "self as acoustical existence" (194). This clearly shows that we have a distance between self and other if we regard the other as "an individual existence" (193). In comparison with this, Washida continues to explain "a universal other" (193) in our attitude to writing/reading. In the case of psychiatrist Mari Nagai, her patient could not recognize the conversation with the other as talking/listening. She talks with others in writing/reading. Namely, her attitude toward others concerns written work. She sees them as universal others. According to Washida, she does not touch the voice of the other and therefore is not sent back to the self (193).

Listening has a double structure. Especially in the case of a talker speaking about a dream of the deceased, the talker speaks with something like images of the deceased. What is the image of the deceased? Is it a memory? We listen to the voice of the talker, furthermore to their appearance. Therefore we touch the voice of the deceased through the talker. However this voice is without words. As I mentioned above, one example is the case of Sakichi and Aki. This conversation has a distance between them, in which we can definitely recognize the other or the deceased. We break new ground in this type of listening.

Conclusion: a cultural bridge between philosophy and *shinsaigaku*

The purpose of this study was to examine the relation with the other and the dead through the structure of listening in *shinsaigaku* and philosophy. First in shinsaigaku, we took notice of *reisei no shinsaigaku*, especially Kanebishi's research on the talk of survivors' dreams. According to Kanebishi, the deceased invades the present of survivors and continues to relate to them. In the dream they have a sort of power to turn the past into the present progressive form. We can say that in the case of this research listening is to listen to the appearance of the deceased from the survivor's talk. Next regarding philosophy, we saw the texture of voice in Washida, a proponent of clinical philosophy. Through the texture of voice, we have seen that we make a conversation by listening to an appearance. In both ideas, listening to the voice of the deceased is involved in crying that we never forget the deceased. However, the crier hears only from the survivor (talker) who dreamed about the deceased. We cry that we never forget the deceased through the survivor's dream as well. This brings us back to the purpose of *He Came to My Dream*. Listening to the dream of the survivor through reading makes the experience of the survivor invade the reader's present, to share his experience. Namely the reader becomes a new listener. We cry that we never forget the deceased through the survivor's dream as well.

In conclusion, how can we build a cultural bridge between philosophy and *shinsaigaku*? About this question I would like to say that philosophy has to realize the necessity of considering the texture of voice. Listening in clinical philosophy involves a conversation which does not consist of the meaning of the content spoken, but of the texture of voice. If philosophy applies the same question to *shinsaigaku*, we need to listen to the texture of voice of the immediate problems with which *shinsaigaku* works. Then philosophy can try to face the sense of touching the voice. Philosophy cannot translate *shinsaigaku* for us. When we translate something, we respect each other and keep a distance but gather in the same place. *Shinsaigaku* and clinical philosophy aim to be this kind of study without a border in between.

Bibliography

Honma, Naoki. Nakaoka, Narifumi. Washida, Kiyokazu. 2010. *Document: rinshō tetsugaku* (『ドキュメント 臨床哲学』Document: Clinical Philosophy). Osaka daigaku shuppankai (大阪大学出版会).

Hosomi, Kazuyuki. 1999. *Identity / Tasha sei* (『アイデンティティ/ 他者性』Identity and Otherness). Iwanami shoten (岩波書店).

Kanebishi, Kiyoshi. 2012. *Dōkoku no kiroku: 71 nin no taikan shita ōtsunami / genpatsu / kyodai jishin* (『3.11 慟哭の記録 71人が体感した大津波・原発・巨大地震』3·11 Document of Wailing: The Great Tsunami / Great Earthquake / Nuclear Power Plant Disaster Experience of 71 People). Shinyōsha (新曜社).

Kanebishi, Kiyoshi. 2014. *Shinsai memento mori: daini no tsunami ni kōshite* (『震災メメントモリ

第二の津波に抗して』Memento Mori of the Earthquake: In the Face of the Second Tsunami). Shinyōsha (新曜社).

Kanebishi, Kiyoshi. 2016. *Shinsai-gaku nyumon: shiseikan kara no shakai kōsō* (『震災学入門——死生観からの社会構造』An Introduction to Disaster-Study: the structure of society from viewpoint of life and death). Chikuma shobō (筑摩書房).

Kawai, Hayao. Washida, Kiyokazu. 2010. *Rinshō to kotoba* (『臨床とことば』The Clinical and Words). Asahi shimbun shuppan (朝日新聞出版).

Koda, Aya. 1992. *Daidokoro no oto* (『台所のおと』The Sound in the Kitchen). Kōdansha (講談社).

Oka, Mari. 2000. *Kioku / Monogatari* (『記憶 / 物語』Memory and Narrative). Iwanami shoten (岩波書店).

Okubori, Akiko. 2019. "On the Question of the Dead or "Ghosts": A Meditation for Disaster Victims", *Journal of Innovative Ethics*, Special Issue, Project Innovative Ethics.

Okuno, Shuji. 2017. *Tamashii demo iikara soba ni ite: 3.11 go no reitaiken wo kiku*, (『魂でもいいから、そばにいて 3.11後の霊体験を聞く』Even if [you are] a spirit, stay by my side: listening the spiritual experience after 3.11). Shinchōsha (新潮社).

The Project for Recording the Earthquake at Tohoku Gakuin University. ed. Kiyoshi Kanebishi. 2016. *Yobisamasareru reisei no shinsai-gaku: 3.11 sei to shi no hazamade* (『呼び覚まされる霊性の震災学 3.11 生と死のはざまで』Shinsai-gaku of Spirituality, Resonant: Between Life and Death). Shinyōsha (新曜社).

The Project for Recording the Earthquake at Tohoku Gakuin University. ed. Kiyoshi Kanebishi. 2018. *Watashi no yume made ai ni kite kureta: 3.11 naki hito tono sorekara* (『私の夢まで、会いに来てくれた 3.11 亡き人とのそれから』He Came to My Dream: 3.11 The Future With the Dead). Asahi shimbun shuppan (朝日新聞出版).

Tohoku Gakuin University. 2017. *Shinsai-gaku* (『震災学』Disaster-studies), vol.10 Araemishi (荒蝦夷).

Washida, Kiyokazu. 1999. *Kiku koto no chikara: rinshōtetsugaku shiron* (『「聴く」ことの力 臨床哲学試論』 The Power of Listening: Toward Clinical Philosophy). TBS buritanika (TBS ブリタニカ).

World Literature Today? Reconsidering Goethe's Idea and its Critical Potential[1]

Yuho Hisayama

In June 1993, a colloquium entitled "Weltliteratur heute" was held in Saarbrücken, Germany, which resulted in a book of the same title. In the very beginning of its introduction the editor Manfred Schmeling writes as follows (Schmeling 1995, IX):

> For almost two centuries, the concept [of World Literature; Y.H.] has circulated with undiminishing success. [...] An explanation for this lasting fortune could be its future-oriented character – World Literature as a constantly new task –, another less productive reason would be the extensibility and inaccuracy of the concept.[2]

> Seit fast zwei Jahrhunderten zirkuliert der Begriff [der Weltliteratur; Y.H.] mit nicht nachlassendem Erfolg. [...] Eine Erklärung für diese dauerhafte Fortune könnte die Zukunftsorientiertheit sein – Weltliteratur als immer wieder neue Aufgabe –, eine andere, weniger produktive, die inhaltliche Dehnbarkeit und Ungenauigkeit des Begriffs.

Such an "undiminishing success" of the conception of World Literature can be observed today more clearly than ever. In the age of digitalized globalization, this originally German terminology is experiencing a huge international boom, even though its definition still remains quite problematic, for – particularly

[1] This essay is based on a talk I gave at Darmstädter Goethe-Gesellschaft (Darmstadt Goethe-society) on 11. December 2019 in German. It was, although I did not know this until the day before, the very last talk event in the long history of the society, as it closes in 2020, which has made me think of the role Goethe plays in the actual worldwide context again and again. Here I would like to thank Prof. em. Gernot Böhme for inviting me to the honorable occasion. This study has been supported by JSPS KAKENHI Grant Numbers 17K02255 and 19K12967.

[2] English translation from German by Yuho Hisayama (same below unless noted otherwise).

from postmodern, postcolonial and transartistic perspectives – the answer to the question of what World Literature actually is inarguably becomes more and more elusive (cf. Damrosch 2003; Sturm-Trigonakis 2007; Stam 2019).

In any case, we can still take the concept of World Literature as an extensible new task, as Schmeling wrote; and this is exactly how it is often interpreted in the context of a more and more globalizing world (cf. Lamping 2010; Gossens 2017). The following essay will try to draw some inspiration from one origin of the concept, i.e. from what Johann Wolfgang von Goethe (1749-1832) wrote and said about the term. Although some other authors such as August Ludwig von Schlözer (1735-1809) and Christoph Martin Wieland (1733-1813) had already used the term "Weltliteratur" before Goethe (Weitz 1987; Schamoni 2008), it was the German poet who transformed the term into an inexact and ambiguous, yet also extendable and meaningful idea, which may still contain a vital critical potential for our age.

His well-known statement of 31. January 1827, as conveyed to us by Johann Peter Eckermann, says (cf. Adler 2017): "National literature has not much to say now; the epoch of World Literature has come and everyone must now work to accelerate this epoch (National-Literatur will jetzt nicht viel sagen; die Epoche der Welt-Literatur ist an der Zeit und jeder muß jetzt dazu wirken, diese Epoche zu beschleunigen)" (FA 39, 225).[3] His idea of World Literature does not refer to any static canonized collection of the masterpieces, but rather a dynamic process of "more or less free spiritual trade (mehr oder weniger freye[r] geistige[r] Handelsverkehr)" (FA 22, 870) through literature. In other words, we could say that Goethe perceived the noun of World Literature rather as a verb.

What would be then the fruit of such a spiritual trade of World Literature? According to Eckermann, Goethe also stated in the same conversation that poetry (Poesie) was "a common good of humanity (ein Gemeingut der Menschheit)" (FA 39, 224). This may sound as if there should be only one "Poesie" of World Literature, belonging to the universal "humanity". Quite similarly Goethe wrote in a short text for his own periodical *Arts and Ancients* (*Kunst und Altertum*, vol. VI-

[3] All quotations from Goethe in this paper are from his Frankfurter Ausgabe (=FA), Goethe 1985-2013. In the main text cited as FA with volume and page numbers.

2): "Apparently the endeavor of the best poets and aesthetic writers of all nations has been directed for quite a long time at the universal human. (Offenbar ist das Bestreben der besten Dichter und ästhetischen Schriftsteller aller Nationen schon seit geraumer Zeit auf das allgemein Menschliche gerichtet.)" (FA 22, 433)[4]

All of this should never be understood to mean that Goethe had ignored cultural specificity. On the contrary, his idea of World Literature clearly premises the coexistence of many various cultures and languages. It is only with such cultural and linguistic variety that the universal human is able to – more or less indirectly – manifest itself, as the foregoing quotation from *Arts and Ancients* (*Kunst und Altertum*) continues: "In every particular [cultural/linguistic phenomenon], whether it be historical, mythological or fabulous, or more or less arbitrarily devised, you can see more and more, through nationality and personality, that universality shines out. (In jedem Besonderen, es sey nun historisch, mythologisch, fabelhaft, mehr oder weniger willkürlich ersonnen, wird man durch Nationalität und Persönlichkeit hin jenes Allgemeine immer mehr durchleuchten und durchscheinen sehen.)" (FA 22, 433) Following this idea, German philologist Erich Auerbach stated at the beginning of his widely read essay *Philology of World Literature* (*Philologie der Weltliteratur*)[5]: "Our earth, which is the world of world literature, is becoming ever smaller and losing its manifoldness. World literature, however, does not simply refer to the common and the human in general, but rather to the reciprocal fertilization of the manifold. (Unsere Erde, die die Welt der Weltliteratur ist, wird kleiner und verliert an Mannigfaltigkeit. Weltliteratur aber bezieht sich nicht einfach auf das Gemeinsame und Menschliche überhaupt, sondern auf dieses als wechselseitige Befruchtung des Mannigfaltigen.)" (Auerbach 1992, 83)

The general can only be perceived through the particular, and in this sense the idea of World Literature corresponds closely with Goethe's concept of the symbol,

[4] In another context, in which the "newest Serbian literature" was discussed, he also spoke about the existence of "the general World Poetry (die allgemeine Weltpoesie)" (FA 22, 386).

[5] This essay was translated into English by Maire and Edward Said in *The Centennial Review* XIII, No. 1 (1969), pp. 1-17 with the title "Philology and *Weltliteratur*". According to Gossens (Gossens 2017, 40), intensive work with this text of Auerbach may have supplied the basic idea for Edward Said's epoch-making book *Orientalism* (1978). Here English translation by Yuho Hisayama.

in which "something special represents something general, not as a dream or a shadow, but as a living momentary revelation of the unknowable (das Besondere das Allgemeinere repräsentiert, nicht als Traum und Schatten, sondern als lebendig augenblickliche Offenbarung des Unerforschlichen)" (FA 13, 33). As regards the method to find such a symbol, Goethe mentioned so-called "repeated mirroring (wiederholte Spiegelungen)", an image that comes originally from his scientific research on entoptic colors. When colorless reflected light shines into the glass placed between two black-painted mirrors, it creates a vivid color phenomenon in that glass through the "repeated mirroring" of the mirrors facing each other (cf. FA 25, 693-694). This appears but in Goethe's text being used in a wider context, in an essay on his memory of his own young days with Friederike Brion, itself titled *Repeated Mirroring* (*Wiederholte Spiegelungen*, 1823) by Eckermann (cf. FA 17, 710). In the same way as the "repeated mirroring" in an entoptic phenomenon, the past memories are enhanced by mirroring each other, and the hidden colors will be revealed in the middle of the repeated mirroring in-between. In this context Goethe says that one can see through such a repeated mirroring "the past not merely being kept alive, but actually elevated to a higher life (das Vergangene nicht allein lebendig erhalten, sondern sogar zu einem höheren Leben empor steigern)" (FA 17, 371), so that one is able to "gain a symbol of what has repeatedly repeated in the history of the arts and sciences, of the church, and probably of the political world, and is still repeating daily. (ein Symbol gewinnen dessen was in der Geschichte der Künste und Wißenschaften, der Kirche, auch wohl der politischen Welt sich mehrmals wiederholt hat und noch täglich wiederholt.)" (FA 17, 371) Here symbols are regarded as a result of the "elevating" of past images mirroring each other (cf. FA 37, 548), and according to this method, one could also understand the image of World Literature as manifold literary activities being "elevated to a higher life" through their "repeated mirroring" (cf. FA 22, 428).

Goethe's earliest use of the term "Weltliteratur" in January 1827 can be closely connected with such an image of "repeated mirroring" (cf. Matsumura 2009, 246-251). His first public mention of "Weltliteratur" appears in his short text *Le Tasse, drame historique en cinq actes, par M. Alexander Duval* ("Tasso, historical drama in five acts by M. Alexander Duval"; FA 22, 353-357),[6] which was prompted by two French reviews of Pineux-Duval's drama based on Goethe's earlier work

Torquato Tasso (first published in 1790): the German poet saw, so to speak, the repeated mirroring of his old work in the French adaptation as the "reception of the reception" (Bohnenkamp 2000). The dynamic exchange in-between emerges here the new vivid colorful phenomena of free spiritual trade. The old Goethe then became more and more interested in such transnational communication through literature. He wrote many critiques of literary works, ranging from ancient Greek to contemporary European works, and published these texts in *Arts and Ancients* (*Kunst und Altertum*), from which I have already quoted some passages above, the magazine, which was published by Goethe himself and played a very important role as the medium through which he expounded upon his idea of World Literature (cf. Birus 1995 and Birus 2017). The poet also had a strong interest in especially French and English literary journals and magazines such as *Le Globe* (1824-1832) for their potential to act as mediums of literary communication throughout Europe.

At the same time Goethe emphasized the importance of translation again and again in the context of such cross-cultural communication, and he himself was an active translator throughout almost his entire life, producing translations of such pieces as Voltaire's *Mahomet* and *Tancrède*, Benvenuto Cellini's autobiography, Denis Diderot's *Le Neveu de Rameau*, Lord Byron's *Manfred* and several Greek poems and dramas.[7]

When Goethe wrote or talked about World Literature, he sometimes seems to have been thinking of European literature. But not only had this tradition interested Goethe, as John Pizer states regarding this topic: "[G]iven the infrastructural and geopolitical realities of the age, world literature on a broad scale was largely restricted to Europe. Goethe's fascination with Asian literature [...] attests to his trans-European cosmopolitanism" (Pizer 2011, 5). Not to be forgotten in this context are especially his works such as the *West-Eastern Diwan* (*West-östlicher Divan*, first version 1819, expanded version 1827) and *Sino-German annual and daily calendar* (*Chinesisch-deutsche Jahres- und Tageszeiten*,

---

[6] The first private usage of this term by Goethe can be found in his diary on 15. January 1827, which itself again might have something to do with the text *Le Tasse*.

[7] Goethe's most important theoretical text on literal and cultural translation can be found in his own commentary for *West-Eastern Diwan* (FA 3-1, 280-283).

1829). Below I will shortly pick up the former, from which a specific example of Goethe's attitude towards dealing with different cultures can be inferred.

Goethe, in his mid-sixties, nurtured an interest in the 14th century Persian poet Hafiz (Hafez), whose poetry he had encountered some years previously, and was inspired by this spiritual "twin" across time and space. This experience then came to be combined with his subtle feeling of affection for a young talented girl in Frankfurt am Main, Marianne (1784-1860, from 1814 the wife of Johann Jakob Willemer), resulting in the famous poems that were crafted in the form of co-authorship through correspondence between the two. Not only did they create original poetry, but they also let the Persian poet speak about their own feelings by entrusting their corresponding letters with the numbers of Hafiz' poems as ciphers. Within the pair's communication, modern Germany was layered upon medieval Persia, and parallel to that Goethe himself was layered upon Hatem, the hero in Hafiz' poetry, and Marianne upon Suleika, the heroine. The two worlds mirrored one another, suggesting their fundamental identity, and at the same time, an analogue of this mirrored relationship was to be found between the two admirers. Goethe's well-known short poem "Gingo Biloba" in *Diwan* shows us the kind of image he created from the specific form this tree leaf takes (FA 3-1, 78-79):

> The leaf of this tree, entrusted from the east / to my garden / gives a secret meaning to taste / which can please those who know.
>
> Is this *one* living being / which separates into two by itself? / Or are they two, which are chosen / so that they are recognized as one?
>
> In order to answer such questions / I found the right sense. / Don't you feel from my songs / that I am *one* and at the same time double?

> Dieses Baum's Blatt, der von Osten / Meinem Garten anvertraut, / Giebt geheimen Sinn zu kosten, / Wie's den Wissenden erbaut.
>
> Ist es Ein lebendig Wesen? / Das sich in sich selbst getrennt, / Sind es zwey? die sich erlesen, / Daß man sie als eines kennt.
>
> Solche Frage zu erwiedern / Fand ich wohl den rechten Sinn; / Fühlst du nicht an meinen Liedern / Daß ich Eins und doppelt bin?

This poetical "one and double" image contains a hint that might help us reach a philosophical understanding of World Literature, and arrive at a new method of grasping the "otherness". Here I will just shortly suggest that one possible way to achieve this could be found via the neo-phenomenological concept of situation by Hermann Schmitz (see Schmitz 1977, 411-444; Schmitz 1994, 67-84; Schmitz 2005, 22). According to Schmitz, a *situation* is "an absolutely or relatively chaotic-manifold wholeness, to which at least facts belong". In such a "chaotic-manifold", the identity and diversity of the elements contained therein cannot be determined. As a result, a situation cannot be equated with Schmitz' conception of the *constellation*, in which the individual elements are clearly separated from each other and then assembled. It would be interesting to apply Schmitz' concept of the situation to Goethe's idea of World Literature, for it can be understood as being "situational" in the sense of Schmitz. Above all, the chaotic-manifold nature of the situation is especially relevant, for the contents of World Literature cannot be clearly separated from each other: They rather reciprocally mirror each other amid the chaotic-manifold communication that takes place between many very different entities. With such a terminology, World Literature is to be found not in a constellational network of information, but in a situational chaotic-manifold of "mutual fertilization" through literature, as expressed by Auerbach. In other words, this kind of relationship should not be envisaged as a network of individual cultural and linguistic units. "Gingo Biloba" showed us an image of being "one and at the same time double": this contradictory mode of being could be considered anew in the contemporary context of transcultural communication.

Concerning what I have introduced so far, Goethe's idea of World Literature might sound too naïve and utopian. On the other hand, however, he considered the realization of this ideal a very difficult task. Quite realistically – or almost pessimistically – he said again and again that mutual intercultural understanding can only rarely succeed, writing for example in May 1828 in relation to the literary journals being published in Edinburgh, which he regarded as having the potential to carry him and his contemporaries "most effectively to a hoped general World Literature (zu einer gehofften allgemeinen Weltliteratur auf das wirksamste)" (FA 22, 491):

> Let us but repeat that the idea that nations should all think the same is out of the question; rather they should only become aware of each other, understand each other, and if they do not love each other, at least learn to tolerate each other.

> [N]ur wiederholen wir, daß nicht die Rede seyn könne, die Nationen sollen übereindenken, sondern sie sollen nur einander gewahr werden, sich begreifen, und wenn sie sich wechselseitig nicht lieben mögen, sich einander wenigstens dulden lernen.

Similarly, Goethe had already stated in the above quoted text *Le Tasse*, the text in which he officially used the term "Weltliteratur" for the first time: "Why should nations be united with each other, even when their fellow-citizens do not understand how to agree with one another. (warum sollten die Nationen unter sich einig seyn, wenn die Mitbürger nicht mit einander übereinzukommen verstehen.)" (FA 22, 357)

Notably it was just in this context that Goethe pays special attention to the necessary length of time: "But this can only be effected *through time* (Dieses kann aber nur *durch die Zeit* bewirkt werden)" (FA 22, 357, italic by Y.H.).[8] The "repeated mirroring" requires a lasting process in order to mature, even to approach national literature, let alone World Literature. Now this tendency seems to be getting more and more critical than ever in the present more and more accelerating globalizing world. This actual problem as the fate of modernity[9] had already been often discussed in connection with Goethe himself. According to Manfred Osten, Goethe's contemporary relevance is to be found in his aversion to the process of acceleration already underway at the time he lived in - that is, in his "discovery of slowness (Entdeckung der Langsamkeit)" (Osten 2003). In order to avoid this modern tendency which surrounded him, the old Goethe

[8] For Goethe's specific image of time see for example Matussek 1998.

[9] German sociologist Hartmut Rosa says that we should strive to free ourselves from the alienation produced by the acceleration of society which is the inevitable consequence of late-modern capitalism by aiming to rediscover everyday experiences that are "resonant" with the world (Rosa 2005; Rosa 2016).

repeatedly expressed what he saw as the need for a slowed and closed form of communication – also in the context in which he spoke about World Literature (cf. Matsumura 2009, 251-254).

His deep doubts about the coming epoch cannot be overlooked when he writes: "The vast world [...] will [...] give us no more than what the native base also gave; what appeals to the crowd will spread without borders [...]. The serious ones must therefore form a quiet, almost depressed church, as it would be in vain to oppose the broad flood of the day; however, one must try to maintain one's position until the current has passed (Die weite Welt [...] wird [...] uns nicht mehr geben als was der einheimische Boden auch verlieh; was der Menge zusagt, wird sich gränzenlos ausbreiten [...]. Die Ernsten müssen deshalb eine stille, fast gedrückte Kirche bilden, da es vergebens wäre der breiten Tagesfluth sich entgegen zu setzen; standhaft aber muß man seine Stellung zu behaupten suchen bis die Strömung vorüber gegangen ist)" (FA 22, 866-7; cf. FA 38, 550-551). What Goethe says here would remind us of our globalized and accelerated age directly: In "the broad flood" of the globalized market, "what appeals to the crowd spreads without borders", so that we might have to "maintain [our] position until the current has passed" forming "a quiet, almost depressed church". From his individualistic and pessimistic feelings about his contemporary world, Goethe then had to speak of a "purest and strictest egoism" in the future (FA 22, 867):

> The question of whether this or that occupation which man dedicates to himself would be useful repeats itself far too often in the course of time and now surfaces again, where no one is allowed to live quietly, contentedly, moderately and without request, as one would like to be. [...] Here, there is nothing left but to say to oneself: only the purest and strictest egoism could save us; but this must be a self-conscious, well-sensed and calm decision.
>
> Die Frage ob diese oder jene Beschäftigung welche[r] sich der Mensch widmet auch nützlich sey? wiederholt sich oft genug im Laufe der Zeit und muß jetzt besonders wieder hervortreten, wo es niemanden mehr erlaubt ist nach Belieben ruhig, zufrieden, mäßig und ohne Anforderung zu leben. [...] Hier bleibt nun nichts übrig als sich selbst zu sagen: nur der reinste und

strengste Egoismus könne uns retten; dieser aber muß ein selbstbewußter, wohlgefühlter und ruhig ausgesprochener Entschluß seyn.

The process of globalization and acceleration has developed much more intensively since the death of Goethe, and not only in the economic world, but also - with the economy closely connected – in the fields of culture and academia. The cross-cultural communication through literature, which Goethe might have once aimed towards, seems to have become at least partly real in a digitally globalized world, but not as he had hoped, rather in the form of the worldwide networking process of acceleration. The old Goethe in the 1820s and 1830s had already been too busy to get along with every new wave in Germany, Scotland, France and Italy, so much that he wrote in a letter dated 21. May 1828 to his good friend Carl Friedrich Zelter (1758-1832), quoting a well-known figure from his own poem, "the World Literature I called for is about to rush to me as if to the Sorcerer's Apprentice and I am now drowning. (daß die von mir angerufenen Weltliteratur auf mich, wie auf den Zauberlehrling, zum Ersäufen zuströmt.)" (FA 37, 611) The addressee of this letter was living in Berlin, but Goethe himself had been staying in a much smaller town, Weimar, until the end of his life. In order to save himself from drowning, he apparently felt he needed a quiet shelter.

Should we say then that the old German poet chose to close his door to the contemporary world? In a certain sense, yes. But from another perspective, we could understand Goethe's swaying ambivalent positioning between openness and closeness itself as the polarity which is necessary for the dynamism of an ever-lasting process of World Literature. In his worldview, a polarity of centrifugal and centripetal directions, something he had learnt from hermetical or alchemical books in his young age (cf. Zimmermann 1969 and 1979), plays a central role, as he used the schema of polarity to try to understand every natural phenomenon (see for example FA 25, 142-175). For him, the dynamism of life occurred as a moving process in between two points, so long as a polarity existed, and it would not be impossible to adapt this model to the idea of World Literature as a dynamic process, in which every culture mirrors each other repeatedly to be "elevated to a higher life", maturing over a long time. In this sense, the idea of World Literature is an on-going metamorphosis between both poles, between the general and the specific, between openness and closure. Once in his diary on 17. May 1808, Goethe noted that metamorphosis is "systole and diastole of the World Spirit (Systole und Diastole des Weltgeistes)", and "from the former the specification emerges, from the latter the progression into infinity (aus jener geht die Spezifikation hervor, aus dieser das Fortgehn in's Unendlich)" (FA 33, 306). Important in the worldview of Goethe was a balance between the tendencies of both specification and generalization, through which he perceived a living, unceasing movement appearing.

As Schmeling states, World Literature in the sense of Goethe should be regarded as a constantly new, endless task. His idea allows us to see cross-cultural communication not as a process of networking but of "repeated mirroring", and "this can only be effected through time", so that one might sometimes need a shelter to avoid the process of unbound acceleration. All of these aspects of World Literature suggest a very opposite image to that offered by the present networking and accelerating world. In this way, with its critical potential, Goethe's ambiguous and elastic idea of Weltliteratur shows us an alternative model to struggle with the world in which we now find ourselves.

Bibliography

Adler, Jeremy. 2017. »die Epoche der Welt-Literatur ist an der Zeit«. Goethe und die Erfindung der modernen Dichtung. In: *Goethe-Jahrbuch* 134: 27-38.

Auerbach, Erich. 1992 [at first 1967]. *Philologie der Weltliteratur. Sechs Versuche über Stil und Wirklichkeitswahrnehmung*. Frankfurt a.M.: Fischer.

Birus, Hendrik. 1995. Goethes Idee der Weltliteratur. Eine historische Vergegenwärtigung. In *Weltliteratur heute. Konzepte und Perspektiven*, ed. by Manfred Schmeling, 5-28. Würzburg: Königshausen & Neumann.

Birus, Hendrik. 2017. Goethes Zeitschrift »Ueber Kunst und Altertum« als Kontext seiner Idee der Weltliteratur. In: *Goethe-Jahrbuch* 134: 90-98.

Bohnenkamp, Anne. 2000. Rezeption der Rezeption. Goethes Entwurf einer Weltliteratur im Kontext seiner Zeit¬schrift ‚Über Kunst und Alterthum'. In *Spuren, Signaturen, Spiegelungen. Zur Goethe-Rezeption in Europa*, ed by Anke Bosse and Bernhard Beutler, 187-205. Köln: Böhlau.

Damrosch, David. 2003. *What is world literature?* Princeton: Princeton UP.

Goethe, Johann Wolfgang von. 1985-2013. *Sämtliche Werke. Briefe, Tagebücher und Gespräche*, ed. by Friedmar Apel, Hendrik Birus, Anne Bohnenkamp, Dieter Borchmeyer et. al. 40 Vol. Frankfurt a.M.: Deutscher Klassiker Verlag (cited as FA with volume and page

numbers).
Gossens, Peter. 2017. »Neue Weltliteratur«? Goethes Weltliteratur-Begriff im Kontext der Globalisierung. In: *Goethe-Jahrbuch* 134: 39-46.
Lamping, Dieter. 2010. *Die Idee der Weltliteratur. Ein Konzept Goethes und seine Karriere*. Stuttgart: Kröner.
Matsumura, Tomohiko. 2009. *Ekkyô to Naisei. Kindai Doitsu-Bungaku no Ibunka-zô*. Suwa and Tokyo: Chôeisha.
Matussek, Peter (ed.). 1998. *Goethe und die Verzeitlichung der Natur*. München: Beck.
Osten, Manfred. 2003. *'Alles veloziferisch' oder Goethes Entdeckung der Langsamkeit*. Frankfurt am Main: Wallstein.
Pizer, John. 2011. Johann Wolfgang von Goethe. Origins and relevance of *Weltliteratur*. In *The Routledge Companion to World Literature*, ed. By Theo D'haen, David Damrosch and Djelal Kadir, 3-11. London and New York: Routledge.
Rosa, Hartmut. 2005. *Beschleunigung. Die Veränderung der Zeitstrukturen in der Moderne*. Frankfurt am Main: Suhrkamp.
Rosa, Hartmut. 2016. *Resonanz. Eine Soziologie der Weltbeziehung*. Frankfurt am Main: Suhrkamp.
Schamoni, Wolfgang. 2008. ‚Weltliteratur' - zuerst 1773 bei August Ludwig Schlözer. In *Arcadia. Internationale Zeitschrift für Literaturwissenschaft* 43: 288-298.
Schmeling, Manfred (ed.). 1995. *Weltliteratur heute. Konzepte und Perspektiven*. Würzburg: Königshausen & Neumann.
Schmitz, Hermann. 1977. *System der Philosophie*, Vol. III-4: *Das Göttliche und der Raum*. Bonn: Bouvier 1977
Schmitz, Hermann. 1994. *Neue Grundlagen der Erkenntnistheorie*. Bonn: Bouvier.
Schmitz, Hermann. 2005. *Situationen und Konstellationen. Wider die Ideologie totaler Vernetzung*. Freiburg und München: Karl Alber.
Stam, Robert. 2019. *World Literature, Transnational Cinema, and Global Media. Towards a Transartistic Commons*. London and New York: Routledge.
Sturm-Trigonakis, Elke. 2007. *Global playing in der Literatur. Ein Versuch über die Neue Weltliteratur*. Würzburg: Königshausen & Neumann.
Weitz, Hans-J. 1987. ‚Weltliteratur' zuerst bei Wieland. In *Arcadia. Internationale Zeitschrift für Literaturwissenschaft* 22: 206-208.
Zimmermann, Rolf Christian. 1969 and 1979. *Das Weltbild des jungen Goethe. Studien zur hermetischen Tradition des deutschen 18. Jahrhunderts*. 2 vols. München: Fink.

Medium, Message and Misinterpretation in "The Signal-Man"

Mizuki Tsutsui

Introduction

Throughout his life, the Victorian novelist Charles Dickens consistently showed an eager curiosity in contemporary science and technology, and such an abiding interest is often directly or indirectly reflected in his full-length novels, Christmas novellas, magazine articles, and even ghost stories. This essay will particularly focus on "The Signal-Man", "the best short story that Dickens ever wrote" (Slater 2009, 554), from the view point of the Victorian information systems—railway signalling, the electric telegraph, as well as spiritualism, a more controversial form of communication, aiming to examine what they can reveal about the issues involved in the mediation and communication between self and other.[1]

The story was first published as a part of *Mugby Junction*, a set of short stories written collaboratively and published as the 1866 Christmas edition of *All the Year Round*, a weekly literary magazine founded and owned by Dickens himself. He wrote half of the whole issue, including the frame narrative in which a retired gentleman, Jackson (known as "the Gentleman for Nowhere") decides to explore the rail lines that connect with a fictional railway station, Mugby Junction. In the subsequent story, "No. 1 Branch Line: The Signal-man", a part of Jackson's "CAREFUL STUDY OF JUNCTION" (Dickens, 1954b, 515), the narrator

[1] There are several studies on "The Signal-Man" that take a similar approach but with different aims. Norris Pope focuses on the story as a starting point for his discussion of "public understandings of the varieties of operational intelligence necessary for railway safety" (Pope 2001, 461). Takashi Harada analyses the text employing media theory, and concludes that ghosts in the nineteenth century were "a piece to fill an unexplainable space in a complex of lines of information" (Harada 2016, 39). The chief purpose of this paper, on the other hand, is to elucidate the fundamental source of the fear evoked by the story by focusing on its sociohistorical context.

encounters a railway signalman haunted by a mysterious apparition which always foreshadows impending disaster on the line, and whose late repeated appearances finally turn out to be a warning about the signalman's own death.

1. Spiritualism

"The Signal-Man" is one of Dickens's rare attempts to create a genuinely uncanny, macabre story. Like other Victorian novelists, Dickens had written many ghost stories before, but for him they were only of value so long as they illustrated a "particular state of mind and processes of the imagination" (Dickens 1988, 546). Indeed, though *All the Year Round* carried many ghost stories and apparently Dickens was responding to "the climate of supernaturalism" (Henson 2004, 59), he himself was no believer in ghosts, and always maintained a sceptical attitude towards mediums and séances. For instance, in 1863, three years prior to the publication of "The Signal-Man", Dickens wrote two articles against spiritualism. In "Rather a Strong Dose", he criticizes *The History of the Supernatural in All Ages and Nations, and in all Churches, Christian and Pagan, Demonstrating a Universal Faith* written by William Howitt (an advocate of spiritualism and an occasional contributor to *Household Words*, the predecessor of *All the Year Round*), and concludes that "it is high time to protest against Mr. Howitt's spiritualism" (Dickens 1863b, 87). The other article, "The Martyr Medium", is a review of *Incidents in My Life*, an autobiography by Daniel Dunglas Home, the most celebrated spiritual medium in the nineteenth century. Dickens extracts a dozen passages from it, apologizing to the reader for "sullying our paper with this nauseous matter" (Dickens 1863a, 134) and finally denounces it as an "odious book" (Dickens 1863a, 135). Other articles written by him on this subject include "The Ghost of the Cock Lane Ghost Wrong Again" (1853), "The Spirit Business" (1853), "Stores for the First of April" (1857) and "Well-Authenticated Rappings" (1858). Dickens consistently attacked spiritualism, often with a tongue-in-cheek comment: "It certainly is very extraordinary that, [. . .] any men can assail their rapping and tipping brothers and sisters, from any sort of pulpit, as void of common sense. The spirit business cannot fail to be regarded by all dispassionate persons as the last great triumph of common sense" (Dickens 1853, 220).

Dickens made fun of spiritualists (known as "Rappers") in his fictional work, too. In another collaborative work *The Haunted House* (1859), a gentleman whom the narrator encounters in a railway coach is absorbed in what he calls "spiritual intercourse" (Dickens 1956a, 227), and attentively tries to write down the received messages. However, the narrator, like Dickens, is quite incredulous of its authenticity, and inwardly dismisses him as "one of a sect for (some of) whom I have the highest respect, but whom I don't believe in" (Dickens 1956a, 226-27), while the gentleman with so much earnestness records the spirit's inexplicable misspelling:

> "'A bird in the hand,'" said the gentleman, reading his last entry with great solemnity, "'is worth two in the Bosh.'"
> "Truly I am of the same opinion," said I; "but shouldn't it be Bush?"
> "It came to me, Bosh," returned the gentleman. (Dickens 1956a, 227)

Here, the gentleman's misinterpretation of the spiritual message is reduced into a mere ridiculous joke. In "Well-Authenticated Rappings", Dickens again mockingly mentions the "bad spelling" of "immaterial Beings" (Dickens 1858, 217). Likewise, Henry Morley, one of the regular contributors to Dickens's publications, also refers to the "mistakes in spelling" in his report of séance with the American medium Mrs. Hayden (Morley 1852, 221). It appears that for those who did not believe in ghosts, such incompleteness of messages, or, in other words, lack of intelligibility of communication could be regarded as evidence against spiritual intercourse. However, in "The Signal-Man", the very theme of the failure of conveying and interpreting messages becomes a very serious concern, and even a source of inexplicable horror. Indeed, as we will see, the function of the title character is analogous to that of a spiritual medium, since he alone can hear and see the ghost, and is obsessed with the idea that the ghost is trying to send warning to someone or somewhere in the railway *through* him. In order to understand the uncommon seriousness with which Dickens dealt with this theme, we must take into account another important aspect of the story's cultural background, the electric telegraph.

2. The Electric Telegraph

In “The Signal-Man”, the ghost’s mysterious messages are often associated with the electric telegraph. At his second meeting with the signalman, the narrator attempts to give a rational explanation for the apparition, by attributing its voice to the vibration of the telegraph wires: “As to an imaginary cry [. . .], do but listen for a moment to the wind in this unnatural valley while we speak so low, and to the wild harp it makes of the telegraph wires” (Dickens 1954b, 530). Far from being persuaded by this reasoning, the signalman firmly insists that the apparition rings the electric bell in his box, while the narrator cannot hear it. According to the signalman, the little bell is not “rung in the natural course of physical things by the station”, but in a distinctively different way: “I have never made a mistake as to that yet, Sir. I have never confused the spectre’s ring with the man’s. The ghost’s ring is a strange vibration in the bell that it derives from nothing else, and I have not asserted that the bell stirs to the eye. I don’t wonder that you failed to hear it. But I heard it” (Dickens 1954b, 532).

Such an association between spiritualism and the electric telegraph, however, is not a new notion. In fact, many scholars note that there exists a close affinity between the two phenomena. In contemporaneous magazine articles, spiritual intercourse was often described with a telegraph metaphor, and at the same time, electrical communication was explained through the imagery of ghosts and spirits. For example, Dickens himself depicts a spiritual medium using a metaphor of telegraph in the above-cited essay “Well-Authenticated Rappings”, whereby a self-proclaimed medium conducts himself “like a telegraph before the invention of the electric one” (Dickens 1858, 219). On the other hand, in an essay named “Wings of Wire” published in *Household Words* in 1850, the author Frederick Knight Hunt uses the concept of “the spirit” in elucidating “electricity, or electro-magnetism” (Hunt 1850, 241). Jeffrey Sconce points out that “[t]he historical proximity and intertwined legacies of these two founding ‘mediums,’ one material and the other spiritual, is hardly a coincidence. Certainly, the explicit connections between the two communication technologies were not lost on the Spiritualists themselves, who eagerly linked Spiritualist phenomena with the similarly fantastic discourses of electromagnetic telegraphy” (Sconce 2000, 24). Certainly they were both newly-developed—and therefore somewhat enigmatic—methods of communication, and each process similarly consisted of sending, receiving and deciphering information.

Exactly like the apparition in "The Signal-Man", the early use of the electric telegraph was initially used to convey news about "occasions of disaster and surprise" (Hunt 1850, 245). For example, during the prevalence of the cholera, the telegraph messages "related principally to sudden sickness and death" (Hunt 1850, 245). In another case, when a murderer named John Hutchings was to be executed in Maidstone in 1847, the telegraph functioned as "the messenger of death" on behalf of the authorities (Hunt 1850, 245).

In order to avoid confusion on these occasions, telegraph messages were to be clear, short and concise, as one small mistake in transmission or interpretation could cause serious consequences, as mentioned by Mr. Walker in Anthony Trollope's *The Last Chronicle of Barset* in 1867—"It is so easy, you know, to misunderstand a telegram, and the wrong copying of a word may make such a mistake!" (Trollope 1929, 111). In fact, while in spiritualism, a misreading of a spiritual message was merely a source of laughter and ridicule for non-believers, similar error in understanding a telegraph message could result in a terrible disaster. A famous episode introduced in *The London Anecdotes for All Readers: The Electric Telegraph* will illustrate this: in 1845, John Tawell, a suspected murderer, attempted to escape by train from Slough to Paddington, having wrapped himself in a Quaker garment. The superintendent of the Slough station immediately sent off a full description of Tawell to Paddington by electric telegraph. However, since there was no separate sign for "Q" in the two-needle instrument in use at the time, the superintendent had to use the letter "K" in order to spell the word "Quaker". This apparent misspelling of course had a high possibility of leading to confusion, and, consequently, Tawell might have escaped capture before the message was properly understood. Fortunately, the person working at Paddington station comprehended this at once, and the murderer was identified and successfully arrested. The article concludes that anyone who noticed the act of interpretation in this case would feel "the immense importance of this novel application of man's philosophy to the protection of his race" (Archer 1848, 108). Thus, unlike the mistake of "Bosh" for "Bush" by the spiritualist gentleman in *The Haunted House*, the misunderstanding of a single letter in an electric telegraph might trigger a serious outcome. It is easy to imagine, therefore, that those who handled electric telegraphs as professionals had to endure heavy responsibilities and accompanying an enormous mental pressure. A railway signalman was one of such profession, and their delinquencies, carelessnesses, or miscommunications in fact did cause some memorable accidents in British railway history.

3. The Signalling System and Railway Accidents

There are two notorious railway accidents that might have had a significant influence on Dickens.[2] In "The Signal-Man", the first disaster forewarned by the ghost is referred to by the signalman as "the memorable accident on this Line" (Dickens 1954b, 531). Presumably this is based upon the Clayton tunnel rail crash of 1861, in which 23 were killed and 176 were injured—the worst train accident on record at the time. The rail crash was caused by the misreading of a telegraph message by a signalman. The signalman Henry Killick, who was at the south entrance of the tunnel, after allowing the first train to enter into the tunnel, realized the malfunctioning of the alarm bell and tried to stop the second train by waving a red flag as it was passed. Being unsure whether the driver of the second train had perceived his warning, Killick sent a telegram to his counterpart at the north end of the tunnel, asking if the tunnel was clear. However, a fatal miscommunication arose here: while the signalman at the opposite end, having seen the *first* train getting out of the tunnel, replied that the train was "out", Killick interpreted that as meaning the *second* train had cleared the tunnel, and thought the tunnel was now empty. Therefore, when a third train approached to the southern entrance of the tunnel, Killick mistakenly allowed it to proceed, without being aware that the driver of the second train had actually seen his signal, and that the train had stopped in the tunnel and now was backing to the southern end. As a consequence of this, the second train and the third train collided in the tunnel with great force,

[2] The following description of the two railway accidents is chiefly based on "Dickens's 'The Signalman' and Information Problems in the Railway Age" by Norris Pope.

killing some instantaneously, while many others were mortally wounded.

There are a couple of underlying causes for the accident—the intervals between the trains were dangerously short, and Killick was at the time working at 24-hour shift, which far exceeded the regulated hours of work. These circumstances undoubtedly strained the nerves of the signalman to the limit. We can easily appreciate just how nerve-wracking it must have been, especially considering the fact that the electric telegraph, of which every signalman was expected to gain a perfect command, was itself none other than "the nervous system of the railway" (Smiles 1879, xv), as Samuel Smiles famously noted. "It is a painful reflection", *The Annual Register* of 1861 says, "that the terrible disaster that happened in a few moments was the result of the mistaken reasoning of the one man and the quick intelligence of the other" (*The Annual Register* 1862, 162). In fact, a large part of all railway accidents arose similarly from "the neglect of the signal-man, and not of the driver" (Head 1856, 180).

The other incident which possibly influenced "The Signal-Man" was the Staplehurst rail crash, also caused by "confusion and poor communication on the line" (Menke 2008, 166), though, strictly speaking, not by the fault of a signalman. The accident occurred at the Beult viaduct on the main line of the South Eastern Railway in 1865. The train derailed while crossing a viaduct which was under repair and whose track had been removed, with the result that ten passengers were killed and forty were injured. Dickens himself was on that train, with his secret mistress Ellen Ternan and her mother.[3] Fortunately his carriage did not fall into the river bed, but he never recovered from the shock he received from this accident. In a letter to John Forster, his friend and biographer, Dickens confesses his unconquerable fear of trains: "I cannot bear railway travelling yet. A perfect conviction, against the senses, that the carriage is down on one side [. . .], comes upon me with anything like speed, and is inexpressibly distressing" (Dickens 1999, 65). The causes of this disaster were twofold. Firstly, the foreman misread the timetable and did not realize that the train would cross the viaduct under repair at that time. The other cause was the position of the flagman. He was supposed to

[3] Shigeru Koike suggests that Dickens wrote "The Signal-Man" in order to "exorcise" his personal fear of trains. See Koike, 5-55.

be away 1000 yards away from the construction site, but he was actually standing only about 500 yards away from there. And due to this lack of enough distance, his warning was given too late, and the train did not have sufficient time to stop before crashing into the construction site.

These two accidents, namely the Clayton tunnel rail crash and the Staplehurst rail crash, as Norris Pope points out, "raised issues about information management and the limits of information systems in markedly revealing ways" (Pope 2001, 447). Both were caused by the miscommunication and misunderstanding of information—in the former case, the signalman's error in interpreting the telegraph message, and in the latter case, the foreman's misreading of the timetable and the incorrectly timed warning of the flagman. These two accidents thus exposed the problems concerning the transmission and interpretation of messages that forms the foundation of modern technology and science. And this appears to be the key to understanding "The Signal-Man"—as Pope observes, the story "touches upon issues of railway operation and railway safety that closely concerned Dickens's mid-Victorian readers, the first generation to experience high-speed railway travel and high-density railway traffic" (Pope 2001, 447). The terror represented in this story is created not simply by the ghost, but through the complex interaction between all these elements—spiritualism, the electric telegraph, and railway accidents, which all share the same concern, the act of correctly interpreting messages.

4. "The Signal-Man": A Story of Failed Communication

Regarding the singularity of this short story, David Seed notes that "[t]he ghosts themselves are strikingly 'modern' in presentation. [. . .] the figure is particularly mysterious because it is performing a realistic action without any real context" (Seed 1981, 54). The ghost's message is conveyed as a cipher or a code, like a telegraph message, and its receiver is required to decipher or decode the message in order to understand its true meaning. However, despite the repeated appearances of the ghost, the signalman cannot understand the meaning of the message, which for him has a fatal consequence: "What is the danger? Where is the danger? There is danger overhanging somewhere on the Line. Some dreadful calamity will happen. It is not to be doubted this third time, after what has gone before. But surely this is a cruel haunting of *me*. What can *I* do?" (Dickens 1954b, 533). Furthermore, there is a fundamental confusion about the roles in the communication. The signalman seems to think of himself as a medium of the spiritual message, rather than the final receiver of it, for he persists in believing that the ghost's warning is to be given to someone else, someone not himself. And this makes him worry about to whom the message should be given, and why he has been chosen as a medium: "If it came, on those two occasions, only to show me that its warnings were true, and so to prepare me for the third, why not warn me plainly now? And I, Lord help me! A mere poor signal-man on this solitary station! Why not go to somebody with credit to be believed, and power to act!" (Dickens 1954b, 534). Ironically, this question resolves when the final disaster happens—it is to the signalman himself that the warning was addressed. He is a medium and at the same time a receiver of the message, and his inability to recognize his own role is the crucial factor in the final catastrophe.

Then, it is notable that in "The Signal-Man", misunderstanding and miscommunication prevail throughout the whole story. In the very first scene of the story, the signalman mistakes the narrator for the ghost: "instead of looking up to where I stood on the top of the steep cutting nearly over his head, he turned himself about and looked down the Line" (Dickens 1954b, 524). Besides this, the signalman, while mistakenly interpreting the meaning of the ghost's message as we have seen, fully recognizes the fact that nobody would believe his spiritual revelation. Talking about the apparition itself is only a source of further confusion: "If I telegraph Danger, on either side of me, or on both, I can give no reason for it, [. . .] I should get into trouble, and do no good. They would think I was mad" (Dickens 1954b, 533). Until the fatal moment of the final accident, this chain of miscommunication is never severed. The engine-driver calls to the signalman as loud as he can, but his voice of warning is not able to reach the signalman's ear: "I never left off calling to him. I put this arm before my eyes, not to see, and I waved this arm to the last; but it was no use" (Dickens 1954b, 536). Thus in this story of "missed signals and failed connections" (Matus 2009, 100), virtually every communication is a doomed failure.

Even the narrator is no exception. the narrator (Jackson) and the signalman never reach mutual understanding in the story. The narrator is surely sympathetic towards the signalman, but he is very sceptical of the existence of the ghost, and never takes it seriously. At first, all he can do is to offer a banal explanation: "I showed him how that this figure must be a deception of his sense of sight; and how that figures, originating in disease of the delicate nerves that minister to the functions of the eye, were known to have often troubled patients, some of whom had become conscious of the nature of their affliction, and had even proved it by experiments upon themselves" (Dickens 1954b, 530). Even when he successes in helping the signalman to compose his mind a little, he carefully avoids attaching any meaning to the ghost and its warning: "Therefore, setting aside all question of reality or unreality between us, I represented to him that whoever thoroughly discharged his duty, must do well, and that at least it was his comfort that he understood his duty, though he did not understand these confounding Appearances" (Dickens 1954b, 534). In the close of the narrative, he similarly refuses to interpret the meaning of the whole story. He only points out the curious coincidence that the engine-driver's words ("Below there!" (Dickens 1954b, 524)) and gestures (waving his right arm) exactly correspond with those of the ghost as described by the signalman, leaving the reader totally confused:

> "Without prolonging the narrative to dwell on any one of its curious circumstances more than on any other, I may, in closing it, point out the coincidence that the warning of the Engine-Driver included, not only the words which the unfortunate Signal-man had repeated to me as haunting him, but also the words which I myself—not he—had attached, and that only in my own mind, to the gesticulation he had imitated." (Dickens 1954b, 536)

Thus, towards the end of the story, Jackson begins to abandon his attempts to explain, interpret, or solve the mystery of the ghost. Instead, he gradually turns into a transparent narrator, who passes on what he has seen or heard, without attaching any meaning to what he is relating. He, as it were, transmits the code without decoding or sends the cipher without deciphering, and shifts the responsibility of interpreting the message to the reader. And this is the only way for the narrator to avoid the risk of misunderstanding or misinterpreting the message, which ultimately means the dire consequence, terrible disaster, or unexpected death in this story.

Another distinguishing feature of the story is the fact that the ghost is never directly described. As Helmut Bonheim points out, in "The Signal-Man", the ghost is presented through a somewhat complicated process:

> In fact he [the narrator] himself never sees the spectre; nor it is introduced to the reader, who stands at the end of a perspective chain, for the story presents:
>
> 1. a spectre who is seen by the
> 2. signal-man, who is met by the
> 3. narrator, who is a fictive creation of the
> 4. author, who presents his story to the
> 5. reader. (Bonheim 1995, 814)

The ghost is only witnessed by the signalman, and in this sense he functions as a spiritual medium, as well as the receiver of the message. Then, the signalman reveals his experience to the narrator, and finally the whole story is told to the reader, via the narrator's first-person narrative. Therefore, there are two forms of mediation between the ghost and the reader: the signalman as a spiritual medium and Jackson as the narrator of the novel. Furthermore, it is significant to note that neither of the mediators provides a "right" or satisfying interpretation: the former fails to interpret the message, and the latter avoids the act of interpreting itself. And that is why the reader is left feeling uneasy or even dismayed at the end of the story—due to these two frustrating mediators, the story itself is delivered as an unintelligible cipher to the reader. It is in this way that Dickens's serious apprehension about the miscommunication and misinterpretation of messages caused by the modern technology is masterly integrated with a supernatural element, and through this technique "The Signal-Man" succeeds in making the reader feel the same way as its narrator.

5. "The Signal-Man" in a Globalizing World

In a letter to W. H. Wills dated 22 August in 1851, Dickens refers to railway construction and the discovery of the Electric Telegraph as "the great progress of the country", and a "contribution to the happiness of mankind" (Dickens 1988, 468). Since Dickens always believed in social progress, it would be against his principles if he were to deny the benefits of new inventions to civilization openly. His vague uneasiness about modern science and technology, therefore, had no choice but to take the form of inexplicable fear, and found an outlet in expressing itself as a ghost story which refuses to allow any rational explanation.

Another significant aspect of the story is that its underlying concerns—the railway and the electric telegraph—are both major technologies of globalization, through which the wide and diverse world was linked together. As Herbert L. Sussman notes, "From the 1840s, England began to be knit together by the railway and the electric telegraph. With the progressive dynamic of technological change, the expansion of these inventions continued in a nineteenth-century form of globalization" (Sussman 2009, 74). In Thomas Hardy's *A Laodicean; or, The Castle of the De Stancys. A Story of To-Day* (1881), the electric telegraph is described as "a machine which beyond everything may be said to symbolize cosmopolitan views and the intellectual and moral kinship of all mankind" (Hardy 1907, 22). And it appears that herein partly lies the reason why "The Signal-Man" has attracted innumerable readers including those abroad since its publication, and has not become an obsolete, old-fashioned ghost story even today.

About forty years after the publication of *Mugby Junction* in England, Lafcadio Hearn, the Greek-born and Irish-American writer, who contributed greatly to the development of English literature studies in Japan, made an interesting comment on it in a lecture at Tokyo Imperial University (where he taught from 1896 to 1903). While he regarded Dickens as one of the greatest literary figures of the nineteenth century, he strongly dissuaded Japanese students from reading him, on the grounds that his works were too difficult for those who were not familiar with London life, while specifically naming *Mugby Junction* as an exception.[4]

Nevertheless I must tell you that they are not to be recommended in a general way to Japanese students. On the contrary I should advise you to read very little of Dickens for the present. Dickens can only be properly understood by a person who has lived a long time in England, and lived there from childhood. To understand the scenes and the characters one should have been especially in London. Having read Dickens in London I could feel the charm of him in a very vivid way; but I doubt extremely whether you could find any charm in his whimsical English middle class life. It was for some time a custom to read "The Cricket on the Hearth" in Japanese schools; but I doubt whether a worse choice could have been made for the sake of Japanese students. [. . .] Infinitely better would have been such stories as the wonderful railroad stories, collected under the title of "Mugby Junction". Those could be tolerably well understood by any one familiar with railroad life. (Hearn 1927, 577-78)

As Toru Sasaki points out, curiously Hearn does not mention "The Signal-Man" in his lecture on Dickens.[5] However, according to another written record of Hearn's lecture, he further explained his choice in more detail. He mentioned the stories of *Mugby Junction* "chiefly because they show in a very strong way the power of Dickens to put ghosts into inanimate objects, to make even railroads and telegraphs become alive" (Hearn 1932, 336). Although he thus highly praised *Mugby Junction*, it is likely that Hearn especially had "The Signal-Man" in mind, considering the fact that there is virtually no mention of the telegraph in the other three chapters written by Dickens, and, more importantly, later in the same lecture, Hearn speaks highly of Dickens's ability to "give us sensations of fear of a very strange kind—ghostly fear" (Hearn 1932, 338). Certainly it might not be necessarily within the scope of Dickens's original intention, but by foregrounding these globalizing technologies, it is safe to say that "The Signal-Man" achieved an enduring and universal appeal for its readers. It is a remarkable fact that even in Japan in the early twentieth century, nothing more was necessary than a familiarity

[4] Masaie Matsumura points out that "English novels were too difficult for most of the young literary men of Japan; and the morality and social consciousness so characteristic of them were not qualities that provoked envy" (Matsumura 1995, 543).
[5] See Sasaki, 188.

with "railroad life" to comprehend this story (by the end of the nineteenth century, railway had already spread all over the country), in spite of many other huge cultural differences.

It is interesting to point out, then, that there is no proper noun at all to be found in "The Signal-Man". Of course, the reader who has read the earlier chapters knows that the narrator's real name is "Jackson", and the railway tunnel where he encounters the signalman is one of the branch lines of "Mugby Junction" (apparently modelled on Rugby in Warwickshire), but in this story these specific names are carefully excluded from the narrative—as if the story itself, exactly like the ghost's message, is devoid of any clear and explicit contexts. Such obscurity does not allow the reader to fix the story in any specific time or place. While the narrator Jackson is the gentleman for *nowhere*, the ghost of "The Signal-Man" can appear *everywhere* in a globalized world, linked together by enormous networks of rail and other varieties. Even today when the electric telegraph is no longer in frequent use, and no doubt in the future too, the story will not lose its hold, as long as the latent, fundamental fear about miscommunication and misunderstanding between self and others lingers in people's minds.

* This article was supported by JSPS KAKANHI Grant Number 20J10967.
** This article is based on a paper I presented at the workshop "Mediation and Message" on 27 July 2018 at Kobe University.

Bibliography

The Annual Register, or a View of the History and Politics of the Year 1861. 1862. London: Woodfall and Kinder.

Archer, Charles Maybury, ed. 1848. *The London Anecdotes for All Readers: The Electric Telegraph*. London: David Bogue.

Bonheim, Helmut. 1995. "The Principle of Cyclicity in Charles Dickens' 'The Signalman'." In *Charles Dickens: Dickens's Later Work: Assessments Since 1870*, edited by Michael Hollington, 811-21. Vol. 3 of, *Charles Dickens: Critical Assessments*. Reprint, Mountfield: Helm Information.

Dickens, Charles. (1859) 1956a. "The Haunted House." In *Christmas Stories*, 223-252. Oxford: Oxford University Press, 1956.

---. (1866) 1956b. "Mugby Junction." In *Christmas Stories*, 473-536. Oxford: Oxford University Press, 1956.

---. 1863a. "The Martyr Medium." *All the Year Round*, April 4, 1863.
---. 1988. *The Pilgrim Edition of the Letters of Charles Dickens: Volume 6: 1850-1852*. Oxford: Clarendon Press.
---. 1999. *The Pilgrim Edition of the Letters of Charles Dickens: Volume 11: 1865-1867*. Oxford: Clarendon Press.
---. 1863b. "Rather a Strong Dose." *All The Year Round*, March 21.
---. 1853. "The Spirit Business." *Household Words*, May 7.
---. 1858. "Well-Authenticated Rappings." *Household Words*, February 20.
Harada, Takashi. 2016 "The Media and Medium in Charles Dickens's "The Signalman": The Junction of Electricity and Spirit" (in Japanese) *Eibeibunka*, 46: 39-53.
Hardy, Thomas. (1881) 1907. *A Laodicean: A Story of To-day*. London: Macmillan.
Head, John Oswald. 1856. "Signals and Engine Drivers." *Household Words*, September 6.
Hearn, Lafcadio. 1927. *History of English Literature: in a Series of Lectures*. Vol. 2. Tokyo: Hokuseido Press.
---. 1932. *On Art, Literature and Philosophy*, Tokyo: Hokuseido Press.
Henson, Louise. 2004. "Investigations and Fictions: Charles Dickens and Ghosts." In *The Victorian Supernatural*, edited by Nicola Bown, Carolyn Burdett and Pamela Thurschwell, 44-66. Cambridge: Cambridge University Press.
Hunt, Frederick Knight. 1850. "Wings of Wire." *Household Words*, December 7.
Koike, Shigeru. 1979. *Dikenzu: jukyuseiki Shingoshu (Dickens: A Signalman of the Nineteenth Century)*. Tojyusya.
Matus, Jill L. 2009. *Shock, Memory and the Unconscious in Victorian Fiction*. Cambridge: Cambridge University Press.
Matsumura, Masaie. 1995. "Dickens in Japan." In *General Assessments since 1945: Biographical, Critical and Thematic*, edited by Michael Hollington, 541-561. Vol. 4 of, *Charles Dickens: Critical Assessments*. Reprint, Mountfield: Helm Information.
Menke, Richard. 2008. *Telegraphic Realism: Victorian Fiction and Other Information Systems*. Stanford: Stanford University Press.
Morley, Henry. 1852. "The Ghost of the Cock Lane Ghost." *Household Words*, November 20.
Pope, Norris. 2001. "Dickens's 'The Signalman' and Information Problems in the Railway Age." *Technology and Culture*, 42 (3): 436-461.
Sconce, Jeffrey. 2000. *Haunted Media: Electronic Presence from Telegraphy to Television*, Durham: Duke University Press.
Seed, David. 1981. "Mystery in Everyday Things: Charles Dickens' 'Signalman.'" *Criticism*, 23 (1): 42-57.
Slater, Michael. 2009. *Charles Dickens*. New Haven: Yale University Press.
Smiles, Samuel. 1879. *Lives of the Engineers: The Locomotive: George and Robert Stephenson*, London: John Murray.
Sussman, Herbert L. 2009. *Victorian Technology: Invention, Innovation, and the Rise of the Machine*, Santa Barbara: Prager.
Trollope, Anthony. (1867) 1929. *The Last Chronicle of Barset*. Vol. 2, Stratford-Upon-Avon: Shakespeare Head Press.

Toru, Sasaki. 1996. "Ghosts in *A Christmas Carol*: A Japanese View." *The Dickensian*, vol. 92, no. 440: 187-194.

Abstracts (alphabetical order)

要旨（アルファベット順）

The Experimental Self: On the Manifestation of Difference in the Early Careers of Tawada Yoko and Levy Hideo

Thomas Brook

Levy Hideo and Tawada Yoko, whose literary careers began in earnest in 1987, are recognized as the pioneers and most critically acclaimed practitioners of "border-crossing literature", a term used mainly to refer to contemporary transnational writing in the Japanese context. Their works are characterized by, above all, a focus on their own otherness or difference in respect to the linguistic and literary cultures they take part in, and they are often seen, and often present themselves, as being in an intermediate position, belonging neither here nor there. Because of this positioning, the "border-crossing literature" of "border-crossing writers" has sometimes been read for its potential to rethink pre-existing notions of national literature and individual belonging (Sakamoto 2006, Miyata 2015). The major drawback of such inquiries is that, because they conceptualize a perpetually intermediate state, they tend to overlook the way "difference" actually manifests in the authors' writing.

In this paper, I try to address this issue by considering the specific experimentation in style, format, and presentation of the "self" in the early careers of Levy and Tawada, and how it relates to the manifestation of difference. In particular, I consider the use of German and Japanese on adjacent pages in Tawada's debut poetry collection, *Only There Where You Are There is Nothing* (1987), and Levy's rewriting of the same visit to mainland China in the non-fiction "At Tiananmen" (1993-4) and subsequent novel "Tiananmen" (1996). Based upon this analysis, I suggest that both authors are taking part in a complex process of "self-translation", through which they attempt to reveal and create forms of difference that are connected to, but not reducible to, their own originary difference as "foreigners".

Keywords
Tawada Yoko
Levy Hideo
border-crossing writers
self-translation
difference

実験的な自己——多和田葉子とリービ英雄の初期キャリアにおける差異の表出

トーマス・ブルック

1987年に本格的にデビューを遂げたリービ英雄と多和田葉子は現代日本の「越境文学」の先駆者かつ牽引者として知られる。両者の作品は、作者が関わっている言語・文学的伝統に対する自らの他者性や差異の顕在化によって特徴づけられ、作家自身も、どこにも属さない中間的な位置にあると認識されてきた。先行研究において、「越境作家」または「越境文学」のこのような位置関係は、従来の国民文学や個人の国家に対する所属関係を問い直し、それに取って代わりうるオルタナティヴを構想するきっかけとして期待を寄せられてきた（Sakamoto 2006、宮田 2015）。だが、こうした試みに付きまとう問題は、永遠に続く中間的な位置を構想することにより、「差異」が個々の作品において実際にどのように生じているかということを見落としがちな点にある。

本稿では、この問題に対処すべく、リービと多和田の初期キャリアにおける実験的な「自己」表象と、それが作品間の差異の表出とどのように関わるかを検討する。具体的には、多和田のデビュー詩集である Nur da wo du bist da ist nichts『あなたのいるところだけなにもない』(1987) における日本語とドイツ語訳との間で生じる差異と、リービが同じ体験をまず「ノンフィクション」で書き、その後「私小説」として書き直し同じ単行本で収録した「天安門にて」（1993-4）と「天安門」（1996）の間の差異を検討する。作品分析を通じて、この差異の表出を、両作家が自らの「外国人」としての元来の差異を出発点としつつ、それに還元され得ない差異を表出させる「自己翻訳」的過程として解釈する。

キーワード
リービ英雄
多和田葉子
越境作家
自己翻訳
差異

World Literature Today? Reconsidering Goethe's Idea and its Critical Potential

Hisayama Yuho

The concept of World Literature is now enjoying a huge international boom. According to J. W. v. Goethe, who transformed the term into an extendable and meaningful idea, it refers to a dynamic process of "free spiritual trade" through literature. This paper will reveal the critical potential of this idea that premised a cultural variety through which the universal human would be able to – more or less indirectly – manifest itself symbolically. Goethe once regarded symbols as the result of entoptic color phenomena, and parallel to this, the image of World Literature can be grasped as a result of so-called "repeated mirroring". An example of it is to find in his work *West-Eastern Diwan* (esp. in the poem titled "Gingko Biloba"), which could philosophically be characterized through the neo-phenomenological concept of "situation" by Hermann Schmitz.

Goethe states, however, that mutual intercultural understanding will only rarely succeed, and in order to reach that ideal the process of World Literature requires a long time to mature. In his last years, the German poet sometimes tended to deny the openness of cultures, which seems at first glance to suggest the failure of his idea of World Literature, but from another perspective his swaying ambivalent positioning itself may be understood as the polarity which is necessary for the dynamism of an ever-lasting process of World Literature, in which every culture repeatedly mirrors one another, maturing over a long period.

Keywords
World Literature
Goethe
repeated mirroring
slowness

今日の世界文学とは――ゲーテの理念とその潜在的批判性

久山 雄甫

ゲーテは世界文学を「精神の自由な交易」として動詞的に捉えた。これを具体的にイメージする手がかりは内視的色彩の現象に見つかる。黒塗りの合わせ鏡のあいだに置かれたガラスに、一方の鏡に反射した無色の光が射し込むとき、無限の鏡同士の「うつしがさね」により、あいだにあるガラスの中では鮮やかな色彩現象が生じる。その様子は、異文化同士が互いのイメージをうつしあい、個別的なもののなかに普遍性を浮かび上がらせる運動としての世界文学とパラレルに捉えられよう。ゲーテの文学作品における一例には、近代ドイツと中世ペルシアが時空をこえて互いに互いをうつしあう『西東詩集』(なかでも詩「銀杏」)がある。これらに見られる関係性は、哲学的にはヘルマン・シュミッツのいう「状況」概念に相当するものであり、分断された個別文化が切り結ぶネットワークとしてではなく、ひとつの全体的「状況」における「うつしがさね」として理解できる。

ただしゲーテは、世界文学の理想の実現が極めて困難であり、それには長い時間がかかることを指摘してもいた。晩年の彼は、加速度的に生のテンポを上げていく近代社会を批判的に捉え、ついには世界への扉を閉じるかのような文章を綴るようになる。しかし開放と閉鎖の両極のあいだで揺れ動く彼の態度それ自体が、終わることのない世界文学のダイナミズムを示すものではなかろうか。そのように捉えるとき、ゲーテの世界文学論は、ますます緊密にネットワーク化し加速化する現代社会を批判し、それとは異なる世界の見方をさぐる手がかりとなる。

キーワード
世界文学
ゲーテ
うつしがさね
近代批判(反・加速化)

Japan's Charm Offensive – NHK World and Soft Power

Griseldis Kirsch

Japan's soft power is undisputable. With manga and anime being consumed around the world, Japanese popular cultural products have become household names. In that context, NHK World has often been overlooked. Broadcast as the English-language outlet of the Japanese public broadcasting station NHK on satellite around the world, this television station has considerable outreach when it comes to the propagation of Japanese (popular) culture. As a 24-hour channel, NHK World does not just broadcast news from Japan and the rest of Asia, it also has several general interest programmes introducing Japanese culture, or reportages on current issues, making it more than a news channel such as BBC World News or CNN.

Focussing on an analysis of several programmes on NHK World, the aim of this paper is to work out which images of Japan are being conveyed to the wider world. Following on from that, I will analyse to what extent these programmes contribute to a greater understanding of Japan among the intended audiences, or whether they do not in fact over-exoticise Japan and thus create boundaries between Japan and 'the Other'.

Keywords
soft power
NHK World
propaganda
Cool Japan

日本の魅力攻勢——NHKワールドとソフトパワー

グリゼルディス・キルシュ（ロンドン大学 SOAS）

日本のソフトパワーは紛れもなく絶大である。漫画やアニメが世界中で消費され、日本の大衆文化作品はどこの国でも馴染み深いものとなっている。そうした状況の中、NHKワールドの存在は見過ごされることが多い。日本の公共放送局 NHK によって全世界に衛星放送される英語放送である NHK ワールドは、日本の（大衆）文化の伝達に関してそれなりに広い射程を持つものとして想定できる。24 時間放送で、日本および他のアジア諸国のニュースに加え、日本文化を紹介する大衆向けの番組の放送や時事問題の報道も行う NHK ワールドは、BBC ワールドニュースや CNN のようなニュース放送局を超える特性を持つ。

本稿の目的は、NHK ワールドで放送されている数種類の番組の分析に重点を置き、日本のどのようなイメージが広く世界中に伝達されているかを解明することにある。その議論を踏まえ、それらの番組が、対象とする視聴者の日本理解の深まりに果たしてどの程度寄与しているかを分析する。すなわち、実際は日本を過度にエキゾチシズムの対象として眺め、その結果、日本と「他者」を隔てる境界を形成してしまっている可能性について検討する。　（日本語訳：尾田知子）

キーワード
ソフトパワー
NHKワールド
プロパガンダ
クールジャパン

The Image Strategy and Rituals of the Monarchy of Thailand in Thai Cinema: Kings, the Emperor, and 'Ritual Space'

Norihiko Nakamura

The purpose of this paper is to examine the image strategy of the monarchy of Thailand and the formation of a ritual space. Previous studies on the Thai monarchy have not covered many cases of portraits or film works. In this context, I would like to take a new look at the image of the Thai king from the perspective of concrete images.

In order to understand the strategic use of image by the King of Thailand and his royal authority, it is necessary to bypass the Japanese emperor's propagation of the image of the emperor and the ceremonial nature of the state through the image of the Goshin-ei (imperial portrait and film). According to a previous study by Koji Taki and others, courtesy refers to a situation in which the sacredness and authority of a person in power are enhanced in a specific process. The current Thai rituals and their representation is one of the main points of interest in this paper. First, I analyze the image of the king's admiration, which is always shown in Thai movie theaters, and reveal how a ceremonial space for the king will be created. Second, I compare the characteristics of Japanese and Thai cinema histories in terms of how the highest authority of the state is represented in films. At the end of the paper, I reveal the characteristics of the ritual space constructed by the monarchy of Thailand, which has been crafted with various image strategies.

Keywords
Thai cinema
Thai monarchy
Apichatpong Weerasethakul
Japanese emperor
ritual

タイ映画におけるタイ王政のイメージ戦略と儀礼——国王、天皇、儀礼的空間

中村 紀彦

本論文の目的は、タイ国王のイメージ戦略や儀礼的空間の形成について検討する。タイ国王についてのこれまでの研究は、肖像写真や映画作品の事例を取り上げることがあまりなかった。そうしたなかで本論では、具体的なイメージの次元からタイ国王のイメージ研究を新たに掘り下げたいと思う。

多木浩二による天皇イメージについての先行研究によれば、儀礼とは、ある権力者の神聖性や権威性を特定のプロセスにおいて高める状況をいう。本論は、タイ国王や王権がイメージをどう戦略的に用いてきたかを知るために、日本の天皇が御真影などを通じて天皇イメージと国家の儀礼性を伝播させた事例を迂回する。こうした本論文の関心は、第一に、現在のタイにおける儀礼はいかに存在するのか、第二にタイの儀礼はイメージとどのように結びついているのか、という点にある。まず本論は、タイの映画館で必ず上映される国王讃美の映像を分析し、国王のための儀礼的空間がいかに構築されるかを明らかにする。そして国家の最高権力者がいかに映画において表象されるかという観点から、日本映画史とタイ映画史の特徴を比較する。さいごに、タイ国王の構築する儀礼的空間が、映画を含めたさまざまなイメージ戦略で巧妙に作り上げられてきた、その特質を明らかにしていく。

キーワード
タイ映画
タイ国王
アピチャッポン・ウィーラセタクン
天皇
儀礼

"Semitic-Celtic Oriental" Seymour: "The Orient" as Counter Culture in J.D. Salinger's Glass Family Saga

Tomoko Oda

Eight stories featuring Seymour Glass—one of the most important characters created by J. D. Salinger—and his six siblings are commonly known as the "Glass family saga." These stories include frequent instances of words and deeds of Seymour that correspond to Eastern thought, providing an impression of him being surrounded by an "Oriental" ambience. On the other hand, Buddy Glass, the second eldest of the Glass siblings, describes Seymour as a "Semitic-Celtic Oriental," in light of his half-Jewish, half-Irish ethnic background. This phrase associates the Jewish-Irish Glass family with "Orientals," who are thrust into the periphery of American society, in which precedence has been taken by WASPs (White Anglo-Saxon Protestants). This tendency of Salinger to regard Jewish and Irish origins as "Oriental" has long been in scholarly neglect despite the fact that Salinger himself was highly conscious of his own half-Jewish, half-Irish ethnicity.

Through close readings of two Glass family stories—"Raise High the Roof Beam, Carpenters" and "Seymour: An Introduction," I will reconsider representations of "the Orient" from the perspective of ethnicity in order to explore the way in which otherness is expressed in Salinger's literary works. Then, by analyzing the links between the Jewish, Irish and "Oriental" imagery seen in "Semitic-Celtic" Seymour as a passionate devotee of Eastern thought and culture, I will argue that Seymour plays a mediating role of embodying "Oriental" otherness as a countervailing measure against WASP-centrism in America. I will also indicate the extent to which "the Orient" is juxtaposed in the same literary space among multiple kinds of religious imagery of the West and East, comparing the pluralistic use of different religious themes to one of the important features of world literature as explained by Homi K. Bhabha. Finally I will argue that the adoption of such pluralistic religions is in significant harmony with the counter culture against hegemonic culture mainly performed by WASP people in terms of a counter message being conveyed through the "Oriental" otherness.

Keywords
J. D. Salinger
Glass family saga
the Orient
otherness
counter culture

「ユダヤ・アイルランド系東洋人」シーモア——J. D. Salingerのグラース家物語におけるカウンター・カルチャーとしての「東洋」

尾田 知子

J. D. サリンジャーによって創造された最重要人物の一人、シーモア・グラース（Seymour Glass）が登場する八編の物語は、一般的に「グラース家物語」（Glass family saga）と呼ばれている。これらの物語では東洋思想に精通するシーモアの言動が頻繁に描かれ、彼を取り巻く「東洋的」な雰囲気を印象付けている。他方、グラース家の次男バディ・グラース (Buddy Glass) は、兄シーモアの「半分ユダヤ系、半分アイルランド系」（half-Jewish, half-Irish）の民族的背景から、彼を「ユダヤ・アイルランド系東洋人（Semitic-Celtic Oriental）と呼ぶ。この呼称は、「ユダヤ・アイルランド系」のグラース家を、WASP（White Anglo-Saxon Protestant）中心に形成されてきたアメリカ社会で周縁に追いやられてきた「東洋人」と関連づけている。作者サリンジャーも自身の「半分ユダヤ系、半分アイルランド系」の家系を強く意識していたにもかかわらず、ユダヤ系とアイルランド系の出自を「オリエンタル」と見なす傾向は、長年議論の俎上に挙げられてこなかった。

本稿では、"Raise High the Roof Beam, Carpenters" と "Seymour: An Introduction" という二編のグラース家物語の精読を通じて、エスニシティの観点からサリンジャーの「東洋」表象を再考し、サリンジャーの文学作品において他者性がいかに表現されているかを考察する。そして、東洋思想・文化に傾倒するシーモアによって体現されるユダヤ系・アイルランド系・「東洋」のイメージの連関を分析し、彼がアメリカのWASP中心主義に対抗する手段としての「東洋的」他者性を体現するという媒介的役割を果たしていることを主張する。さらに、「東洋」が東西の複数の宗教的事項と同一の文学空間において並列されていることを指摘し、そうした異なる宗教モチーフの多元的な使用を、ホミ・K・バーバによって説明される「世界文学」（world literature）に照らし合わせる。対抗のメッセージが「東洋的」他者性を通じて伝達されている点で、こうした複数の宗教イメージの使用は、主にWASPによって主導権を握られてきた主流文化に対抗するカウンター・カルチャーといみじくも響き合うものであることを主張する。

キーワード
J.D.サリンジャー
グラース家物語
東洋
他者性
カウンター・カルチャー

Nostalgia as a Modern Myth: From Modern Europe to Contemporary Japan

Kantaro Ohashi

This paper aims to interpret the meaning of the nostalgic movement in Japanese contemporary culture, referring to worldwide tendencies and to the historical development of this notion in modern Europe. On the one hand, in the European cultural tradition, the feeling of nostalgia has existed from the time of Homer in ancient Greece, and it has always progressed in parallel with the modernization process of the outer world. In this sense, nostalgia functions as one of the primary notions throughout Western history. But on the other, it shows local and specific development in recent Japan, where from the Meiji era influences from the West have played a decisive role in modernization/westernization. Furthermore, especially after the beginning of the new millennium, many cultural products such as novels, popular songs, animation films, etc. reflect a recent preference for nostalgia.

Beginning with a historical review of the birth of the notion of nostalgia in early modern Europe in the first section, in the second section this paper examines Adorno and Horkheimer's arguments in their work Dialectics of the Enlightenment about Ulysses, before in the third section referring to the arguments on the relationship between nostalgia and language posed by French critic Barbara Cassin. After surveying modern arguments on nostalgia in this way, in the final section, an object to understand modern aspects of nostalgia in Japan is presented through the example presented by the novelist Ango Sakaguchi. He began his literary career with an authentic notion of nostalgia, but his idea of nostalgia also showed a radical change after the experience of total defeat and destruction in WWII. In conclusion, I try to indicate that this rediscovered nostalgia by Sakaguchi in the postwar ruins functions as a severe critique toward recent commercialized nostalgic trends that dominate our cultural surroundings still now.

Keywords
nostalgia
modernization
critical theory
European literature
Japanese literature

現代神話としての「望郷」——西洋近代から現代日本へ

大橋 完太郎

本論は、今日の社会、文化情勢における特徴的な現象内に見出される「ノスタルジー（ノスタルジア）」の美学について、近年の文化理論および批評理論による研究を踏まえた上で、その一つの批判的な展開を戦後日本の作家坂口安吾の思想から提示する試みである。この研究を通じて、ノスタルジアが近代化の運動に必然的に伴うことであることを示し、またその意識がとりわけ近年の文化産業の一潮流を形成するに至るメカニズムを明らかにするとともに、文化の産業化を促進するノスタルジアとは異なる批判的形象としてのノスタルジアのあり方を示唆したく思う。

第一節では西洋の近代初期に病ないしは性向としての「ノスタルジア」が発生した歴史的経緯を振り返り、第二節ではアドルノとホルクハイマーの『啓蒙の弁証法』の議論を参照し、現代におけるノスタルジアと西洋における近代化の運動とが不可分であることを検討する。第三節はフランスの文藝批評家バーバラ・カッサンの議論をもとに、ノスタルジアと言語、詩との関係について考察する。最後の第四節では日本の作家坂口安吾による二種類の「ふるさと」論を対象に、安吾が戦後に展開した「望郷（＝ノスタルジア）」の概念が、近代的かつロマン主義的なノスタルジア概念とは異なり、存在論的なレベルでの批判的射程を持つものであることを示す。

キーワード
ノスタルジー（ノスタルジア）
近代化
批判理論
ヨーロッパ文学
戦後日本文化

Listening: The Other in the Dream

Akiko Okubori

How can we listen to the voice of the other? This essay will look at the relationship shared with the other and the dead through the structure of listening in *shinsaigaku* (disaster studies) and philosophy. I approach this question by considering the Great East Japan Earthquake. This earthquake happened on March 11, 2011. The magnitude was 9.0, the biggest one in the recorded history of Japan. Especially many coastal towns in the Tohoku region were visited by the great tsunami, and then the towns disappeared with their people. We had an acute feeling that all ordinary things stop being ordinary in front of the supernatural. New academic fields are now being developed in the disaster victim areas of the Great East Japan Earthquake. I will take notice of "*reisei no shinsaigaku*" (disaster studies on spirituality) by sociologist Kiyoshi Kanebishi, and the "texture of voice" by philosopher Kiyokazu Washida. They have one key thing in common. The key thing is the relationship shared with the other in listening. Kanebishi listens to the deceased of the earthquake by first listening to the stories of survivors. On the other hand, Washida considers listening from the viewpoint of the "texture of voice", through which the listener touches the appearance of the other. Furthermore, he says there is a distance between ourselves and the other even "in conversation". Thus the voice of the other is carried to me. Neither of these ideas about listening analyze the meaning of words. *Reisei no shinsaigaku* and philosophy belong to different academic fields, but both have the same goal when they consider listening. Their goal is to interpret the heaviness of the existence of things that lie behind words. Their common point might be a basic focus on the origin of the act of listening.

Keywords
The Great East Japan Earthquake
listening
disaster studies on spirituality
clinical philosophy

聴くということ――夢の中の他者

奥堀 亜紀子

本論文が論じているのは、震災学と哲学の領域を軸に考察された、他者あるいは死者との関係性である。2011年3月11日に起きた東日本大震災。地震の規模は日本観測史上最大のマグニチュード9.0で、とりわけ地震による津波の被害は甚大であった。東北地方の太平洋沿岸部の町は破壊的な被害を受け、人びとや町が津波に呑み込まれていく様子は、直接的に被害に遭った人びとのあいだだけで語られるのではなく、メディアを通して日本、また世界各地の人びとへと伝えられた。人知を超えた出来事を前に、私たちはこれまで当たり前だと考えていた事柄の不確かさを痛感したのであった。東日本大震災以降、日本では東北発信の新しい学問がつくられている。本論文が注目しているのは金菱清が取り組んでいる霊性の震災学である。霊性の震災学と、哲学者である鷲田清一が論じている「声の肌理」という概念の比較を通して導き出される両者の共通問題が、「聴く」という行為における他者との関係性である。震災、津波の被害に遭った人びとの夢の話を聴き、それを記録することで彼らの話の背景にいる死者について論じている金菱と、一般的な聴くという場面における表面的な言葉の意味ではなく、話し手である他者と聴き手である自己のあいだの距離によって生み出される「他者の気配」を通して、声に触れると論じている鷲田。「聴く」という行為に対する二つの見解は、両者とも、会話をしている者の言葉を分析しているのではない。二つの相異なった学問領域が「聴く」という概念によって目指しているのは、言葉になるものの背後にある何かの存在の重さを引き受ける態度と言えるのではないだろうか。彼らの共通点は決して学問領域の異質性を批判するものではなく、むしろ両者の垣根をなくすもの、私たちの「聴く」という行為の原点となるものなのかもしれない。

キーワード
東日本大震災
聴くということ
霊性の震災学
臨床哲学

Medium, Message and Misinterpretation in "The Signal-Man"

Mizuki Tsutsui

This essay will examine "The Signal-Man" (1866), a short story written by the Victorian novelist Charles Dickens, from the view point of the Victorian information systems—spiritual intercourse, the electric telegraph and railway signalling, aiming to examine what they can reveal about issues involved in the mediation and communication between self and other. These three aspects of cultural backgrounds share a same concern with message and interpretation, and Dickens's serious apprehension about miscommunication and misunderstanding of information caused by the modern technology is masterly integrated with a supernatural element in "The Signal-Man", a story in which failure of communication prevails. Furthermore, due to the two frustrating mediators (the signalman and the narrator), the text itself is delivered as an unintelligible cipher to the reader, and in this way Dickens succeeded in creating a genuinely uncanny, macabre story. I will then discuss "The Signal-Man" in the context of a globalizing world, especially by focusing on its reception in Japan in the early twentieth century. This short story also owes its enduring success to the fact that its underlying concerns—the railway and the electric telegraph—are both technologies of globalization, through which the wide and diverse world was linked together. Certainly it might not be necessarily within the scope of Dickens's original intention, but by foregrounding these predominant worldwide technologies, "The Signal-Man" achieved a universal appeal for many readers, including even those not familiar with English culture or London life.

Keywords
Charles Dickens
spiritualism
the electric telegraph
railway signalling system

『信号手』における媒体、メッセージ、誤解

筒井 瑞貴

本論文はヴィクトリア朝の小説家チャールズ・ディケンズによる短篇「信号手」(1866)を、交霊術、電信、鉄道信号といった同時代の「情報システム」の観点から分析し、「自己」と「他者」との間の媒介作用やコミュニケーションといった問題を考察する。上記三つの文化的背景に共通するのは「メッセージ」と「解釈」への関心であり、ディケンズが抱いていた、近代的技術によって生じる情報の誤読や誤った伝達といった懸念は、コミュニケーションの失敗に貫かれる「信号手」において超自然的要素の中に巧みに織り込まれつつ投影されている。さらに、信号手と語り手という二人の不完全な「媒介者」によって、テクストそのものがいわば一種の解読不能な暗号として読み手に伝達されることで、ディケンズは純粋に不可解で不気味な物語を構築することに成功していると論じる。さらに、20世紀初頭の日本での受容にも焦点を当て、グローバル化する世界というコンテクストにおける本作品の位置づけを考察する。この短篇の成功の要因として、作品の根底にある関心事である鉄道と電信が、いずれも多様で広大な世界を一体化し、グローバル化をもたらした技術であったことを指摘する。ディケンズの当初の意図ではなかったかもしれないが、この広く世界に普及した二つの技術を前景化することによって、「信号手」はイギリスの文化やロンドンの生活になじみのない読者にさえも強く訴求する普遍的な魅力を持つに至ったといえる。

キーワード
チャールズ・ディケンズ
心霊主義
電信
鉄道信号システム

About the Authors (alphabetical order)
著者紹介（アルファベット順）

Thomas Brook is a Ph.D. student at the Graduate School of Humanities, Kobe University, and Research Fellow (DC1) of the Japan Society for the Promotion of Science. B.A. in Japanese Studies from SOAS, University of London (2015) and M.A. in Japanese Language and Literature from Kobe University (2018). His research concerns contemporary "border-crossing" writers of Japanese, with a particular focus on the work and life of Levy Hideo. Publications include "Strung between worlds apart: A lyrical moment in *A Room Where the Star-Spangled Banner Cannot Be Heard*" (Hikaku bungaku, vol. 61, 2018) and "Mizumura Minae ni okeru "bungaku no shinri" to "shōsetsu ga mochiuru "shinjitsu no chikara": sakuhin no eiyaku wo tōshite kangaeru" (*Bigakugeijutsu ronshū*, vol. 16, 2020). He also created the English subtitles for the documentary film *A Home Within Foreign Borders* (Keiko Okawa, 2013) and has translated several short works of fiction by Wen Yuju.

トーマス・ブルック

神戸大学大学院人文学研究科博士課程後期課程、日本学術振興会特別研究員DC1。ロンドン大学SOAS卒業、神戸大学大学院人文学研究科博士課程前期課程修了。リービ英雄を中心に、日本語で創作活動を行う「越境作家」に関する研究。研究論文に"Strung between worlds apart: A lyrical moment in *A Room Where the Star-Spangled Banner Cannot Be Heard*"『比較文学』第61巻（2018)、「水村美苗における「文学の真理」と「小説が持ちうる「真実の力」」――作品の英訳を通して考える」『美学芸術学論集』第16号（2020)。研究論文の他、大川景子監督『異境の中の故郷』（2013）の英語字幕作成（英語題：*A Home Within Foreign Borders*)、温又柔による短編作品の英訳など、日英翻訳も行う。

Akiho Hayashi is a Ph.D. student at the Graduate School of Humanities, Kobe University. She specializes in the relationship between tourism and art theory/aesthetics, particularly the phenomenon of tourism (taking pictures or mobility etc.) based on 'The Tourist Gaze 3.0' written by co-authors John Urry and Jonas Larsen. Research presentations include: "Tourist Photographs and Place Image: From the Perspective of the Tourist Photographs on Instagram" (*Research Proceedings of Japan Society for Tourism Studies 2020*, Japan society for Tourism study, pp.60-61, July 2020).

林 玲穂（はやし あきほ）

神戸大学大学院人文学研究科博士後期課程。専門は、観光学と美学・芸術学の関係性について。とりわけ、ジョン・アーリ、ヨーナス・ラースン共著『観光のまなざし〔増補改訂版〕』をもとに観光をとりまく現象（写真撮影や移動といった観光者の経験など）についての研究。研究発表として「観光写真と場所のイメージ ――Instagram における観光写真の観点から」（『2020 年度研究報告要旨集』、観光学術学会第 9 回大会、60-61 頁、2020 年 7 月）など。

Yuho Hisayama, associate professor of German Studies at the Graduate School of Humanities, Kobe University, received his B.A. (2006) and M.A. (2008) form Kyoto University, then his Ph.D. (2013) from TU Darmstadt (Germany). His publications include: "Goethes Gewalt-Begriff im Kontext seiner Auffassung von Natur und Kunst" in *Goethe-Jahrbuch* 129 (2012), pp. 64-74; *Erfahrungen des ki. Leibessphäre, Atmosphäre, Pansphäre*. Freiburg und München: Karl Alber 2014; "Individuum und Atmosphäre. Überlegungen zum Distanzproblem am Beispiel des japanischen Wortes *kûki*" in Michael Großheim et. al. (eds.): *Leib, Ort, Gefühl. Perspektiven der räumlichen Erfahrung*. Freiburg und München: Karl Alber 2015, pp. 56-70; "Krankheit, Spiegel und Hoffnung. Makarie als eine „geistige" Figur in Goethes *Wilhelm Meisters Wanderjahre*" in Gernot Böhme (ed.): *Über Goethes Romane*. Bielefeld: Aisthesis 2016, pp. 69-79; "Weltseele, Weltgeist und das Ungesagte in Goethes Altersgedicht *Eins und Alles*" in *Goethe-Jahrbuch* 135 (2018), pp. 39-46. (For his publications in Japanese, see the Japanese version.)

久山 雄甫（ひさやま ゆうほ）

神戸大学大学院人文学研究科／神戸大学文学部准教授（ヨーロッパ文学／ドイツ文学専修）。京都大学総合人間学部卒業（学士）、京都大学大学院人間・環境学研究科修了（修士）、ダルムシュタット工科大学博士課程修了（Ph.D.）。日本語論文に「ゲーテとフィチーノのスピリトゥス論」『モルフォロギア』30 号（2008），52-69 頁；「モナド・エンテレケイア・マカーリエ――ゲーテにおける「個の不滅」の問題」『モルフォロギア』37 号(2015)，49-77 頁；「形態学と想像力――ゲーテのナマケモノ論における「詩的表現」の意味」『モルフォロギア』38 号 (2016), 59-88 頁；「ゲーテの「現在」概念―― 『ファウスト第二部』ヘレナ劇の解釈のために」『ドイツ文学論攷』58 号（2016），5-23 頁；「色彩としての生命――ゲーテの自然観とプロティノス批判」『モルフォロギア』40 号(2018)，35-59 頁など。（ドイツ語論文については英語での著者紹介を参照。）

Griseldis Kirsch is Reader in Contemporary Japanese Culture at SOAS, University of London. Ph.D. (Trier). Publications include *Contemporary Sino-Japanese Relations on Screen, A History, 1989-2005* (London: Bloomsbury, 2015).

グリゼルディス・キルシュ

ロンドン大学SOASで現代日本文化准教授。トリーア大学（ドイツ）博士課程後期課程修了（Ph.D.）。著作に*Contemporary Sino-Japanese Relations on Screen, A History, 1989-2005*（London: Bloomsbury, 2015）など。

Norihiko Nakamura is an independent scholar in Kobe. He is currently working at Kobe municipal office after completing an MA at Kobe University, Graduate School of Humanities. He researches Southeast Asian cinema with a focus on the work of Apichatpong Weerasethakul. His publications include: "From the Reversing 'Site' to the Ghosting of the Viewer: About Apichatpong Weerasethakul's *Phantoms of Nabua*" (*Bigaku*, The Japanese Society for Aesthetics, vol. 69, no. 253, pp. 49-60, December 2018), *Apichatpong Weerasethakul: Artist of Memory and Splendor* (Film Art Inc., Miyuki Natsume and Yu Kaneko eds., 2016 (in Japanese, co-authored book)), *The Complete Book of OZU Yasujiro* (Asahi Shimbun Publications Inc., Kanji Matsuura and Akiko Miyamoto eds., 2019 (in Japanese, co-authored book)), *Vibrant Southeast Asian Cinema: Multiculture, Border Transgression, Solidarity* (Miyuki Natsume, Kenji Ishizaka, and The Japan Foundation Asia Center eds., 2019 (in Japanese, co-authored book)).

中村 紀彦（なかむら のりひこ）

神戸を拠点に在野研究者として活動している。神戸大学大学院博士後期課程を退学後、神戸市役所で勤務。専門は映像研究、とくに東南アジア映画およびタイの映像作家アピチャッポン・ウィーラセタクンの研究をおこなっている。主な論文に「反転する「場」から観者の亡霊化へ——アピチャッポン《ナブアの亡霊》をめぐって」（『美学』、美学会、第69巻、253号、49-60頁、2018年12月）、主な共著書に『アピチャッポン・ウィーラセタクン：光と記憶のアーティスト』（夏目深雪・金子遊編、フィルムアート社、2016年）、『小津安二郎 大全』（松浦莞二、宮本明子編、朝日新聞出版社、2019年）、『躍動する東南アジア映画：多文化・越境・連帯』（夏目深雪、石坂健治、国際交流基金編、論創社、2019年）など。

Tomoko Oda completed a Ph.D. at the Graduate School of Humanities, Kobe University in March 2021, and is a research fellow of the Japan Society for the Promotion of Science. She specializes in contemporary American literature, particularly the literary works of J. D. Salinger. Publications include: "Crying over the marginalization of a 'Semitic-Celtic-Oriental' family: the representation of multiple religions and cultures in J. D. Salinger's 'Franny' and 'Zooey'" (*Letters and Essays*, Bungaku to Hyoron Sha, vol. 3, no. 13, pp. 22-35, December 2020); "Is the Virgin Mary blessed? Revisiting Christian symbolism in three of J. D. Salinger's short stories" (Creativity, Addleton Academic Publishers, vol. 3, no. 1, pp. 51-67, September 2020).

尾田 知子（おだ ともこ）

神戸大学大学院人文学研究科博士課程後期課程修了。博士（文学）。日本学術振興会特別研究員。専門は現代アメリカ文学、とりわけJ. D. サリンジャーの文学作品。主な論文に "Crying over the marginalization of a 'Semitic-Celtic-Oriental' family: the representation of multiple religions and cultures in J. D. Salinger' s 'Franny' and 'Zooey'"（『文学と評論』第3集・第13号（総50号）、22-35頁、2020年12月）、"Is the Virgin Mary blessed? Revisiting Christian symbolism in three of J. D. Salinger' s short stories"（*Creativity*、Addleton Academic Publishers、第3集・第1号、51-67頁、2020年9月）など。

Kantaro Ohashi is Associate Professor of Art Theory at the Graduate School of Humanities, Kobe University. Ph.D. (2009) in International Cultural Studies from University of Tokyo. Research Fellow and Part-time Assistant Professor of University of Tokyo Center for Philosophy from 2009 to 2010. Lecturer and Associate Professor of Kobe College from 2011 to 2015. Publications include *Diderot's Materialism*, Housei-Daigaku-Syuppankyoku, Tokyo, 2011 (in Japanese).

大橋 完太郎（おおはし かんたろう）

神戸大学大学院人文学研究科准教授（芸術学）。博士（学術）。京都大学文学部卒。京都大学大学院文学研究科修士課程（フランス語学フランス文学）および東京大学大学院総合文化研究科修士課程（表象文化論コース）修了。東京大学大学院総合文化研究科博士課程単位取得退学後、2009年同課程博士取得。その後ベルギー・ブリュッセル自由大学研究員、東京大学特任研究員、同特任講師、神戸女学院大学文学部専任講師、同准教授を経て、2015年10月より現職。専門はフランスを中心とした近現代の感覚論・文化理論。著書に『ディドロの唯物論』法政大学出版局、2011年（第3回表象文化論学会賞受賞)、翻訳にジャック・デリダ『スクリッブル』月曜社、2020年など。

Akiko Okubori completed a Ph.D. at the Graduate School of Humanities, Kobe University in 2017. After getting her Ph.D., she started to do fieldwork as a research fellow of the Japan Society for the Promotion of Science in the disaster area, especially in Ishinomaki city until March 2020. She continues to conduct research there. Her field of specialization is 20th-century French philosophy and thanatology. Publications include: "Jankélévitch" in *Gendai Furansu tetsugaku nyumon* (「ジャンケレヴィッチ」『現代フランス哲学入門』Introduction to Contemporary French Philosophy, Mineruva shobō, 2020), "On the Question of the Dead or "Ghosts": A Meditation for Disaster Victims" (*Journal of Innovative Ethics Special Issue*, Project Innovative Ethics, March 2019).

奥堀 亜紀子（おくぼり あきこ）

2017年3月神戸大学大学院人文学研究科文化構造専攻博士課程後期課程修了。同年4月より日本学術振興会特別研究員PDの採用に伴い、大阪大学大学院人間科学研究科を拠点に東日本大震災後の喪の作業に関するフィールドワークを開始。任期終了後も石巻市で研究を継続。専門はフランス現代思想、死生学。著書には、『現代フランス哲学入門』(分担執筆「ジャンケレヴィッチ」、ミネルヴァ書房、2020年7月)、「On the Question of the Dead or "Ghosts" : A Meditation for Disaster Victims」『Journal of Innovative Ethics』Special Issue (Project Innovative Ethics, 2019)』など。

Mizuki Tsutsui completed a Ph.D. at the Graduate School of Humanities, Kobe University in 2021 and is a research fellow of the Japan Society for the Promotion of Science. His publications include "Disguise and Deception in *Barnaby Rudge*" (*Dickens Studies Annual*, Penn State University Press, vol. 51, no. 1, 2020) and "*Nicholas Nickleby*: Dickens's Anti-Melodramatic Strategy" (*Dickens and the Anatomy of Evil: Sesquicentennial Essays*, edited by Mitsuharu Matsuoka, Athena Press, 2020).

筒井 瑞貴（つつい みずき）

神戸大学大学院人文学研究科博士課程後期課程修了。博士（文学)。日本学術振興会特別研究員。主要業績に "Disguise and Deception in *Barnaby Rudge*" (*Dickens Studies Annual*, ペンシルベニア州立大学出版局, vol. 51, no. 1, 2020) and "*Nicholas Nickleby*: Dickens' s Anti-Melodramatic Strategy" (*Dickens and the Anatomy of Evil: Sesquicentennial Essays*, Athena Press, 松岡光治編, 2020) など。

あとがき

本書は、神戸大学大学院人文学研究科において、過去4年に渡って継続して企画されたロンドン大学東洋アフリカ学院（SOAS）東アジアの文化・言語学部日本・韓国セクションとの共同研究交流の成果をもとに構成されている。SOASから寄稿者の一人でもあるグリゼルディス・キルシュ氏（現在は同セクションの長を務めている）が毎年来日し、神戸大学を会場として、在籍する博士課程学生や若手教員とともに、現代日本の文化事象を題材にしたワークショップや研究発表会を開催してきた。複数回のセッションを通じて各人が研究を進め、今回、さまざまな協力や助力を得て、ここにそれらの考察を収録した本書を刊行する運びとなった。お世話になった各人へのお礼は最後にするとして、こうした論文集を刊行する意義について、編者の一人として思うところを述べてみたい。

＊　＊　＊

本書の第一の特徴は——神戸大学出版会が設立されて初の試みということだが——英語・日本語二言語を併用する形で制作されている点にあるだろう。「日本からの視点」を英語話者にもわかる形で発信することには、実のところ、今日の人文学、とりわけ文学・芸術などを含めた文化研究が置かれた複雑かつ困難な状況が反映されている。本書所収のトーマス・ブルック氏による論考において言及されている水村美苗『日本語が亡びるとき』の議論を参照してもよい。今日の世界における〈世界通貨〉〈普遍語〉としての地位を揺るぎないものとした英語の前で、英語以外の言語、すなわち英語圏以外の地域で生まれた人々の「自分たちの言語」は「亡びる」宿命に置かれるのではないか、「国民文学」の一翼を担う作家としての意識をもつ水村は、そうした不安を打ち明けている。だがこの不安は作家だけのものではない。自分の知る限りではあるが、日本で活動する人文学の研究者の多くも、自らの研究成果を日本語で発表することに今日どれだけの意味があるのか、ということを自問せざるを得ない状況にある。大学の行政システムにおいて国際的な研究活動の方が実績として評価されやすいということだけが理由ではない。それは大きな意味では、今日の日本に生きて住み、何かを考えることを仕事にしている者たちが、文化・芸術・文学という地平で、世界に対して（あるいは世界に伍して）問いかけるべきなにかを持つことができるだろうか、という、自らの思考と感性の存在理由に関わるものでもある。

日本文学そのものとそれに関する文学研究・人文学研究とのあいだにさえ大きな違いがある。水村は日本文学が欧米圏において「主要な文学（major literature)」とみなされている（少なくともごく近い過去においてそうみなされていた）と述べているが、それに比べると、研究成果の日本語による発信をもとにして、それが英訳されることで世界の研究情勢において枢軸的な役割を担うといった例を私は寡聞にして知らない。先端的な分野においては、成果を英語で発表することが常識となって久しいように思われる。英語化されていく学術世界の中で、日本「発」のもの、とりわけ「日本」「アジア」など歴史的には「英語」「英語化」から離れて長い時間を生きてきた国を対象にした議論を通じて、わたしたちは何を「発信」することになるのだろうか？ 結局、この書物によって、受け取られるべきものとして差し出されているものは、いったい何なのだろうか？ 本書における各種の論考や読み物のなかには、こうしたメタ的な問いが常に反響しているということを編者として付言しておきたい。これに加えて、日本から離れた地で日本の文学や文化を志向し、繊細な眼差しによって此の地を捉えつづけてきた人々には、また別種の（だが、おそらくどこか共通したところをもつ）問いがあるに違いない。大学の国際交流という、詩的なものとはほど遠い枠組みを通してではあるが、私はそうした視点をもつ卓越した人々に出会い、そのうちの一人が力強い企画者・編者として働き、本書を世に出すに至った。私はそれらの人々を軽々しく代弁することは差し控える。そうした人たちの眼差しはおそらく本書に書き込まれているだろうし、私はそれを後でもう一度読み、考えることになるだろう。

立場や出自、生い立ちが異なる本書の執筆者たち、とりわけ若い書き手が、実際の執筆や校正の作業を経るなかで、日本語の作品や日本語での思考、日本発の思考が「英語化」されることの意味を、あるいは「英語化」されることで獲得されるものや失われてしまうものの存在を感じ取ることができれば、作り手としては一定の意義があったのではないかと思う。「他者」に対して差し向けられた「他者の言語」が、実際の「他者」とどのような対話を織りなすことになるのか、それが「自己」にどのような意識の変容を迫り、「他者としての自己」を発見させることになるのか。こうした問いも、刊行後の楽しみにとっておくことにしよう。

＊　＊　＊

本書の刊行においては数えきれない人たちにお世話になった。
人文学研究科・研究科長の奥村弘教授からは、本企画に対する全面的な理解とバックアップをいただき、わたしたちは神戸大学出版会との企画進行において言葉に尽くせないほどの助力にあずかることができた。副研究科長である長坂一郎教授、樋口大祐教授も計画の進捗を常々気にかけてくださり、折々に企画運用を円滑かつ効果的にする助言や働きかけをいただいた。前研究科長の増本浩子教授は、キルシュ教授との研究会に毎回出席され、その発言で共同研究の質を高めるのみならず、若い参加学生を大いに励ましてくださった。才能にあふれた同僚である久山雄甫准教授に執筆者として参加してもらったことは、この論集の価値を一段と高めることになった。なによりこの企画は、人文学研究科全体から認めてもらわないことには成立し得なかった。研究科長筆頭に、研究科のすべての人たちに改めて御礼を申し上げたく思う。

また、言うまでもなく、本書の主たる問題提起は、イギリスから何度も来日し研究会に参加していただいたSOASのグリゼルディス・キルシュ氏に負うところが大きい。現代日本における日々の暮らしの中では見過ごされがちな問題を鋭く指摘して日本研究の先端的なトピックとして提示し、それによってこの共同研究の現代性と国際性を確固たるものにした氏の熱意に心からの敬意と感謝を捧げる。

この書籍を作り上げた学生諸氏にも感謝を述べたい。一々に名をあげることは控えるが、本書は、博士課程に在籍し、博士論文を準備中である者、まもなくそれを完成しようとしている者、あるいはすでに社会に出て活躍を見せている者など、専門分野のみならず研究の段階もそれぞれに異なる学生たちが、何度も議論を繰り返す中で練り上げられたものである。私自身は彼ら彼女らの鋭敏な問題意識をすべて汲み取ることができたわけではなく、大した助力もなし得たとは思えないが、研究に打ち込む若い人々の姿を見て、新しいチャレンジに踏み出すことができた。将来続く思考と実践の中で、若き日の自分たちが作り上げた本が唯一無二の里程標とならんことを、年長世代の一人として心より願う。

最後に、共編者であるトーマス・ブルック氏に。この企画を主導し書籍という最後の形まで結実させたのは間違いなく氏の熱意と誠実さである。皮肉なことに、この書物が完成しつつある現在、コロナウィルスの影響で、グローバル社会の特徴の一つである流動性に対して大きな疑問が投げかけられようとしている。だが、同時代の他者との直接的な接触が制限されつつある時代においてこそ、別の形で別の他者とつながることができる形式——たとえば文学や芸術——はいっそう有効なのではないか？　他者の言語を学ぶことが「今ここ」を超えたつながりや価値を生み出す機縁となるということを、ブルック氏は論考によってのみならず、本書を作るという具体的な実践によって証明してみせた。執筆者を代表して、ブルック氏に与うる限り最大限の感謝と労いを伝えたい。

すべての人たちが、他者との良き出会いのなかで生きんことを。

2021年1月　神戸にて

大橋完太郎

他者をめぐる人文学

グローバル世界における翻訳・媒介・伝達

Adaptation, Mediation and Communication of Otherness in a Globalizing World: Perspectives from Japan

2021年3月31日　初版第1刷発行

編者———大橋完太郎　トーマス・ブルック

発行———神戸大学出版会

〒657-8501 神戸市灘区六甲台町2-1
神戸大学附属図書館社会科学系図書館内
TEL 078-803-7315　FAX 078-803-7320
URL : http://www.org.kobe-u.ac.jp/kupress/

発売———神戸新聞総合出版センター

〒650-0044 神戸市中央区東川崎町1-5-7
TEL 078-362-7140 ／ FAX 078-361-7552
URL : https://kobe-yomitai.jp/

印刷／神戸新聞総合印刷

落丁・乱丁本はお取り替えいたします

ISBN978-4-909364-12-8 C3090